NEW PERSPECTIVES

# Microsoft® Office 365™ & Access® 2016

## INTRODUCTORY

**Mark Shellman**

Gaston College

**Sasha Vodnik**

D1306139

CENGAGE
Learning·

Australia • Brazil • Mexico • Singapore • United Kingdom • United States

CENGAGE
Learning®

**New Perspectives Microsoft® Office 365™ & Access® 2016, Introductory**
**Mark Shellman, Sasha Vodnik**

SVP, GM Skills & Global Product Management: Dawn Gerrain

Product Director: Kathleen McMahon

Senior Product Team Manager: Lauren Murphy

Product Team Manager: Andrea Topping

Associate Product Managers: William Guiliani, Melissa Stehler

Senior Director, Development: Marah Bellegarde

Product Development Manager: Leigh Hefferon

Senior Content Developer: Marjorie Hunt

Developmental Editors: Kim T. M. Crowley, Sasha Vodnik

Product Assistant: Erica Chapman

Marketing Director: Michele McTighe

Marketing Manager: Stephanie Albracht

Senior Production Director: Wendy Troeger

Production Director: Patty Stephan

Senior Content Project Manager: Jennifer Goguen McGrail

Designer: Diana Graham

Composition: GEX Publishing Services

Cover image(s): asharkyu/Shutterstock.com

For product information and technology assistance, contact us at
**Cengage Learning Customer & Sales Support, 1-800-354-9706**

For permission to use material from this text or product, submit all requests online at **www.cengage.com/permissions**. Further permissions questions can be e-mailed to **permissionrequest@cengage.com**

Some of the product names and company names used in this book have been used for identification purposes only and may be trademarks or registered trademarks of their respective manufacturers and sellers.

Windows® is a registered trademark of Microsoft Corporation. © 2012 Microsoft. Microsoft and the Office logo are either registered trademarks or trademarks of Microsoft Corporation in the United States and/or other countries. Cengage Learning is an independent entity from Microsoft Corporation and not affiliated with Microsoft in any manner.

Disclaimer: Any fictional data related to persons or companies or URLs used throughout this text is intended for instructional purposes only. At the time this text was published, any such data was fictional and not belonging to any real persons or companies.

Disclaimer: The material in this text was written using Microsoft Office 365 ProPlus and Microsoft Access 2016 running on Microsoft Windows 10 Professional and was Quality Assurance tested before the publication date. As Microsoft continually updates the Microsoft Office suite and the Windows 10 operating system, your software experience may vary slightly from what is presented in the printed text.

Microsoft product screenshots used with permission from Microsoft Corporation. Unless otherwise noted, all clip art is courtesy of openclipart.org.

Library of Congress Control Number: 2016931128
ISBN: 978-1-305-88028-3

**Cengage Learning**
20 Channel Center Street
Boston, MA 02210
USA

Cengage Learning is a leading provider of customized learning solutions with employees residing in nearly 40 different countries and sales in more than 125 countries around the world. Find your local representative at **www.cengage.com.**

Cengage Learning products are represented in Canada by Nelson Education, Ltd.

To learn more about Cengage Learning, visit **www.cengage.com**

Purchase any of our products at your local college store or at our preferred online store **www.cengagebrain.com**

Printed in the United States of America
Print Number: 01                    Print Year: 2016

# BRIEF CONTENTS

# TABLE OF CONTENTS

# Productivity Apps for School and Work

Corinne Hoisington

Lochlan keeps track of his class notes, football plays, and internship meetings with OneNote.

Zoe is using the annotation features of Microsoft Edge to take and save web notes for her research paper.

Nori is creating a Sway site to highlight this year's activities for the Student Government Association.

Hunter is adding interactive videos and screen recordings to his PowerPoint resume.

© Rawpixel/Shutterstock.com

**Being computer literate no longer means mastery of only Word, Excel, PowerPoint, Outlook, and Access. To become technology power users, Hunter, Nori, Zoe, and Lochlan are exploring Microsoft OneNote, Sway, Mix, and Edge in Office 2016 and Windows 10.**

**In this Module**

**Learn to use productivity apps!**
Links to companion **Sways**, featuring **videos** with hands-on instructions, are located on www.cengagebrain.com.

# Introduction to OneNote 2016

notebook | section tab | To Do tag | screen clipping | note | template | Microsoft OneNote Mobile app | sync | drawing canvas | inked handwriting | Ink to Text

As you glance around any classroom, you invariably see paper notebooks and notepads on each desk. Because deciphering and sharing handwritten notes can be a challenge, Microsoft OneNote 2016 replaces physical notebooks, binders, and paper notes with a searchable, digital notebook. OneNote captures your ideas and schoolwork on any device so you can stay organized, share notes, and work with others on projects. Whether you are a student taking class notes as shown in **Figure 1** or an employee taking notes in company meetings, OneNote is the one place to keep notes for all of your projects.

Figure 1: OneNote 2016 notebook

Each **notebook** is divided into sections, also called **section tabs**, by subject or topic.

Use **To Do tags**, icons that help you keep track of your assignments and other tasks.

Type on a page to add a **note**, a small window that contains text or other types of information.

Personalize a page with a **template**, or stationery.

Write or draw directly on the page using drawing tools.

Pages can include pictures such as **screen clippings**, images from any part of a computer screen.

Attach files and enter equations so you have everything you need in one place.

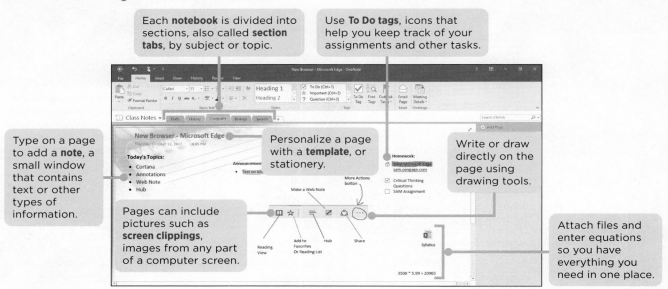

## Creating a OneNote Notebook

OneNote is divided into sections similar to those in a spiral-bound notebook. Each OneNote notebook contains sections, pages, and other notebooks. You can use One-Note for school, business, and personal projects. Store information for each type of project in different notebooks to keep your tasks separate, or use any other organization that suits you. OneNote is flexible enough to adapt to the way you want to work.

When you create a notebook, it contains a blank page with a plain white background by default, though you can use templates, or stationery, to apply designs in categories such as Academic, Business, Decorative, and Planners. Start typing or use the buttons on the Insert tab to insert notes, which are small resizable windows that can contain text, equations, tables, on-screen writing, images, audio and video recordings, to-do lists, file attachments, and file printouts. Add as many notes as you need to each page.

## Syncing a Notebook to the Cloud

OneNote saves your notes every time you make a change in a notebook. To make sure you can access your notebooks with a laptop, tablet, or smartphone wherever you are, OneNote uses cloud-based storage, such as OneDrive or SharePoint. **Microsoft OneNote Mobile app**, a lightweight version of OneNote 2016 shown in **Figure 2**, is available for free in the Windows Store, Google Play for Android devices, and the AppStore for iOS devices.

If you have a Microsoft account, OneNote saves your notes on OneDrive automatically for all your mobile devices and computers, which is called **syncing**. For example, you can use OneNote to take notes on your laptop during class, and then open OneNote on your phone to study later. To use a notebook stored on your computer with your OneNote Mobile app, move the notebook to OneDrive. You can quickly share notebook content with other people using OneDrive.

**Figure 2:** Microsoft OneNote Mobile app

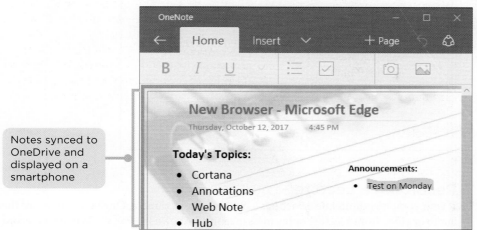

Notes synced to OneDrive and displayed on a smartphone

## Taking Notes

Use OneNote pages to organize your notes by class and topic or lecture. Beyond simple typed notes, OneNote stores drawings, converts handwriting to searchable text and mathematical sketches to equations, and records audio and video.

OneNote includes drawing tools that let you sketch freehand drawings such as biological cell diagrams and financial supply-and-demand charts. As shown in **Figure 3**, the Draw tab on the ribbon provides these drawing tools along with shapes so you can insert diagrams and other illustrations to represent your ideas. When you draw on a page, OneNote creates a **drawing canvas**, which is a container for shapes and lines.

### On the Job Now

OneNote is ideal for taking notes during meetings, whether you are recording minutes, documenting a discussion, sketching product diagrams, or listing follow-up items. Use a meeting template to add pages with content appropriate for meetings.

**Figure 3:** Tools on the Draw tab

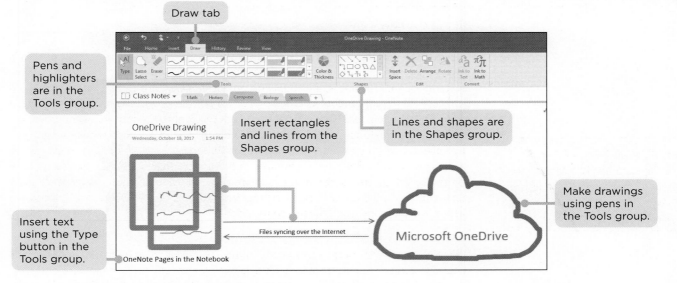
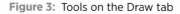

Draw tab

Pens and highlighters are in the Tools group.

Insert text using the Type button in the Tools group.

Insert rectangles and lines from the Shapes group.

Lines and shapes are in the Shapes group.

Make drawings using pens in the Tools group.

## Converting Handwriting to Text

When you use a pen tool to write on a notebook page, the text you enter is called **inked handwriting**. OneNote can convert inked handwriting to typed text when you use the **Ink to Text** button in the Convert group on the Draw tab, as shown in **Figure 4**. After OneNote converts the handwriting to text, you can use the Search box to find terms in the converted text or any other note in your notebooks.

**Figure 4:** Converting handwriting to text

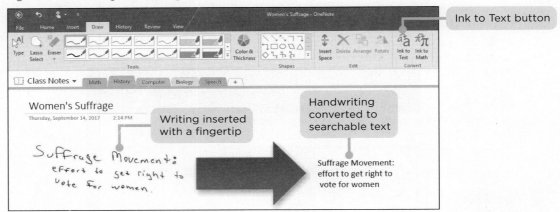

Ink to Text button

Women's Suffrage

Thursday, September 14, 2017    2:14 PM

Writing inserted with a fingertip

Suffrage Movement: effort to get right to vote for women.

Handwriting converted to searchable text

Suffrage Movement: effort to get right to vote for women

## Recording a Lecture

If your computer or mobile device has a microphone or camera, OneNote can record the audio or video from a lecture or business meeting as shown in **Figure 5**. When you record a lecture (with your instructor's permission), you can follow along, take regular notes at your own pace, and review the video recording later. You can control the start, pause, and stop motions of the recording when you play back the recording of your notes.

**Figure 5:** Video inserted in a notebook

Record Video button

Audio & Video Recording tab

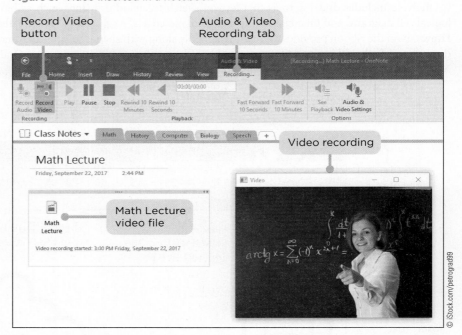

Video recording

Math Lecture

Friday, September 22, 2017    2:44 PM

Math Lecture

Math Lecture video file

Video recording started: 3:00 PM Friday, September 22, 2017

© iStock.com/petrograd99

# Try This Now

**Learn to use OneNote!**
Links to companion **Sways**, featuring **videos** with hands-on instructions, are located on www.cengagebrain.com.

## 1: Taking Notes for a Week

As a student, you can get organized by using OneNote to take detailed notes in your classes. Perform the following tasks:

a. Create a new OneNote notebook on your Microsoft OneDrive account (the default location for new notebooks). Name the notebook with your first name followed by "Notes," as in **Caleb Notes**.

b. Create four section tabs, each with a different class name.

c. Take detailed notes in those classes for one week. Be sure to include notes, drawings, and other types of content.

d. Sync your notes with your OneDrive. Submit your assignment in the format specified by your instructor.

## 2: Using OneNote to Organize a Research Paper

You have a research paper due on the topic of three habits of successful students. Use OneNote to organize your research. Perform the following tasks:

a. Create a new OneNote notebook on your Microsoft OneDrive account. Name the notebook **Success Research**.

b. Create three section tabs with the following names:

- **Take Detailed Notes**
- **Be Respectful in Class**
- **Come to Class Prepared**

c. On the web, research the topics and find three sources for each section. Copy a sentence from each source and paste the sentence into the appropriate section. When you paste the sentence, OneNote inserts it in a note with a link to the source.

d. Sync your notes with your OneDrive. Submit your assignment in the format specified by your instructor.

## 3: Planning Your Career

*Note*: This activity requires a webcam or built-in video camera on any type of device.

Consider an occupation that interests you. Using OneNote, examine the responsibilities, education requirements, potential salary, and employment outlook of a specific career. Perform the following tasks:

a. Create a new OneNote notebook on your Microsoft OneDrive account. Name the notebook with your first name followed by a career title, such as **Kara - App Developer**.

b. Create four section tabs with the names **Responsibilities, Education Requirements, Median Salary**, and **Employment Outlook**.

c. Research the responsibilities of your career path. Using OneNote, record a short video (approximately 30 seconds) of yourself explaining the responsibilities of your career path. Place the video in the Responsibilities section.

d. On the web, research the educational requirements for your career path and find two appropriate sources. Copy a paragraph from each source and paste them into the appropriate section. When you paste a paragraph, OneNote inserts it in a note with a link to the source.

e. Research the median salary for a single year for this career. Create a mathematical equation in the Median Salary section that multiplies the amount of the median salary times 20 years to calculate how much you will possibly earn.

f. For the Employment Outlook section, research the outlook for your career path. Take at least four notes about what you find when researching the topic.

g. Sync your notes with your OneDrive. Submit your assignment in the format specified by your instructor.

# Introduction to Sway

Sway site | responsive design | Storyline | card | Creative Commons license | animation emphasis effects | Docs.com

Expressing your ideas in a presentation typically means creating PowerPoint slides or a Word document. Microsoft Sway gives you another way to engage an audience. Sway is a free Microsoft tool available at Sway.com or as an app in Office 365. Using Sway, you can combine text, images, videos, and social media in a website called a **Sway site** that you can share and display on any device. To get started, you create a digital story on a web-based canvas without borders, slides, cells, or page breaks. A Sway site organizes the text, images, and video into a **responsive design**, which means your content adapts perfectly to any screen size as shown in **Figure 6**. You store a Sway site in the cloud on OneDrive using a free Microsoft account.

**Figure 6:** Sway site with responsive design

You can display a Sway presentation in a web browser.

Sway uses responsive design to make sure pages fit perfectly on any device.

## Creating a Sway Presentation

You can use Sway to build a digital flyer, a club newsletter, a vacation blog, an informational site, a digital art portfolio, or a new product rollout. After you select your topic and sign into Sway with your Microsoft account, a **Storyline** opens, providing tools and a work area for composing your digital story. See **Figure 7**. Each story can include text, images, and videos. You create a Sway by adding text and media content into a Storyline section, or **card**. To add pictures, videos, or documents, select a card in the left pane and then select the Insert Content button. The first card in a Sway presentation contains a title and background image.

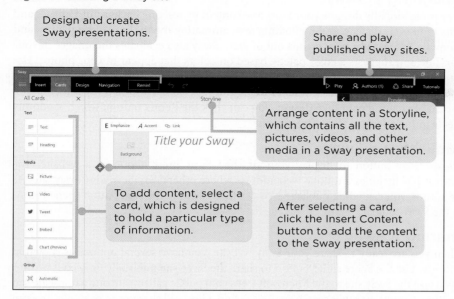

Design and create Sway presentations.

Share and play published Sway sites.

Arrange content in a Storyline, which contains all the text, pictures, videos, and other media in a Sway presentation.

To add content, select a card, which is designed to hold a particular type of information.

After selecting a card, click the Insert Content button to add the content to the Sway presentation.

## Adding Content to Build a Story

As you work, Sway searches the Internet to help you find relevant images, videos, tweets, and other content from online sources such as Bing, YouTube, Twitter, and Facebook. You can drag content from the search results right into the Storyline. In addition, you can upload your own images and videos directly in the presentation. For example, if you are creating a Sway presentation about the market for commercial drones, Sway suggests content to incorporate into the presentation by displaying it in the left pane as search results. The search results include drone images tagged with **Creative Commons license** at online sources as shown in **Figure 8**. A Creative Commons license is a public copyright license that allows the free distribution of an otherwise copyrighted work. In addition, you can specify the source of the media. For example, you can add your own Facebook or OneNote pictures and videos in Sway without leaving the app.

**On the Job Now**

If you have a Microsoft Word document containing an outline of your business content, drag the outline into Sway to create a card for each topic.

Figure 8: Images in Sway search results

Select the source of media objects

Information about Creative Commons licenses

Storyline title

The Market for Commercial Drones

Drag an image to the picture placeholder box

Suggested images in the search results

**On the Job Now**

If your project team wants to collaborate on a Sway presentation, click the Authors button on the navigation bar to invite others to edit the presentation.

## Designing a Sway

Sway professionally designs your Storyline content by resizing background images and fonts to fit your display, and by floating text, animating media, embedding video, and removing images as a page scrolls out of view. Sway also evaluates the images in your Storyline and suggests a color palette based on colors that appear in your photos. Use the Design button to display tools including color palettes, font choices, **animation emphasis effects**, and style templates to provide a personality for a Sway presentation. Instead of creating your own design, you can click the Remix button, which randomly selects unique designs for your Sway site.

## Publishing a Sway

Use the Play button to display your finished Sway presentation as a website. The Address bar includes a unique web address where others can view your Sway site. As the author, you can edit a published Sway site by clicking the Edit button (pencil icon) on the Sway toolbar.

## Sharing a Sway

When you are ready to share your Sway website, you have several options as shown in Figure 9. Use the Share slider button to share the Sway site publically or keep it private. If you add the Sway site to the Microsoft **Docs.com** public gallery, anyone worldwide can use Bing, Google, or other search engines to find, view, and share your Sway site. You can also share your Sway site using Facebook, Twitter, Google+, Yammer, and other social media sites. Link your presentation to any webpage or email the link to your audience. Sway can also generate a code for embedding the link within another webpage.

**Figure 9:** Sharing a Sway site

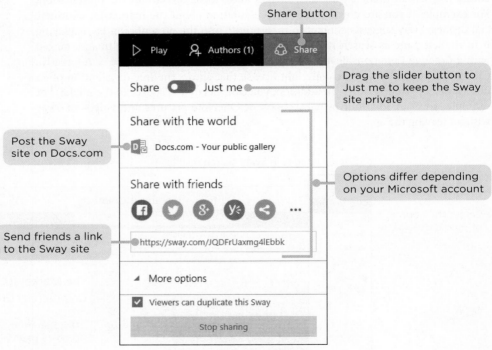

# Try This Now

## 1: Creating a Sway Resume

Sway is a digital storytelling app. Create a Sway resume to share the skills, job experiences, and achievements you have that match the requirements of a future job interest. Perform the following tasks:

> **Learn to use Sway!**
> Links to companion **Sways**, featuring **videos** with hands-on instructions, are located on www.cengagebrain.com.

  a. Create a new presentation in Sway to use as a digital resume. Title the Sway Storyline with your full name and then select a background image.
  b. Create three separate sections titled **Academic Background, Work Experience**, and **Skills**, and insert text, a picture, and a paragraph or bulleted points in each section. Be sure to include your own picture.
  c. Add a fourth section that includes a video about your school that you find online.
  d. Customize the design of your presentation.
  e. Submit your assignment link in the format specified by your instructor.

## 2: Creating an Online Sway Newsletter

Newsletters are designed to capture the attention of their target audience. Using Sway, create a newsletter for a club, organization, or your favorite music group. Perform the following tasks:

  a. Create a new presentation in Sway to use as a digital newsletter for a club, organization, or your favorite music group. Provide a title for the Sway Storyline and select an appropriate background image.
  b. Select three separate sections with appropriate titles, such as Upcoming Events. In each section, insert text, a picture, and a paragraph or bulleted points.
  c. Add a fourth section that includes a video about your selected topic.
  d. Customize the design of your presentation.
  e. Submit your assignment link in the format specified by your instructor.

## 3: Creating and Sharing a Technology Presentation

To place a Sway presentation in the hands of your entire audience, you can share a link to the Sway presentation. Create a Sway presentation on a new technology and share it with your class. Perform the following tasks:

  a. Create a new presentation in Sway about a cutting-edge technology topic. Provide a title for the Sway Storyline and select a background image.
  b. Create four separate sections about your topic, and include text, a picture, and a paragraph in each section.
  c. Add a fifth section that includes a video about your topic.
  d. Customize the design of your presentation.
  e. Share the link to your Sway with your classmates and submit your assignment link in the format specified by your instructor.

# Introduction to Office Mix

add-in | clip | slide recording | Slide Notes | screen recording | free-response quiz

To enliven business meetings and lectures, Microsoft adds a new dimension to presentations with a powerful toolset called Office Mix, a free add-in for PowerPoint. (An **add-in** is software that works with an installed app to extend its features.) Using Office Mix, you can record yourself on video, capture still and moving images on your desktop, and insert interactive elements such as quizzes and live webpages directly into PowerPoint slides. When you post the finished presentation to OneDrive, Office Mix provides a link you can share with friends and colleagues. Anyone with an Internet connection and a web browser can watch a published Office Mix presentation, such as the one in **Figure 10**, on a computer or mobile device.

Figure 10: Office Mix presentation

## Adding Office Mix to PowerPoint

To get started, you create an Office Mix account at the website mix.office.com using an email address or a Facebook or Google account. Next, you download and install the Office Mix add-in (see **Figure 11**). Office Mix appears as a new tab named Mix on the PowerPoint ribbon in versions of Office 2013 and Office 2016 running on personal computers (PCs).

Figure 11: Getting started with Office Mix

## Capturing Video Clips

A **clip** is a short segment of audio, such as music, or video. After finishing the content on a PowerPoint slide, you can use Office Mix to add a video clip to animate or illustrate the content. Office Mix creates video clips in two ways: by recording live action on a webcam and by capturing screen images and movements. If your computer has a webcam, you can record yourself and annotate the slide to create a **slide recording** as shown in **Figure 12**.

**Figure 12:** Making a slide recording

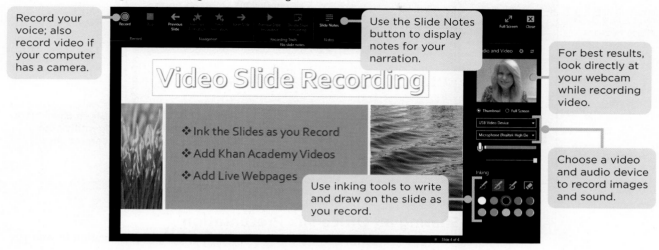

Record your voice; also record video if your computer has a camera.

Use the Slide Notes button to display notes for your narration.

For best results, look directly at your webcam while recording video.

Choose a video and audio device to record images and sound.

Use inking tools to write and draw on the slide as you record.

When you are making a slide recording, you can record your spoken narration at the same time. The **Slide Notes** feature works like a teleprompter to help you focus on your presentation content instead of memorizing your narration. Use the Inking tools to make annotations or add highlighting using different pen types and colors. After finishing a recording, edit the video in PowerPoint to trim the length or set playback options.

The second way to create a video is to capture on-screen images and actions with or without a voiceover. This method is ideal if you want to show how to use your favorite website or demonstrate an app such as OneNote. To share your screen with an audience, select the part of the screen you want to show in the video. Office Mix captures everything that happens in that area to create a **screen recording**, as shown in **Figure 13**. Office Mix inserts the screen recording as a video in the slide.

**Figure 13:** Making a screen recording

Record the action on the screen within the red dashed outline.

Record audio while capturing your on-screen actions.

Select Area button

## Inserting Quizzes, Live Webpages, and Apps

To enhance and assess audience understanding, make your slides interactive by adding quizzes, live webpages, and apps. Quizzes give immediate feedback to the user as shown in **Figure 14**. Office Mix supports several quiz formats, including a **free-response quiz** similar to a short answer quiz, and true/false, multiple-choice, and multiple-response formats.

**Figure 14:** Creating an interactive quiz

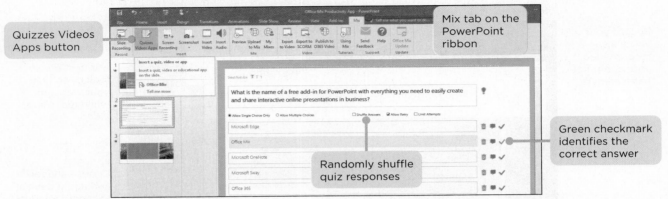

Quizzes Videos Apps button

Mix tab on the PowerPoint ribbon

Green checkmark identifies the correct answer

Randomly shuffle quiz responses

## Sharing an Office Mix Presentation

When you complete your work with Office Mix, upload the presentation to your personal Office Mix dashboard as shown in **Figure 15**. Users of PCs, Macs, iOS devices, and Android devices can access and play Office Mix presentations. The Office Mix dashboard displays built-in analytics that include the quiz results and how much time viewers spent on each slide. You can play completed Office Mix presentations online or download them as movies.

**Figure 15:** Sharing an Office Mix presentation

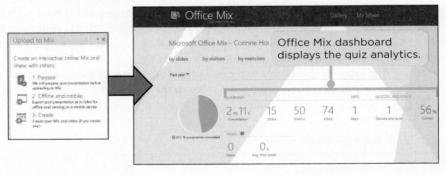

Office Mix dashboard displays the quiz analytics.

# Try This Now

## 1: Creating an Office Mix Tutorial for OneNote

*Note*: This activity requires a microphone on your computer.

Office Mix makes it easy to record screens and their contents. Create PowerPoint slides with an Office Mix screen recording to show OneNote 2016 features. Perform the following tasks:

a. Create a PowerPoint presentation with the Ion Boardroom template. Create an opening slide with the title **My Favorite OneNote Features** and enter your name in the subtitle.
b. Create three additional slides, each titled with a new feature of OneNote. Open OneNote and use the Mix tab in PowerPoint to capture three separate screen recordings that teach your favorite features.
c. Add a fifth slide that quizzes the user with a multiple-choice question about OneNote and includes four responses. Be sure to insert a checkmark indicating the correct response.
d. Upload the completed presentation to your Office Mix dashboard and share the link with your instructor.
e. Submit your assignment link in the format specified by your instructor.

## 2: Teaching Augmented Reality with Office Mix

*Note:* This activity requires a webcam or built-in video camera on your computer.

A local elementary school has asked you to teach augmented reality to its students using Office Mix. Perform the following tasks:

a. Research augmented reality using your favorite online search tools.
b. Create a PowerPoint presentation with the Frame template. Create an opening slide with the title **Augmented Reality** and enter your name in the subtitle.
c. Create a slide with four bullets summarizing your research of augmented reality. Create a 20-second slide recording of yourself providing a quick overview of augmented reality.
d. Create another slide with a 30-second screen recording of a video about augmented reality from a site such as YouTube or another video-sharing site.
e. Add a final slide that quizzes the user with a true/false question about augmented reality. Be sure to insert a checkmark indicating the correct response.
f. Upload the completed presentation to your Office Mix dashboard and share the link with your instructor.
g. Submit your assignment link in the format specified by your instructor.

## 3: Marketing a Travel Destination with Office Mix

*Note*: This activity requires a webcam or built-in video camera on your computer.

To convince your audience to travel to a particular city, create a slide presentation marketing any city in the world using a slide recording, screen recording, and a quiz. Perform the following tasks:

a. Create a PowerPoint presentation with any template. Create an opening slide with the title of the city you are marketing as a travel destination and your name in the subtitle.
b. Create a slide with four bullets about the featured city. Create a 30-second slide recording of yourself explaining why this city is the perfect vacation destination.
c. Create another slide with a 20-second screen recording of a travel video about the city from a site such as YouTube or another video-sharing site.
d. Add a final slide that quizzes the user with a multiple-choice question about the featured city with five responses. Be sure to include a checkmark indicating the correct response.
e. Upload the completed presentation to your Office Mix dashboard and share your link with your instructor.
f. Submit your assignment link in the format specified by your instructor.

# Introduction to Microsoft Edge

Reading view | Hub | Cortana | Web Note | Inking | sandbox

Bottom Line

**Bottom Line**
- Microsoft Edge is the name of the new web browser built into Windows 10.
- Microsoft Edge allows you to search the web faster, take web notes, read webpages without distractions, and get instant assistance from Cortana.

Microsoft Edge is the default web browser developed for the Windows 10 operating system as a replacement for Internet Explorer. Unlike its predecessor, Edge lets you write on webpages, read webpages without advertisements and other distractions, and search for information using a virtual personal assistant. The Edge interface is clean and basic, as shown in **Figure 16**, meaning you can pay more attention to the webpage content.

**Figure 16:** Microsoft Edge tools

Forward button | New tab button | Web address in the Address bar | Add to favorites or reading list button

Back button | Reading view button | More button

Refresh (F5) button | Hub (Favorites, reading list, history, and downloads) button | Share Web Note button | Make a Web Note button

**Learn to use Edge!**
Links to companion **Sways**, featuring **videos** with hands-on instructions, are located on www.cengagebrain.com.

**On the Job Now**

Businesses started adopting Internet Explorer more than 20 years ago simply to view webpages. Today, Microsoft Edge has a different purpose: to promote interaction with the web and share its contents with colleagues.

## Browsing the Web with Microsoft Edge

One of the fastest browsers available, Edge allows you to type search text directly in the Address bar. As you view the resulting webpage, you can switch to **Reading view**, which is available for most news and research sites, to eliminate distracting advertisements. For example, if you are catching up on technology news online, the webpage might be difficult to read due to a busy layout cluttered with ads. Switch to Reading view to refresh the page and remove the original page formatting, ads, and menu sidebars to read the article distraction-free.

Consider the **Hub** in Microsoft Edge as providing one-stop access to all the things you collect on the web, such as your favorite websites, reading list, surfing history, and downloaded files.

## Locating Information with Cortana

**Cortana**, the Windows 10 virtual assistant, plays an important role in Microsoft Edge. After you turn on Cortana, it appears as an animated circle in the Address bar when you might need assistance, as shown in the restaurant website in **Figure 17**. When you click the Cortana icon, a pane slides in from the right of the browser window to display detailed information about the restaurant, including maps and reviews. Cortana can also assist you in defining words, finding the weather, suggesting coupons for shopping, updating stock market information, and calculating math.

**Figure 17:** Cortana providing restaurant information

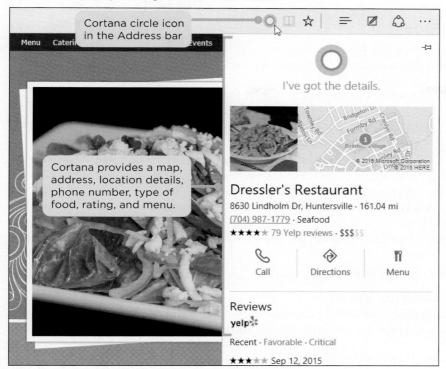

Cortana circle icon in the Address bar

I've got the details.

© 2015 Microsoft Corporation © 2015 HERE

Cortana provides a map, address, location details, phone number, type of food, rating, and menu.

**Dressler's Restaurant**
8630 Lindholm Dr, Huntersville · 161.04 mi
(704) 987-1779 · Seafood
★★★★ 79 Yelp reviews · $$$$$

Call | Directions | Menu

Reviews
yelp

Recent · Favorable · Critical
★★★ Sep 12, 2015

## Annotating Webpages

One of the most impressive Microsoft Edge features are the **Web Note** tools, which you use to write on a webpage or to highlight text. When you click the Make a Web Note button, an **Inking** toolbar appears, as shown in **Figure 18**, that provides writing and drawing tools. These tools include an eraser, a pen, and a highlighter with different colors. You can also insert a typed note and copy a screen image (called a screen clipping). You can draw with a pointing device, fingertip, or stylus using different pen colors. Whether you add notes to a recipe, annotate sources for a research paper, or select a product while shopping online, the Web Note tools can enhance your productivity. After you complete your notes, click the Save button to save the annotations to OneNote, your Favorites list, or your Reading list. You can share the inked page with others using the Share Web Note button.

**On the Job Now**

To enhance security, Microsoft Edge runs in a partial sandbox, an arrangement that prevents attackers from gaining control of your computer. Browsing within the **sandbox** protects computer resources and information from hackers.

**Figure 18:** Web Note tools in Microsoft Edge

Inking toolbar with Web Note tools for making annotations

Writing and drawing created with the Pen tool

Highlighted text

Save a copy of the webpage with annotations

Work anywhere

The integrated Kickstand features multiple positions so you can work comfortably whether you're on a plane, at your desk, or in front of the television.

I am considering purchasing the new Surface Pro for school

Typed note

# Try This Now

**Learn to use Edge!**

Links to companion **Sways**, featuring **videos** with hands-on instructions, are located on www.cengagebrain.com.

## 1: Using Cortana in Microsoft Edge

*Note*: This activity requires using Microsoft Edge on a Windows 10 computer.

Cortana can assist you in finding information on a webpage in Microsoft Edge. Perform the following tasks:

a. Create a Word document using the Word Screen Clipping tool to capture the following screenshots.

- Screenshot A—Using Microsoft Edge, open a webpage with a technology news article. Right-click a term in the article and ask Cortana to define it.
- Screenshot B—Using Microsoft Edge, open the website of a fancy restaurant in a city near you. Make sure the Cortana circle icon is displayed in the Address bar. (If it's not displayed, find a different restaurant website.) Click the Cortana circle icon to display a pane with information about the restaurant.
- Screenshot C—Using Microsoft Edge, type **10 USD to Euros** in the Address bar without pressing the Enter key. Cortana converts the U.S. dollars to Euros.
- Screenshot D—Using Microsoft Edge, type **Apple stock** in the Address bar without pressing the Enter key. Cortana displays the current stock quote.

b. Submit your assignment in the format specified by your instructor.

## 2: Viewing Online News with Reading View

*Note*: This activity requires using Microsoft Edge on a Windows 10 computer.

Reading view in Microsoft Edge can make a webpage less cluttered with ads and other distractions. Perform the following tasks:

a. Create a Word document using the Word Screen Clipping tool to capture the following screenshots.

- Screenshot A—Using Microsoft Edge, open the website **mashable.com**. Open a technology article. Click the Reading view button to display an ad-free page that uses only basic text formatting.
- Screenshot B—Using Microsoft Edge, open the website **bbc.com**. Open any news article. Click the Reading view button to display an ad-free page that uses only basic text formatting.
- Screenshot C—Make three types of annotations (Pen, Highlighter, and Add a typed note) on the BBC article page displayed in Reading view.

b. Submit your assignment in the format specified by your instructor.

## 3: Inking with Microsoft Edge

*Note*: This activity requires using Microsoft Edge on a Windows 10 computer.

Microsoft Edge provides many annotation options to record your ideas. Perform the following tasks:

a. Open the website **wolframalpha.com** in the Microsoft Edge browser. Wolfram Alpha is a well-respected academic search engine. Type **US$100 1965 dollars in 2015** in the Wolfram Alpha search text box and press the Enter key.

b. Click the Make a Web Note button to display the Web Note tools. Using the Pen tool, draw a circle around the result on the webpage. Save the page to OneNote.

c. In the Wolfram Alpha search text box, type the name of the city closest to where you live and press the Enter key. Using the Highlighter tool, highlight at least three interesting results. Add a note and then type a sentence about what you learned about this city. Save the page to OneNote. Share your OneNote notebook with your instructor.

d. Submit your assignment link in the format specified by your instructor.

MODULE **1**

# Creating a Database

*Tracking Animal, Visit, and Billing Data*

**ACCESS**

## Case | *Riverview Veterinary Care Center*

Riverview Veterinary Care Center, a veterinary care center in Cody, Wyoming, provides care for pets and livestock in the greater Cody area. In addition to caring for household pets, such as dogs and cats, the center specializes in serving the needs of livestock on ranches in the surrounding area. Kimberly Johnson, the office manager for Riverview Veterinary Care Center, oversees a small staff and is responsible for maintaining the medical records for all of the animals the care center serves.

In order to best manage the center, Kimberly and her staff rely on electronic medical records for information on the animals and their owners, billing, inventory control, purchasing, and accounts payable. Several months ago, the center upgraded to **Microsoft Access 2016** (or simply **Access**), a computer program used to enter, maintain, and retrieve related data in a format known as a database. Kimberly and her staff want to use Access to store information about the animals, their owners, billing, vendors, and products. She asks for your help in creating the necessary Access database.

## STARTING DATA FILES

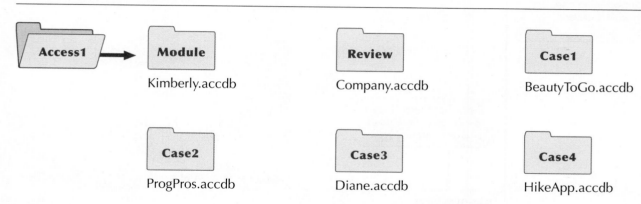

| Access1 → Module | Review | Case1 |
| --- | --- | --- |
| Kimberly.accdb | Company.accdb | BeautyToGo.accdb |

| Case2 | Case3 | Case4 |
| --- | --- | --- |
| ProgPros.accdb | Diane.accdb | HikeApp.accdb |

# Session 1.1 Visual Overview:

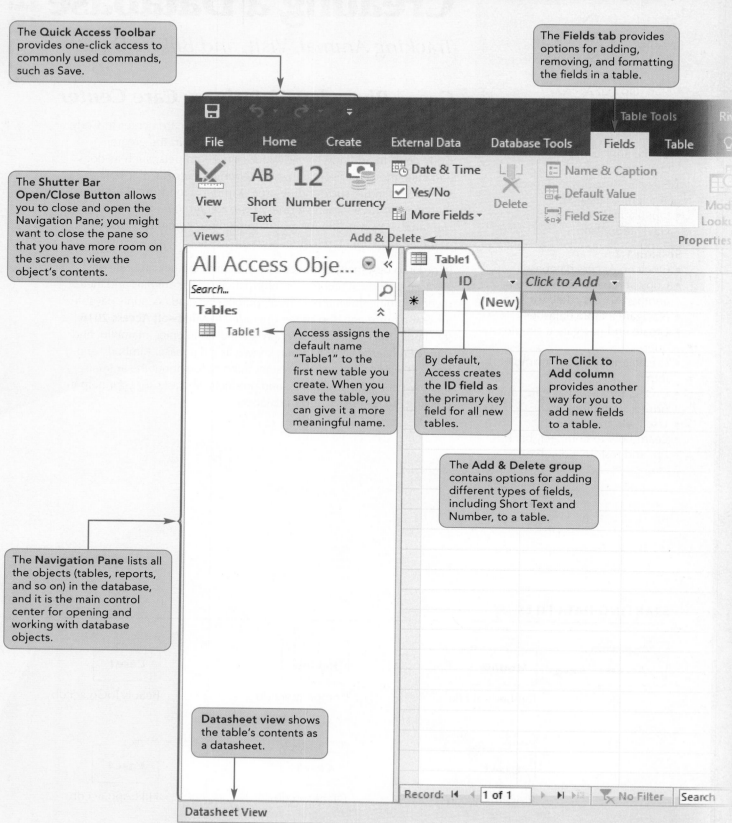

The **Quick Access Toolbar** provides one-click access to commonly used commands, such as Save.

The **Fields tab** provides options for adding, removing, and formatting the fields in a table.

The **Shutter Bar Open/Close Button** allows you to close and open the Navigation Pane; you might want to close the pane so that you have more room on the screen to view the object's contents.

Access assigns the default name "Table1" to the first new table you create. When you save the table, you can give it a more meaningful name.

By default, Access creates the **ID field** as the primary key field for all new tables.

The **Click to Add column** provides another way for you to add new fields to a table.

The **Add & Delete group** contains options for adding different types of fields, including Short Text and Number, to a table.

The **Navigation Pane** lists all the objects (tables, reports, and so on) in the database, and it is the main control center for opening and working with database objects.

**Datasheet view** shows the table's contents as a datasheet.

# The Access Window

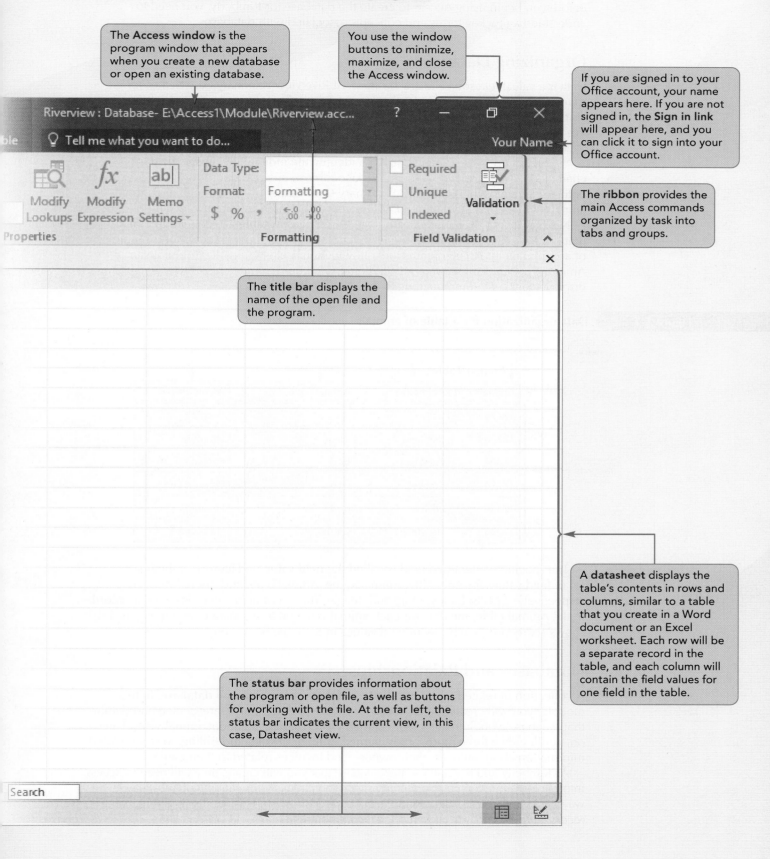

The **Access window** is the program window that appears when you create a new database or open an existing database.

You use the window buttons to minimize, maximize, and close the Access window.

If you are signed in to your Office account, your name appears here. If you are not signed in, the **Sign in link** will appear here, and you can click it to sign into your Office account.

The **ribbon** provides the main Access commands organized by task into tabs and groups.

The **title bar** displays the name of the open file and the program.

A **datasheet** displays the table's contents in rows and columns, similar to a table that you create in a Word document or an Excel worksheet. Each row will be a separate record in the table, and each column will contain the field values for one field in the table.

The **status bar** provides information about the program or open file, as well as buttons for working with the file. At the far left, the status bar indicates the current view, in this case, Datasheet view.

Riverview : Database- E:\Access1\Module\Riverview.acc...

Tell me what you want to do...

Your Name

Data Type:
Format:   Formatting
$  %  ,   ←.0  .00

Required
Unique
Indexed

Validation

Modify Lookups    Modify Expression    Memo Settings

Properties    Formatting    Field Validation

Search

# Introduction to Database Concepts

Before you begin using Access to create the database for Kimberly, you need to understand a few key terms and concepts associated with databases.

## Organizing Data

Data is a valuable resource to any business. At Riverview Veterinary Care Center, for example, important data includes the names of the animals, owners' contact information, visit dates, and billing information. Organizing, storing, maintaining, retrieving, and sorting this type of data are critical activities that enable a business to find and use information effectively. Before storing data on a computer, however, you must organize the data.

Your first step in organizing data is to identify the individual fields. A **field** is a single characteristic or attribute of a person, place, object, event, or idea. For example, some of the many fields that Riverview Veterinary Care Center tracks are the animal ID, animal name, animal type, breed, visit date, reason for visit, and invoice amount.

Next, you group related fields together into tables. A **table** is a collection of fields that describes a person, place, object, event, or idea. Figure 1-1 shows an example of an Animal table that contains the following four fields: AnimalID, AnimalName, AnimalType, and AnimalBreed. Each field is a column in the table, with the field name displayed as the column heading.

| Figure 1-1 | Data organization for a table of animals |
|---|---|

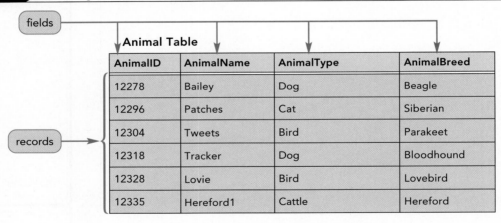

The specific content of a field is called the **field value**. In Figure 1-1, the first set of field values for AnimalID, AnimalName, AnimalType, and AnimalBreed are, respectively: 12278; Bailey; Dog; and Beagle. This set of field values is called a **record**. In the Animal table, the data for each animal is stored as a separate record. Figure 1-1 shows six records; each row of field values in the table is a record.

## Databases and Relationships

A collection of related tables is called a **database**, or a **relational database**. In this module, you will create the database for Riverview Veterinary Care Center, and within that database, you'll create a table named Visit to store data about animal visits. Later on, you'll create three more tables, named Animal, Owner, and Billing, to store related information about animals, their owners, and invoices related to their care.

As Kimberly and her staff use the database that you will create, they will need to access information about animals and their visits. To obtain this information, you must have a way to connect records in the Animal table to records in the Visit table. You connect the records in the separate tables through a **common field** that appears in both tables.

In the sample database shown in Figure 1-2, each record in the Animal table has a field named AnimalID, which is also a field in the Visit table. For example, the beagle named Bailey is the first animal in the Animal table and has an AnimalID field value of 12278. This same AnimalID field value, 12278, appears in two records in the Visit table. Therefore, the beagle named Bailey is the animal that was seen at these two visits.

| Figure 1-2 | Database relationship between tables for animals and visits |

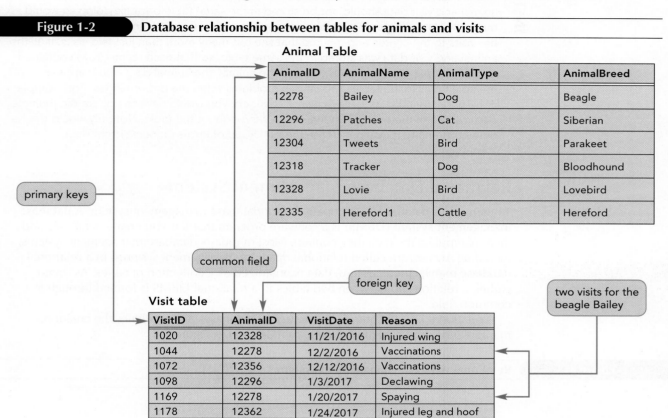

Each AnimalID value in the Animal table must be unique so that you can distinguish one animal from another. These unique AnimalID values also identify each animal's specific visits in the Visit table. The AnimalID field is referred to as the primary key of the Animal table. A **primary key** is a field, or a collection of fields, whose values uniquely identify each record in a table. No two records can contain the same value for the primary key field. In the Visit table, the VisitID field is the primary key because Riverview Veterinary Care Center assigns each visit a unique identification number.

When you include the primary key from one table as a field in a second table to form a relationship between the two tables, it is called a **foreign key** in the second table, as shown in Figure 1-2. For example, AnimalID is the primary key in the Animal table and a foreign key in the Visit table. The AnimalID field must have the same characteristics in both tables. Although the primary key AnimalID contains unique values in the Animal table, the same field as a foreign key in the Visit table does not necessarily contain unique values. The AnimalID value 12278, for example, appears two times in the Visit table because the beagle named Bailey made two visits to the center. Each foreign key value, however, must match one of the field values for the primary key in the other table. In the example shown in Figure 1-2, each AnimalID value in the Visit table must match an AnimalID value in the Animal table. The two tables are related, enabling users to connect the facts about animals with the facts about their visits to the center.

INSIGHT

### Storing Data in Separate Tables

When you create a database, you must create separate tables that contain only fields that are directly related to each other. For example, in the Riverview database, the animal and visit data should not be stored in the same table because doing so would make the data difficult to update and prone to errors. Consider the beagle Bailey and her visits to the center, and assume that she has many more than just two visits. If all the animal and visit data was stored in the same table, so that each record (row) contained all the information about each visit and the animal, the animal data would appear multiple times in the table. This causes problems when the data changes. For example, if the phone number of Bailey's owner changed, you would have to update the multiple occurrences of the owner's phone number throughout the table. Not only would this be time-consuming, it would increase the likelihood of errors or inconsistent data.

## Relational Database Management Systems

To manage its databases, a company uses a database management system. A **database management system (DBMS)** is a software program that lets you create databases and then manipulate the data they contain. Most of today's database management systems, including Access, are called relational database management systems. In a **relational database management system**, data is organized as a collection of tables. As stated earlier, a relationship between two tables in a relational DBMS is formed through a common field.

A relational DBMS controls the storage of databases and facilitates the creation, manipulation, and reporting of data, as illustrated in Figure 1-3.

**Figure 1-3** **Relational database management system**

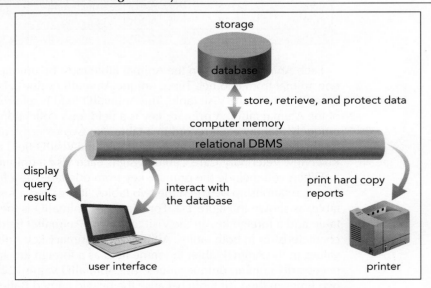

Specifically, a relational DBMS provides the following functions:

- It allows you to create database structures containing fields, tables, and table relationships.
- It lets you easily add new records, change field values in existing records, and delete records.
- It contains a built-in query language, which lets you obtain immediate answers to the questions (or queries) you ask about your data.
- It contains a built-in report generator, which lets you produce professional-looking, formatted reports from your data.
- It protects databases through security, control, and recovery facilities.

An organization such as Riverview Veterinary Care Center benefits from a relational DBMS because it allows users working in different groups to share the same data. More than one user can enter data into a database, and more than one user can retrieve and analyze data that other users have entered. For example, the database for Riverview Veterinary Care Center will contain only one copy of the Visit table, and all employees will use it to access visit information.

Finally, unlike other software programs, such as spreadsheet programs, a DBMS can handle massive amounts of data and can be used to create relationships among multiple tables. Each Access database, for example, can be up to two gigabytes in size, can contain up to 32,768 objects (tables, reports, and so on), and can have up to 255 people using the database at the same time. For instructional purposes, the databases you will create and work with throughout this text contain a relatively small number of records compared to databases you would encounter outside the classroom, which would likely contain tables with very large numbers of records.

## Starting Access and Creating a Database

Now that you've learned some database terms and concepts, you're ready to start Access and create the Riverview database for Kimberly.

**To start Access:**

▶ **1.** On the Windows taskbar, click the **Start** button ⊞. The Start menu opens.

▶ **2.** Click **All apps** on the Start menu, and then click **Access 2016**. Access starts and displays the Recent screen in Backstage view. See Figure 1-4.

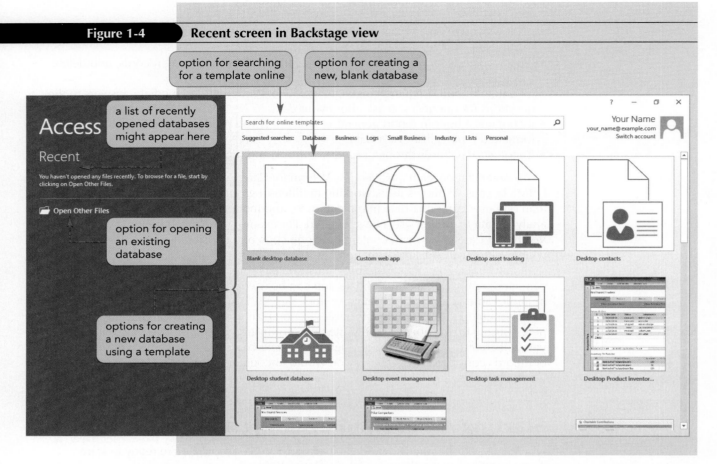

**Figure 1-4**    **Recent screen in Backstage view**

option for searching for a template online

option for creating a new, blank database

a list of recently opened databases might appear here

option for opening an existing database

options for creating a new database using a template

When you start Access, the first screen that appears is Backstage view, which is the starting place for your work in Access. **Backstage view** contains commands that allow you to manage Access files and options. The Recent screen in Backstage view provides options for you to create a new database or open an existing database. To create a new database that does not contain any data or objects, you use the Blank desktop database option. If the database you need to create contains objects that match those found in common databases, such as databases that store data about contacts or tasks, you can use one of the templates provided with Access. A **template** is a predesigned database that includes professionally designed tables, reports, and other database objects that can make it quick and easy for you to create a database. You can also search for a template online using the Search for online templates box.

In this case, the templates provided do not match Kimberly's needs for the center's database, so you need to create a new, blank database from scratch.

### To create the new Riverview database:

 **1.** Make sure you have the Access starting Data Files on your computer.

   **Trouble?** If you don't have the starting Data Files, you need to get them before you can proceed. Your instructor will either give you the Data Files or ask you to obtain them from a specified location (such as a network drive). If you have any questions about the Data Files, see your instructor or technical support person for assistance.

 **2.** On the Recent screen, click **Blank desktop database** (see Figure 1-4). The Blank desktop database screen opens.

Be sure to type **Riverview** or you'll create a database named Database1.

**3.** In the File Name box, type **Riverview** to replace the selected database name provided by Access, Database1. Next you need to specify the location for the file.

**4.** Click the **Browse** button 📁 to the right of the File Name box. The File New Database dialog box opens.

**5.** Navigate to the drive and folder where you are storing your files, as specified by your instructor.

**6.** Make sure the Save as type box displays "Microsoft Access 2007–2016 Databases."

   **Trouble?** If your computer is set up to show filename extensions, you will see the Access filename extension ".accdb" in the File name box.

**TIP**

If you don't type the filename extension, Access adds it automatically.

**7.** Click the **OK** button. You return to the Blank desktop database screen, and the File Name box now shows the name Riverview.accdb. The filename extension ".accdb" identifies the file as an Access 2007–2016 database.

**8.** Click the **Create** button. Access creates the new database, saves it to the specified location, and then opens an empty table named Table1.

   **Trouble?** If you see only ribbon tab names and no buttons, click the Home tab to expand the ribbon, and then in the bottom-right corner of the ribbon, click the Pin the ribbon button 📌.

Refer back to the Session 1.1 Visual Overview and spend some time becoming familiar with the components of the Access window.

**INSIGHT**

### Understanding the Database File Type

Access 2016 uses the .accdb file extension, which is the same file extension used for databases created with Microsoft Access 2007, 2010, and 2013. To ensure compatibility between these earlier versions and the Access 2016 software, new databases created using Access 2016 have the same file extension and file format as Access 2007, Access 2010, and Access 2013 databases. This is why the File New Database dialog box provides the Microsoft Access 2007–2016 Databases option in the Save as type box. In addition, the notation "(Access 2007–2016 file format)" appears in the title bar next to the name of an open database in Access 2016, confirming that database files with the .accdb extension can be used in Access 2007, Access 2010, Access 2013, and Access 2016.

## Working in Touch Mode

**TIP**

On a touch device, you *tap* instead of *click*.

If you are working on a touch device, such as a tablet, you can switch to Touch Mode in Access to make it easier for you to tap buttons on the ribbon and perform other touch actions. Your screens will not match those shown in the book exactly, but this will not cause any problems.

**Note:** The following steps assume that you are using a mouse. If you are instead using a touch device, please read these steps but don't complete them, so that you remain working in Touch Mode.

## To switch to Touch Mode:

▶ **1.** On the Quick Access Toolbar, click the **Customize Quick Access Toolbar** button ⛛. A menu opens listing buttons you can add to the Quick Access Toolbar as well as other options for customizing the toolbar.

**Trouble?** If the Touch/Mouse Mode command on the menu has a checkmark next to it, press the Esc key to close the menu, and then skip to Step 3.

▶ **2.** Click **Touch/Mouse Mode**. The Quick Access Toolbar now contains the Touch/Mouse Mode button 👆, which you can use to switch between Mouse Mode, the default display, and Touch Mode.

▶ **3.** On the Quick Access Toolbar, click the **Touch/Mouse Mode** button 👆. A menu opens with two commands: Mouse, which shows the ribbon in the standard display and is optimized for use with the mouse; and Touch, which provides more space between the buttons and commands on the ribbon and is optimized for use with touch devices. The icon next to Mouse is shaded red to indicate that it is selected.

**Trouble?** If the icon next to Touch is shaded red, press the Esc key to close the menu and skip to Step 5.

▶ **4.** Click **Touch**. The display switches to Touch Mode with more space between the commands and buttons on the ribbon. See Figure 1-5.

| Figure 1-5 | Ribbon displayed in Touch Mode |

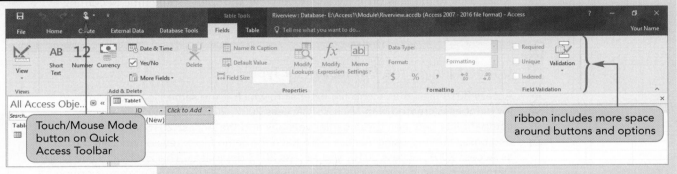

*Touch/Mouse Mode button on Quick Access Toolbar*

*ribbon includes more space around buttons and options*

The figures in this text show the standard Mouse Mode display, and the instructions assume you are using a mouse to click and select options, so you'll switch back to Mouse Mode.

**Trouble?** If you are using a touch device and want to remain in Touch Mode, skip Steps 5 and 6.

▶ **5.** On the Quick Access Toolbar, click the **Touch/Mouse Mode** button 👆, and then click **Mouse**. The ribbon returns to the standard display, as shown in the Session 1.1 Visual Overview.

▶ **6.** On the Quick Access Toolbar, click the **Customize Quick Access Toolbar** button ⛛, and then click **Touch/Mouse Mode** to deselect it. The Touch/Mouse Mode button is removed from the Quick Access Toolbar.

# Creating a Table in Datasheet View

Tables contain all the data in a database and are the fundamental objects for your work in Access. There are different ways to create a table in Access, including entering the fields and records for the table directly in Datasheet view.

### Creating a Table in Datasheet View

- On the ribbon, click the Create tab.
- In the Tables group, click the Table button.
- Rename the default ID primary key field and change its data type, if necessary; or accept the default ID field with the AutoNumber data type.
- In the Add & Delete group on the Fields tab, click the button for the type of field you want to add to the table (for example, click the Short Text button), and then type the field name; or, in the table datasheet, click the Click to Add column heading, click the type of field you want to add from the list that opens, and then press the Tab or Enter key to move to the next column in the datasheet. Repeat this step to add all the necessary fields to the table.
- In the first row below the field names, enter the value for each field in the first record, pressing the Tab or Enter key to move from one field to the next.
- After entering the value for the last field in the first record, press the Tab or Enter key to move to the next row, and then enter the values for the next record. Continue this process until you have entered all the records for the table.
- On the Quick Access Toolbar, click the Save button, enter a name for the table, and then click the OK button.

For Riverview Veterinary Care Center, Kimberly needs to track information about each animal visit at the center. She asks you to create the Visit table according to the plan shown in Figure 1-6.

**Figure 1-6**        **Plan for the Visit table**

| Field | Purpose |
| --- | --- |
| VisitID | Unique number assigned to each visit; will serve as the table's primary key |
| AnimalID | Unique number assigned to each animal; common field that will be a foreign key to connect to the Animal table |
| VisitDate | Date on which the animal visited the center or was seen offsite |
| Reason | Reason/diagnosis for the animal visit |
| OffSite | Whether the animal visit was offsite at a home or ranch |

As shown in Kimberly's plan, she wants to store data about visits in five fields, including fields to contain the date of each visit, the reason for the visit, and if the visit was offsite. These are the most important aspects of a visit and, therefore, must be tracked. Also, notice that the VisitID field will be the primary key for the table; each visit at Riverview Veterinary Care Center has a unique number assigned to it, so this field is the logical choice for the primary key. Finally, the AnimalID field is needed in the Visit table as a foreign key to connect the information about visits to animals. The data about animals, as well as the data about their owners, and the bills for the animals' care, will be stored in separate tables, which you will create later.

Notice the name of each field in Figure 1-6. You need to name each field, table, and object in an Access database.

*Decision Making: Naming Fields in Access Tables*

One of the most important tasks in creating a table is deciding what names to specify for the table's fields. Keep the following guidelines in mind when you assign field names:

- A field name can consist of up to 64 characters, including letters, numbers, spaces, and special characters, except for the period (.), exclamation mark (!), grave accent ('), and square brackets ([ ]).
- A field name cannot begin with a space.
- Capitalize the first letter of each word in a field name that combines multiple words, for example VisitDate.
- Use concise field names that are easy to remember and reference and that won't take up a lot of space in the table datasheet.
- Use standard abbreviations, such as Num for Number, Amt for Amount, and Qty for Quantity, and use them consistently throughout the database. For example, if you use Num for Number in one field name, do not use the number sign (#) for Number in another.
- Give fields descriptive names so that you can easily identify them when you view or edit records.
- Although Access supports the use of spaces in field names (and in other object names), experienced database developers avoid using spaces because they can cause errors when the objects are involved in programming tasks.

By spending time obtaining and analyzing information about the fields in a table, and understanding the rules for naming fields, you can create a well-designed table that will be easy for others to use.

## Renaming the Default Primary Key Field

As noted earlier, Access provides the ID field as the default primary key for a new table you create in Datasheet view. Recall that a primary key is a field, or a collection of fields, whose values uniquely identify each record in a table. However, according to Kimberly's plan, the VisitID field should be the primary key for the Visit table. You'll begin by renaming the default ID field to create the VisitID field.

### To rename the ID field to the VisitID field:

1. Right-click the **ID** column heading to open the shortcut menu, and then click **Rename Field**. The column heading ID is selected, so that whatever text you type next will replace it.

2. Type **VisitID** and then click the row below the heading. The column heading changes to VisitID, and the insertion point moves to the row below the heading. The **insertion point** is a flashing cursor that shows where text you type will be inserted. In this case, it is hidden within the selected field value (New). See Figure 1-7.

   **Trouble?** If you make a mistake while typing the field name, use the Backspace key to delete characters to the left of the insertion point or the Delete key to delete characters to the right of the insertion point. Then type the correct text. To correct a field name by replacing it entirely, press the Esc key, and then type the correct text.

**TIP**

A **shortcut menu** opens when you right-click an object and provides options for working with that object.

**Figure 1-7**          **ID field renamed to VisitID**

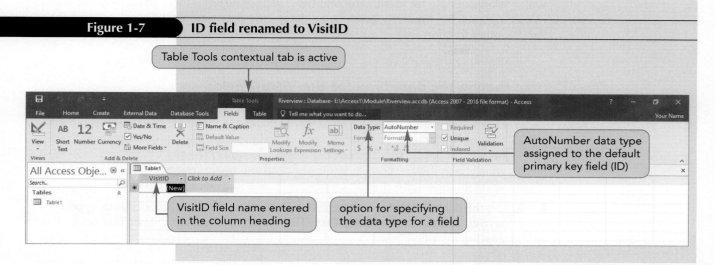

Table Tools contextual tab is active

AutoNumber data type assigned to the default primary key field (ID)

VisitID field name entered in the column heading

option for specifying the data type for a field

Notice that the Table Tools tab is active on the ribbon. This is an example of a **contextual tab**, which is a tab that appears and provides options for working with a specific object that is selected—in this case, the table you are creating. As you work with other objects in the database, other contextual tabs will appear with commands and options related to each selected object.

You have renamed the default primary key field, ID, to VisitID. However, the VisitID field still retains the characteristics of the ID field, including its data type. Your next task is to change the data type of this field.

## Changing the Data Type of the Default Primary Key Field

Notice the Formatting group on the Table Tools Fields tab. One of the options available in this group is the Data Type option (see Figure 1-7). Each field in an Access table must be assigned a data type. The **data type** determines what field values you can enter for the field. In this case, the AutoNumber data type is displayed. Access assigns the AutoNumber data type to the default ID primary key field because the **AutoNumber** data type automatically inserts a unique number in this field for every record, beginning with the number 1 for the first record, the number 2 for the second record, and so on. Therefore, a field using the AutoNumber data type can serve as the primary key for any table you create.

Visit numbers at the Riverview Veterinary Care Center are specific, four-digit numbers, so the AutoNumber data type is not appropriate for the VisitID field, which is the primary key field in the table you are creating. A better choice is the **Short Text** data type, which allows field values containing letters, digits, and other characters, and which is appropriate for identifying numbers, such as visit numbers, that are never used in calculations. So, Kimberly asks you to change the data type for the VisitID field from AutoNumber to Short Text.

### To change the data type for the VisitID field:

▶ 1. Make sure that the VisitID column is selected. A column is selected when you click a field value, in which case the background color of the column heading changes to orange (the default color) and the insertion point appears in the field value. You can also click the column heading to select a column, in which case the background color of both the column heading and the field value changes (the default colors are gray and blue, respectively).

▶ 2. On the Table Tools Fields tab, in the Formatting group, click the **Data Type arrow**, and then click **Short Text**. The VisitID field is now a Short Text field. See Figure 1-8.

---

**Figure 1-8** Short Text data type assigned to the VisitID field

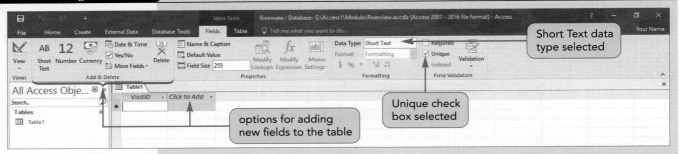

Note the Unique check box in the Field Validation group. This check box is selected because the VisitID field assumed the characteristics of the default primary key field, ID, including the fact that each value in the field must be unique. Because this check box is selected, no two records in the Visit table will be allowed to have the same value in the VisitID field.

With the VisitID field created and established as the primary key, you can now enter the rest of the fields in the Visit table.

## Adding New Fields

When you create a table in Datasheet view, you can use the options in the Add & Delete group on the Table Tools Fields tab to add fields to your table. You can also use the Click to Add column in the table datasheet to add new fields. (See Figure 1-8.) You'll use both methods to add the four remaining fields to the Visit table. The next field you need to add is the AnimalID field. Similar to the VisitID field, the AnimalID field will contain numbers that will not be used in calculations, so it should be a Short Text field.

### To add the rest of the fields to the Visit table:

▶ 1. On the Table Tools Fields tab, in the Add & Delete group, click the **Short Text** button. A new field named "Field1" is added to the right of the VisitID field. See Figure 1-9.

Figure 1-9     New Short Text field added to the table

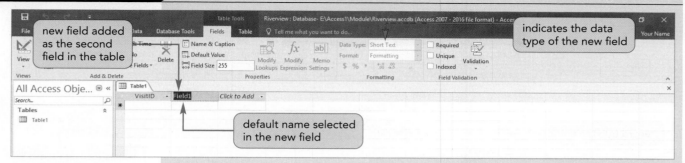

The text "Field1" is selected, so you can simply type the new field name to replace it.

▶ **2.** Type **AnimalID**. The second field is added to the table. Next, you'll add the VisitDate field. Because this field will contain date values, you'll add a field with the **Date/Time** data type, which allows field values in a variety of date and time formats.

▶ **3.** In the Add & Delete group, click the **Date & Time** button. Access adds a third field to the table, this time with the Date/Time data type.

▶ **4.** Type **VisitDate** to replace the selected name "Field1." The fourth field in the Visit table is the Reason field, which will contain brief descriptions of the reason for the visit to the center. You'll add another Short Text field—this time using the Click to Add column.

▶ **5.** Click the **Click to Add** column heading. Access displays a list of available data types from which you can choose the data type for the new field you're adding.

▶ **6.** Click **Short Text** in the list. Access adds a fourth field to the table.

▶ **7.** Type **Reason** to replace the highlighted name "Field1," and then press the **Enter** key. The Click to Add column becomes active and displays the list of field data types.

The fifth and final field in the Visit table is the OffSite field, which will indicate whether or not the visit was at an offsite venue, such as at a home or ranch (that is, not within the center). The **Yes/No** data type is suitable for this field because it is used to define fields that store values representing one of two options—true/false, yes/no, or on/off.

**TIP**

You can also type the first letter of a data type to select it and close the Click to Add list.

▶ **8.** Click **Yes/No** in the list, and then type **OffSite** to replace the highlighted name "Field1."

**Trouble?** If you pressed the Tab or Enter key after typing the OffSite field name, press the Esc key to close the Click to Add list.

▶ **9.** Click in the row below the VisitID column heading. All five fields are now entered for the Visit table. See Figure 1-10.

**Figure 1-10**    **Table with all fields entered**

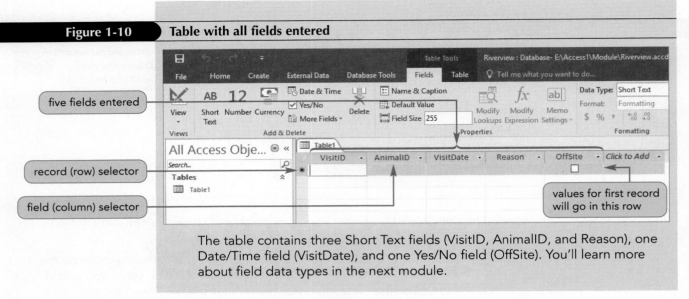

The table contains three Short Text fields (VisitID, AnimalID, and Reason), one Date/Time field (VisitDate), and one Yes/No field (OffSite). You'll learn more about field data types in the next module.

As noted earlier, Datasheet view shows a table's contents in rows (records) and columns (fields). Each column is headed by a field name inside a field selector, and each row has a record selector to its left (see Figure 1-10). Clicking a **field selector** or a **record selector** selects that entire column or row (respectively), which you then can manipulate. A field selector is also called a **column selector**, and a record selector is also called a **row selector**.

## Entering Records

With the fields in place for the table, you can now enter the field values for each record. Kimberly requests that you enter eight records in the Visit table, as shown in Figure 1-11.

**Figure 1-11**    **Visit table records**

| VisitID | AmimalID | VisitDate | Reason | OffSite |
|---------|----------|-----------|--------|---------|
| 1072 | 12356 | 12/12/2016 | Vaccinations | Yes |
| 1169 | 12278 | 1/20/2017 | Spaying | No |
| 1184 | 12443 | 1/25/2017 | Neutering | No |
| 1016 | 12345 | 11/18/2016 | Vaccinations | Yes |
| 1196 | 12455 | 2/1/2017 | Vaccinations | No |
| 1098 | 12296 | 1/3/2017 | Declawing | No |
| 1178 | 12362 | 1/24/2017 | Injured leg and hoof | Yes |
| 1044 | 12278 | 12/2/2016 | Vaccinations | No |

To enter records in a table datasheet, you type the field values below the column headings for the fields. The first record you enter will go in the first row (see Figure 1-10).

### To enter the first record for the Visit table:

Be sure to type the numbers "0" and "1" and not the letters "O" and "I" in the field value.

1. In the first row for the VisitID field, type **1072** (the VisitID field value for the first record), and then press the **Tab** key. Access adds the field value and moves the insertion point to the right, into the AnimalID column. See Figure 1-12.

**Figure 1-12**  First field value entered

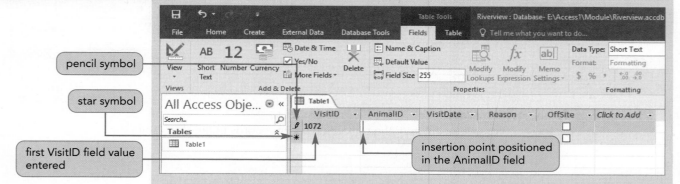

pencil symbol

star symbol

first VisitID field value entered

insertion point positioned in the AnimalID field

**Trouble?** If you make a mistake when typing a value, use the Backspace key to delete characters to the left of the insertion point or the Delete key to delete characters to the right of the insertion point. Then type the correct value. To correct a value by replacing it entirely, press the Esc key, and then type the correct value.

Notice the pencil symbol that appears in the row selector for the new record. The **pencil symbol** indicates that the record is being edited. Also notice the star symbol that appears in the row selector for the second row. The **star symbol** identifies the second row as the next row available for a new record.

2. Type **12356** (the AnimalID field value for the first record), and then press the **Tab** key. Access enters the field value and moves the insertion point to the VisitDate column.

3. Type **12/12/16** (the VisitDate field value for the first record), and then press the **Tab** key. Access displays the year as "2016" even though you entered only the final two digits of the year. This is because the VisitDate field has the Date/Time data type, which automatically formats dates with four-digit years.

4. Type **Vaccinations** (the Reason field value for the first record), and then press the **Tab** key to move to the OffSite column.

   Recall that the OffSite field is a Yes/No field. Notice the check box displayed in the OffSite column. By default, the value for any Yes/No field is "No"; therefore, the check box is initially empty. For Yes/No fields with check boxes, you press the Tab key to leave the check box unchecked, or you press the spacebar to insert a checkmark in the check box. The record you are entering in the table is for an offsite visit, so you need to insert a checkmark in the check box to indicate "Yes."

**TIP**

You can also click a check box in a Yes/No field to insert or remove a checkmark.

5. Press the **spacebar** to insert a checkmark, and then press the **Tab** key. The first record is entered into the table, and the insertion point is positioned in the VisitID field for the second record. The pencil symbol is removed from the first row because the record in that row is no longer being edited. The table is now ready for you to enter the second record. See Figure 1-13.

Figure 1-13 | **Datasheet with first record entered**

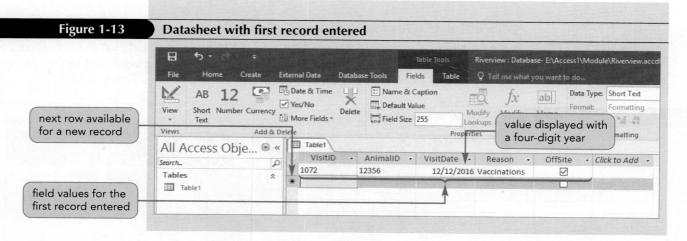

next row available for a new record

value displayed with a four-digit year

field values for the first record entered

Now you can enter the remaining seven records in the Visit table.

**To enter the remaining records in the Visit table:**

1. Referring to Figure 1-11, enter the values for records 2 through 8, pressing the **Tab** key to move from field to field and to the next row for a new record. Keep in mind that you do not have to type all four digits of the year in the VisitDate field values; you can enter only the final two digits, and Access will display all four. Also, for any OffSite field values of "No," be sure to press the Tab key to leave the check box empty.

   **Trouble?** If you enter a value in the wrong field by mistake, such as entering a Reason field value in the VisitDate field, a menu might open with options for addressing the problem. If this happens, click the "Enter new value" option in the menu. You'll return to the field with the incorrect value selected, which you can then replace by typing the correct value.

   Notice that not all of the Reason field values are fully displayed. To see more of the table datasheet and the full field values, you'll close the Navigation Pane and resize the Reason column.

2. At the top of the Navigation Pane, click the **Shutter Bar Open/Close Button** «. The Navigation Pane closes, and only the complete table datasheet is displayed.

3. Place the pointer on the vertical line to the right of the Reason field name until the pointer changes to ↔, and then double-click the vertical line. All the Reason field values are now fully displayed. See Figure 1-14.

**Figure 1-14**  **Datasheet with eight records entered**

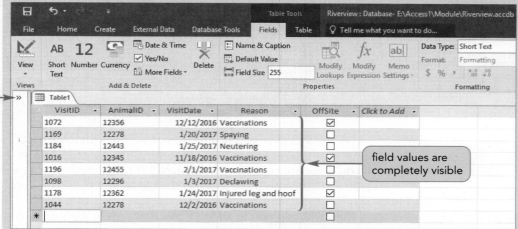

Navigation Pane is closed

field values are completely visible

When you resize a datasheet column by double-clicking the column dividing line, you are sizing the column to its **best fit**—that is, so the column is just wide enough to display the longest visible value in the column, including the field name.

Carefully compare your VisitID and AnimalID values with those in the figure, and correct any errors before continuing.

4. Compare your table to the one in Figure 1-14. If any of the field values in your table do not match those shown in the figure, you can correct a field value by clicking to position the insertion point in the value, and then using the Backspace key or Delete key to delete incorrect text. Then type the correct text and press the Enter key. To correct a value in the OffSite field, simply click the check box to add or remove the checkmark as appropriate. Also, be sure the spelling and capitalization of field names in your table match those shown in the figure exactly and that there are no spaces between words. To correct a field name, double-click it to select it, and then type the correct name; or use the Rename Field option on the shortcut menu to rename a field with the correct name.

## Saving a Table

The records you enter are immediately stored in the database as soon as you enter them; however, the table's design—the field names and characteristics of the fields themselves, plus any layout changes to the datasheet—are not saved until you save the table. When you save a new table for the first time, you should give it a name that best identifies the information it contains. Like a field name, a table name can contain up to 64 characters, including spaces.

**REFERENCE**

*Saving a Table*

- Make sure the table you want to save is open.
- On the Quick Access Toolbar, click the Save button. The Save As dialog box opens.
- In the Table Name box, type the name for the table.
- Click the OK button.

According to Kimberly's plan, you need to save the table with the name "Visit."

### To save and name the Visit table:

1. On the Quick Access Toolbar, click the **Save** button 🖫. The Save As dialog box opens.

2. With the default name Table1 selected in the Table Name box, type **Visit**, and then click the **OK** button. The tab for the table now displays the name "Visit," and the Visit table design is saved in the Riverview database.

Notice that after you saved and named the Visit table, Access sorted and displayed the records in order by the values in the VisitID field because it is the primary key. If you compare your screen to Figure 1-11, which shows the records in the order you entered them, you'll see that the current screen shows the records in order by the VisitID field values.

Kimberly asks you to add two more records to the Visit table. When you add a record to an existing table, you must enter the new record in the next row available for a new record; you cannot insert a row between existing records for the new record. In a table with just a few records, such as the Visit table, the next available row is visible on the screen. However, in a table with hundreds of records, you would need to scroll the datasheet to see the next row available. The easiest way to add a new record to a table is to use the New button, which scrolls the datasheet to the next row available so you can enter the new record.

### To enter additional records in the Visit table:

1. If necessary, click the first record's VisitID field value (**1016**) to make it the current record.

2. On the ribbon, click the **Home** tab.

3. In the Records group, click the **New** button. The insertion point is positioned in the next row available for a new record, which in this case is row 9. See Figure 1-15.

---

**Figure 1-15** | **Entering a new record**

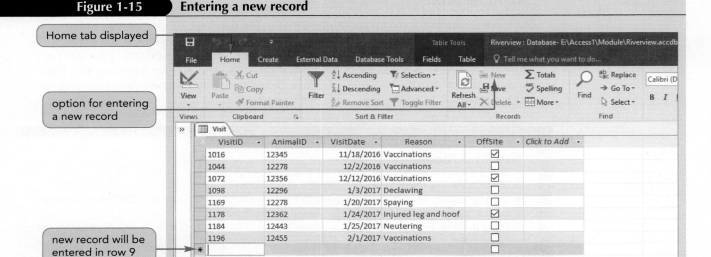

**4.** With the insertion point in the VisitID field for the new record, type **1036** and then press the **Tab** key.

**5.** Complete the entry of this record by entering each value shown below, pressing the **Tab** key to move from field to field:

AnimalID = **12294**

VisitDate = **11/29/2016**

Reason = **Declawing**

OffSite = **No (unchecked)**

**6.** Enter the values for the next new record, as follows, and then press the **Tab** key after entering the OffSite field value:

VisitID = **1152**

AnimalID = **12318**

VisitDate = **1/13/2017**

Reason = **Not eating**

OffSite = **No (unchecked)**

Your datasheet should now look like the one shown in Figure 1-16.

| Figure 1-16 | Datasheet with additional records entered |

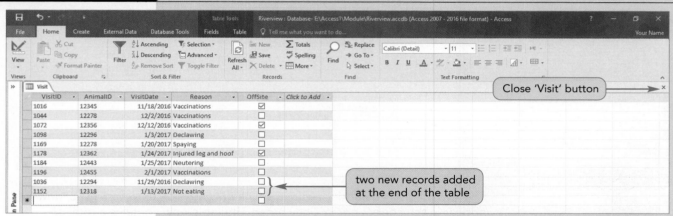

The new records you added appear at the end of the table, and are not sorted in order by the primary key field values. For example, VisitID 1036 should be the second record in the table, placed between VisitID 1016 and VisitID 1044. When you add records to a table datasheet, they appear at the end of the table. The records are not displayed in primary key order until you either close and reopen the table or switch between views.

**7.** Click the **Close 'Visit'** button ⊠ on the object tab (see Figure 1-16 for the location of this button). The Visit table closes, and the main portion of the Access window is now blank because no database object is currently open. The Riverview database file is still open, as indicated by the filename in the Access window title bar.

## Opening a Table

The tables in a database are listed in the Navigation Pane. You open a table, or any Access object, by double-clicking the object name in the Navigation Pane. Next, you'll open the Visit table so you can see all the records you've entered in the correct primary key order.

**To open the Visit table:**

▶ **1.** On the Navigation Pane, click the **Shutter Bar Open/Close Button** ≫ to open the pane. Note that the Visit table is listed.

▶ **2.** Double-click **Visit** to open the table in Datasheet view. See Figure 1-17.

**Figure 1-17** Table with 10 records entered and displayed in primary key order

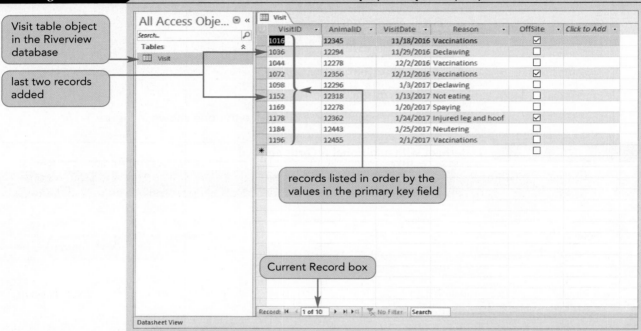

Visit table object in the Riverview database

last two records added

records listed in order by the values in the primary key field

Current Record box

The two records you added, with VisitID field values of 1036 and 1152, now appear in the correct primary key order. The table now contains a total of 10 records, as indicated by the Current Record box at the bottom of the datasheet. The **Current Record box** displays the number of the current record as well as the total number of records in the table.

Each record contains a unique VisitID value because this field is the primary key. Other fields, however, can contain the same value in multiple records; for example, note the four values of "Vaccinations" in the Reason field.

# Closing a Table and Exiting Access

When you are finished working in an Access table, it's a good idea to close the table so that you do not make unintended changes to the table data. You can close a table by clicking its Close button on the object tab, as you did earlier. Or, if you want to close the Access program as well, you can click the program's Close button. When you do, any open tables are closed, the active database is closed, and you exit the Access program.

**To close the Visit table and exit Access:**

**TIP**

To close a database without exiting Access, click the File tab to display Backstage view, and then click Close.

1. Click the **Close** button ✕ on the program window title bar. The Visit table and the Riverview database close, and then the Access program closes.

**INSIGHT**

### Saving a Database

Unlike the Save buttons in other Office programs, the Save button on the Quick Access Toolbar in Access does not save the active document (database). Instead, you use the Save button to save the design of an Access object, such as a table (as you saw earlier), or to save datasheet format changes, such as resizing columns. Access does not have a button or option you can use to save the active database.

Access saves changes to the active database automatically when you change or add a record or close the database. If your database is stored on a removable storage device, such as a USB drive, you should never remove the device while the database file is open. If you do, Access will encounter problems when it tries to save the database, which might damage the database. Make sure you close the database first before removing the storage device.

Now that you've become familiar with database concepts and Access, and created the Riverview database and the Visit table, Kimberly wants you to add more records to the table and work with the data stored in it to create database objects including a query, form, and report. You'll complete these tasks in the next session.

**REVIEW**

### Session 1.1 Quick Check

1. A(n) _____ is a single characteristic of a person, place, object, event, or idea.

2. You connect the records in two separate tables through a(n) _____ that appears in both tables.

3. The _____, whose values uniquely identify each record in a table, is called a(n) _____ when it is placed in a second table to form a relationship between the two tables.

4. The _____ is the area of the Access window that lists all the objects in a database, and it is the main control center for opening and working with database objects.

5. What is the name of the field that Access creates, by default, as the primary key field for a new table in Datasheet view?

6. Which group on the Fields tab contains the options you use to add new fields to a table?

7. What does a pencil symbol at the beginning of a record represent? What does a star symbol represent?

8. Explain how the saving process in Access is different from saving in other Office programs.

# Session 1.2 Visual Overview:

The **Create tab** provides options for creating various database objects, including tables, forms, and reports. The options appear on the tab grouped by object type.

The **Query Wizard button** opens a dialog box with different types of wizards that guide you through the steps to create a query. One of these, the **Simple Query Wizard**, allows you to select records and fields quickly to display in the query results.

You use the options in the Tables group to create a table in Datasheet view or in Design view.

The Forms group contains options for creating a **form**, which is a database object you use to enter, edit, and view records in a database.

The **Form tool** quickly creates a form containing all the fields in the table (or query) on which you're basing the form.

The **Form Wizard** guides you through the process of creating a form.

The Queries group contains options for creating a **query**, which is a question you ask about the data stored in a database. In response to a query, Access displays the specific records and fields that answer your question.

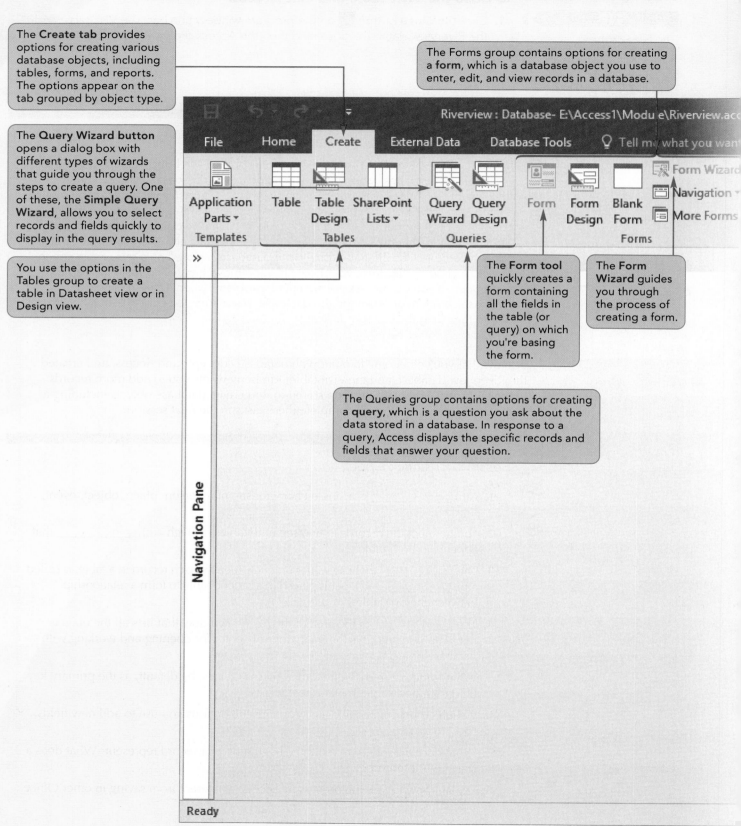

# The Create Tab Options

The Reports group contains options for creating a **report**, which is a formatted printout (or screen display) of the contents of one of more tables (or queries) in a database.

The Microsoft Access Help button opens the **Access 2016 Help** window, where you can find information about Access commands and features as well as instructions for using them.

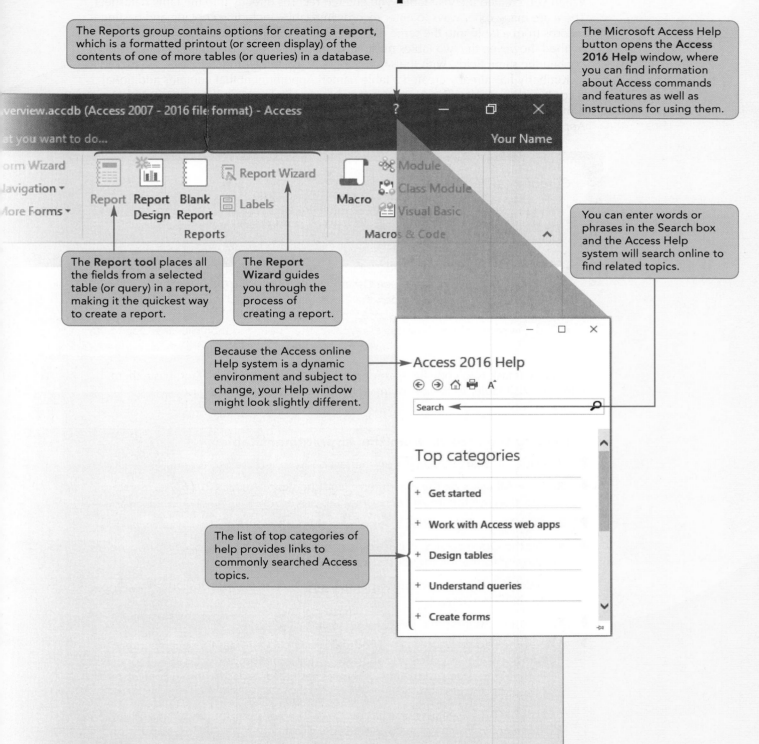

The **Report tool** places all the fields from a selected table (or query) in a report, making it the quickest way to create a report.

The **Report Wizard** guides you through the process of creating a report.

You can enter words or phrases in the Search box and the Access Help system will search online to find related topics.

Because the Access online Help system is a dynamic environment and subject to change, your Help window might look slightly different.

The list of top categories of help provides links to commonly searched Access topics.

# Copying Records from Another Access Database

When you created the Visit table, you entered records directly into the table datasheet. There are many other ways to enter records in a table, including copying and pasting records from a table into the same database or into a different database. To use this method, however, the two tables must have the same structure—that is, the tables must contain the same fields, with the same design, in the same order.

Kimberly has already created a table named Appointment that contains additional records with visit data. The Appointment table is contained in a database named Kimberly located in the Access1 > Module folder included with your Data Files. The Appointment table has the same table structure as the Visit table you created.

**REFERENCE**

### Opening a Database

- Start Access and display the Recent screen in Backstage view.
- Click the name of the database you want to open in the list of recently opened databases.

*or*

- Start Access and display the Recent screen in Backstage view.
- In the navigation bar, click Open Other Files to display the Open screen.
- Click the Browse button to open the Open dialog box, and then navigate to the drive and folder containing the database file you want to open.
- Click the name of the database file you want to open, and then click the Open button.

Your next task is to copy the records from the Appointment table and paste them into your Visit table. To do so, you need to open the Kimberly database.

### To copy the records from the Appointment table:

1. Click the **Start** button ⊞ on the taskbar to open the Start menu.

2. Click **All apps** on the Start menu, and then click **Access 2016**. Access starts and displays the Recent screen in Backstage view.

3. Click **Open Other Files** to display the Open screen in Backstage view.

4. On the Open screen, click **Browse**. The Open dialog box opens, showing folder information for your computer.

   **Trouble?** If you are storing your files on OneDrive, click OneDrive, and then log in if necessary.

5. Navigate to the drive that contains your Data Files.

6. Navigate to the **Access1 > Module** folder, click the database file named **Kimberly**, and then click the **Open** button. The Kimberly database opens in the Access program window. Note that the database contains only one object, the Appointment table.

   **Trouble?** If a security warning appears below the ribbon indicating that some active content has been disabled, click the Enable Content button. Access provides this warning because some databases might contain content that could harm your computer. Because the Kimberly database does not contain objects that could be harmful, you can open it safely. If you are accessing the file over a network, you might also see a dialog box asking if you want to make the file a trusted document; click Yes.

**7.** In the Navigation Pane, double-click **Appointment** to open the Appointment table in Datasheet view. The table contains 65 records and the same five fields, with the same characteristics, as the fields in the Visit table. See Figure 1-18.

| Figure 1-18 | Appointment table in the Kimberly database |

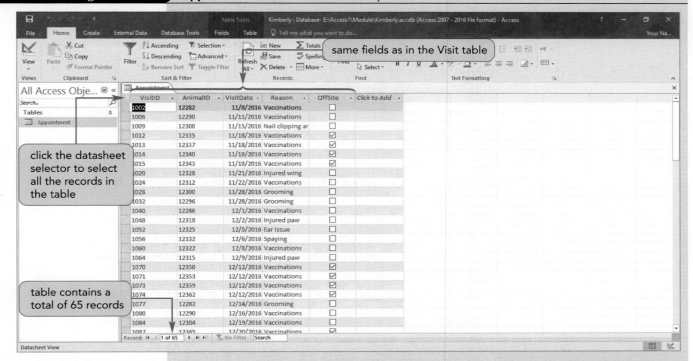

Kimberly wants you to copy all the records in the Appointment table. You can select all the records by clicking the **datasheet selector**, which is the box to the left of the first field name in the table datasheet, as shown in Figure 1-18.

**8.** Click the **datasheet selector** to the left of the VisitID field. All the records in the table are selected.

**9.** On the Home tab, in the Clipboard group, click the **Copy** button. All the records are copied to the Clipboard.

**10.** Click the **Close 'Appointment'** button ☒ on the object tab. A dialog box opens asking if you want to save the data you copied to the Clipboard. This dialog box opens only when you copy a large amount of data to the Clipboard.

**11.** Click the **Yes** button. The dialog box closes, and then the Appointment table closes.

With the records copied to the Clipboard, you can now paste them into the Visit table. First you need to close the Kimberly database while still keeping the Access program open, and then open the Riverview database.

**To close the Kimberly database and then paste the records into the Visit table:**

▶ **1.** Click the **File** tab to open Backstage view, and then click **Close** in the navigation bar to close the Kimberly database. You return to a blank Access program window, and the Home tab is the active tab on the ribbon.

▶ **2.** Click the **File** tab to return to Backstage view, and then click **Open** in the navigation bar. Recent is selected on the Open screen, and the recently opened database files are listed. This list should include the Riverview database.

▶ **3.** Click **Riverview** to open the Riverview database file.

**Trouble?** If the Riverview database file is not in the list of recent files, click Browse. In the Open dialog box, navigate to the drive and folder where you are storing your files, and then open the Riverview database file.

**Trouble?** If the security warning appears below the ribbon, click the Enable Content button, and then, if necessary, click Yes to identify the file as a trusted document.

▶ **4.** In the Navigation Pane, double-click **Visit** to open the Visit table in Datasheet view.

▶ **5.** On the Navigation Pane, click the **Shutter Bar Open/Close Button** ⟨⟨ to close the pane.

▶ **6.** Position the pointer on the star symbol in the row selector for row 11 (the next row available for a new record) until the pointer changes to ➡, and then click to select the row.

▶ **7.** On the Home tab, in the Clipboard group, click the **Paste** button. The pasted records are added to the table, and a dialog box opens asking you to confirm that you want to paste all the records (65 total).

**Trouble?** If the Paste button isn't active, click the ➡ pointer on the row selector for row 11, making sure the entire row is selected, and then repeat Step 7.

▶ **8.** Click the **Yes** button. The dialog box closes, and the pasted records are selected. See Figure 1-19. Notice that the table now contains a total of 75 records—10 records that you entered previously and 65 records that you copied and pasted.

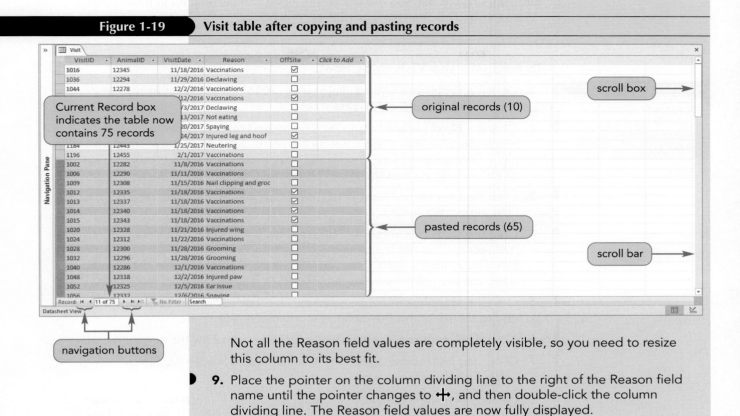

**Figure 1-19**    Visit table after copying and pasting records

Not all the Reason field values are completely visible, so you need to resize this column to its best fit.

**9.** Place the pointer on the column dividing line to the right of the Reason field name until the pointer changes to ✛, and then double-click the column dividing line. The Reason field values are now fully displayed.

# Navigating a Datasheet

The Visit table now contains 75 records, but only some of the records are visible on the screen. To view fields or records not currently visible on the screen, you can use the horizontal and vertical scroll bars to navigate the data. The **navigation buttons**, shown in Figure 1-19 and also described in Figure 1-20, provide another way to move vertically through the records. The Current Record box appears between the two sets of navigation buttons and displays the number of the current record as well as the total number of records in the table. Figure 1-20 shows which record becomes the current record when you click each navigation button. Note the New (blank) record button, which works in the same way as the New button on the Home tab you used earlier to enter a new record in the table.

**Figure 1-20**    Navigation buttons

| Navigation Button | Record Selected | Navigation Button | Record Selected |
|---|---|---|---|
| ◄ | First record | ►| | Last record |
| ◄ | Previous record | ►* | New (blank) record |
| ► | Next record | | |

Kimberly suggests that you use the various navigation techniques to move through the Visit table and become familiar with its contents.

### To navigate the Visit datasheet:

**TIP**

You can make a field the current field by clicking anywhere within the column for that field.

▶ **1.** Click the first record's VisitID field value (**1016**). The Current Record box shows that record 1 is the current record.

▶ **2.** Click the **Next record** button ▶. The second record is now highlighted, which identifies it as the current record. Also, notice that the second record's value for the VisitID field is selected, and the Current Record box displays "2 of 75" to indicate that the second record is the current record.

▶ **3.** Click the **Last record** button ▶|. The last record in the table, record 75, is now the current record.

▶ **4.** Drag the scroll box in the vertical scroll bar up to the top of the bar. Notice that record 75 is still the current record, as indicated in the Current Record box. Dragging the scroll box changes the display of the table datasheet, but does not change the current record.

▶ **5.** Drag the scroll box in the vertical scroll bar back down until you can see the end of the table and the current record (record 75).

▶ **6.** Click the **Previous record** button ◀. Record 74 is now the current record.

▶ **7.** Click the **First record** button |◀. The first record is now the current record and is visible on the screen.

Earlier you resized the Reason column to its best fit, to ensure all the field values were visible. However, when you resize a column to its best fit, the column expands to fully display only the field values that are visible on the screen at that time. If you move through the complete datasheet and notice that not all of the field values are fully displayed after conducting the resizing process on the records initially visible, you need to repeat the resizing process.

▶ **8.** Scroll down through the records and observe if the field values are fully displayed. In this case, all of the fields are fully visible, so there is no need to resize any of the field columns.

The Visit table now contains all the data about animal visits for Riverview Veterinary Care Center. To better understand how to work with this data, Kimberly asks you to create simple objects for the other main types of database objects—queries, forms, and reports.

## Creating a Simple Query

As noted earlier, a query is a question you ask about the data stored in a database. When you create a query, you tell Access which fields you need and what criteria it should use to select the records that will answer your question. Then Access displays only the information you want, so you don't have to navigate through the entire database for the information. In the Visit table, for example, Kimberly might create a query to display only those records for visits that occurred in a specific month. Even though a query can display table information in a different way, the information still exists in the table as it was originally entered.

Kimberly wants to see a list of all the visit dates and reasons for visits in the Visit table. She doesn't want the list to include all the fields in the table, such as AnimalID and OffSite. To produce this list for Kimberly, you'll use the Simple Query Wizard to create a query based on the Visit table.

### To start the Simple Query Wizard:

▶ 1. On the ribbon, click the **Create** tab.

▶ 2. In the Queries group, click the **Query Wizard** button. The New Query dialog box opens.

▶ 3. Make sure **Simple Query Wizard** is selected, and then click the **OK** button. The first Simple Query Wizard dialog box opens. See Figure 1-21.

| Figure 1-21 | First Simple Query Wizard dialog box |

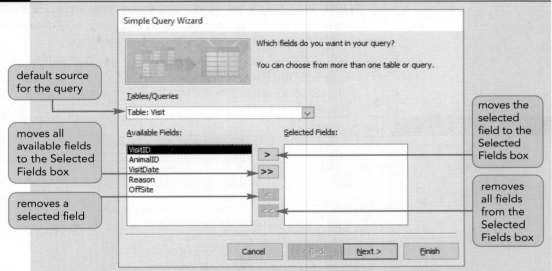

Because the Visit table is the only object in the Riverview database, it is listed in the Tables/Queries box by default. If the database contained more objects, you could click the Tables/Queries arrow and choose another table or a query as the basis for the new query you are creating. The Available Fields box lists all the fields in the Visit table.

You need to select fields from the Available Fields box to include them in the query. To select fields one at a time, click a field and then click the  >  button. The selected field moves from the Available Fields box on the left to the Selected Fields box on the right. To select all the fields, click the  >>  button. If you change your mind or make a mistake, you can remove a field by clicking it in the Selected Fields box and then clicking the  <  button. To remove all fields from the Selected Fields box, click the  <<  button.

Each Simple Query Wizard dialog box contains buttons on the bottom that allow you to move to the previous dialog box (Back button), move to the next dialog box (Next button), or cancel the creation process (Cancel button). You can also finish creating the object (Finish button) and accept the wizard's defaults for the remaining options.

Kimberly wants her query results to list to include data from only the following fields: VisitID, VisitDate, and Reason. You need to select these fields to include them in the query.

**TIP**

You can also double-click a field to move it from the Available Fields box to the Selected Fields box.

## To create the query using the Simple Query Wizard:

▶ 1. Click **VisitID** in the Available Fields box to select the field (if necessary), and then click the  >  button. The VisitID field moves to the Selected Fields box.

▶ 2. Repeat Step 1 for the fields **VisitDate** and **Reason**, and then click the **Next** button. The second, and final, Simple Query Wizard dialog box opens and asks you to choose a name (title) for your query. The suggested name is "Visit Query" because the query you are creating is based on the Visit table. You'll change the suggested name to "VisitList."

▶ 3. Click at the end of the suggested name, use the **Backspace** key to delete the word "Query" and the space, and then type **List**. Now you can view the query results.

▶ 4. Click the **Finish** button to complete the query. The query results are displayed in Datasheet view, on a new tab named "VisitList." A query datasheet is similar to a table datasheet, showing fields in columns and records in rows—but only for those fields and records you want to see, as determined by the query specifications you select.

▶ 5. Place the pointer on the column divider line to the right of the Reason field name until the pointer changes to ↔, and then double-click the column divider line to resize the Reason field. See Figure 1-22.

| Figure 1-22 | Query results |
| --- | --- |

only the three specified fields are displayed in the query datasheet

all 75 records are included in the results

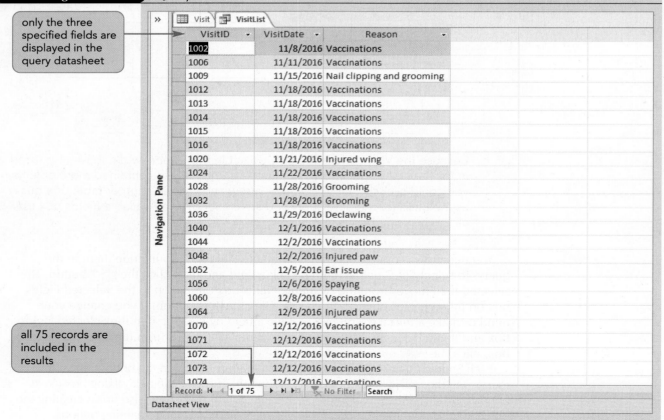

The VisitList query datasheet displays the three fields in the order you selected them in the Simple Query Wizard, from left to right. The records are listed in order by the primary key field, VisitID. Even though the query datasheet displays only the three fields you chose for the query, the Visit table still includes all the fields for all records.

Notice that the navigation buttons are located at the bottom of the window. You navigate a query datasheet in the same way that you navigate a table datasheet.

6. Click the **Last record** button ▶|. The last record in the query datasheet is now the current record.
7. Click the **Previous record** button ◀. Record 74 in the query datasheet is now the current record.
8. Click the **First record** button |◀. The first record is now the current record.
9. Click the **Close 'VisitList'** button ✕ on the object tab. A dialog box opens asking if you want to save the changes to the layout of the query. This dialog box opens because you resized the Reason column.
10. Click the **Yes** button to save the query layout changes and close the query.

The query results are not stored in the database; however, the query design is stored as part of the database with the name you specified. You can re-create the query results at any time by opening the query again. When you open the query at a later date, the results displayed will reflect up-to-date information to include any new records entered in the Visit table.

Next, Kimberly asks you to create a form for the Visit table so that Riverview Veterinary Care Center staff can use the form to enter and work with data in the table easily.

# Creating a Simple Form

As noted earlier, you use a form to enter, edit, and view records in a database. Although you can perform these same functions with tables and queries, forms can present data in many customized and useful ways.

Kimberly wants a form for the Visit table that shows all the fields for one record at a time, with fields listed one below another in a column. This type of form will make it easier for her staff to focus on all the data for a particular visit. You'll use the Form tool to create this form quickly and easily.

## To create the form using the Form tool:

1. Make sure the Visit table is still open in Datasheet view. The table or other database object you're using as the basis for the form must either be open or selected in the Navigation Pane when you use the Form tool.

   **Trouble?** If the Visit table is not open, click the Shutter Bar Open/Close Button » to open the Navigation Pane. Then double-click Visit to open the Visit table in Datasheet view. Click the Shutter Bar Open/Close Button « to close the pane.

2. On the ribbon, click the **Create** tab if necessary.

**3.** In the Forms group, click the **Form** button. The Form tool creates a simple form showing every field in the Visit table and places it on a tab named "Visit" because the form is based on the Visit table. See Figure 1-23.

**Figure 1-23** **Form created by the Form tool**

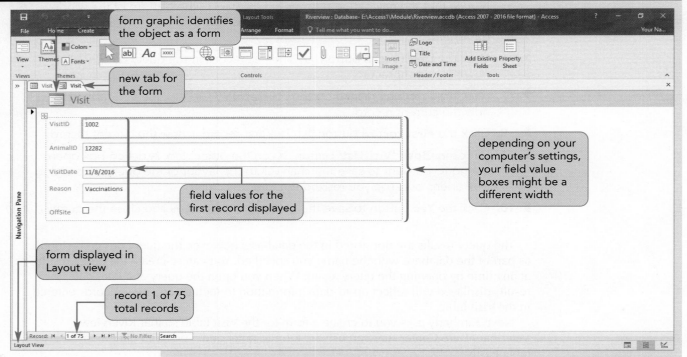

**Trouble?** Depending on the size of your monitor and your screen resolution settings, the fields in your form might appear in multiple columns instead of a single column. This difference will not present any problems.

The form displays one record at a time in the Visit table, providing another view of the data that is stored in the table and allowing you to focus on the values for one record. Access displays the field values for the first record in the table and selects the first field value (VisitID) as indicated by the border that appears around the value. Each field name appears on a separate line and on the same line as its field value, which appears in a box to the right. Depending on your computer's settings, the field value boxes in your form might be wider or narrower than those shown in the figure. As indicated in the status bar, the form is displayed in Layout view. In **Layout view**, you can make design changes to the form while it is displaying data, so that you can see the effects of the changes you make immediately.

To view, enter, and maintain data using a form, you must know how to move from field to field and from record to record. Notice that the form contains navigation buttons, similar to those available in Datasheet view, which you can use to display different records in the form. You'll use these now to navigate the form; then you'll save and close the form.

**To navigate, save, and close the form:**

▶ **1.** Click the **Next record** button ▶. The form now displays the values for the second record in the Visit table.

▶ **2.** Click the **Last record** button ▶I to move to the last record in the table. The form displays the information for VisitID 1196.

▶ **3.** Click the **Previous record** button ◀ to move to record 74.

▶ **4.** Click the **First record** button I◀ to return to the first record in the Visit table.

▶ **5.** Next, you'll save the form with the name "VisitData" in the Riverview database. Then the form will be available for later use.

▶ **6.** On the Quick Access Toolbar, click the **Save** button 🖫. The Save As dialog box opens.

▶ **7.** In the Form Name box, click at the end of the selected name "Visit," type **Data**, and then press the **Enter** key. The dialog box closes and the form is saved as VisitData in the Riverview database. The tab containing the form now displays the name VisitData.

▶ **8.** Click the **Close 'VisitData'** button ✖ on the object tab to close the form.

### Saving Database Objects

In general, it is best to save a database object—query, form, or report—only if you anticipate using the object frequently or if it is time-consuming to create, because all objects use storage space and increase the size of the database file. For example, you most likely would not save a form you created with the Form tool because you can re-create it easily with one mouse click. (However, for the purposes of this text, you usually need to save the objects you create.)

Kimberly would like to see the information in the Visit table presented in a more readable and professional format. You'll help Kimberly by creating a report.

# Creating a Simple Report

As noted earlier, a report is a formatted printout (or screen display) of the contents of one or more tables or queries. You'll use the Report tool to quickly produce a report based on the Visit table for Kimberly. The Report tool creates a report based on the selected table or query.

**To create the report using the Report tool:**

▶ **1.** On the ribbon, click the **Create** tab.

▶ **2.** In the Reports group, click the **Report** button. The Report tool creates a simple report showing every field in the Visit table and places it on a tab named "Visit" because the object you created (the report) is based on the Visit table. See Figure 1-24.

**Figure 1-24** **Report created by the Report tool**

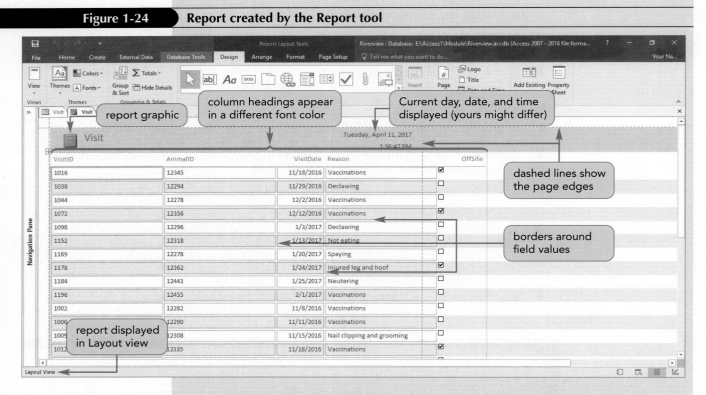

**Trouble?** The records in your report might appear in a different order from the records shown in Figure 1-24. This difference will not cause any problems.

The report shows each field in a column, with the field values for each record in a row, similar to a table or query datasheet. However, the report offers a more visually appealing format for the data, with the column headings in a different color, borders around each field value, a graphic of a report at the top left, and the current day, date, and time at the top right. Also notice the dashed horizontal and vertical lines on the top and right, respectively; these lines mark the edges of the page and show where text will print on the page.

The report needs some design changes to better display the data. The columns are much wider than necessary for the VisitID and AnimalID fields, and the Reason and OffSite field values and borders are not completely displayed within the page area defined by the dashed lines, which means they would not appear on the same page as the rest of the fields in the printed report. You can resize the columns easily in Layout view.

### To resize the VisitID and AnimalID columns:

1. Position the pointer on the right border of any field value in the VisitID column until the pointer changes to ↔.

2. Click and drag the mouse to the left. Notice the dark outlines surrounding the field names and field values indicating the changing column width.

3. Drag to the left until the column is slightly wider than the VisitID field name, and then release the mouse button. The VisitID column is now narrower, and the other four columns have shifted to the left. The Reason and OffSite fields, values, and borders are now completely within the page area. See Figure 1-25.

Figure 1-25   Report after resizing the VisitID column

Figure 1-25   Report after resizing the VisitID column

field values and borders are now within the page border marked by the dashed lines

column is now narrower

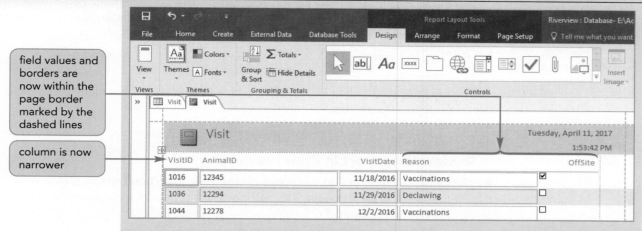

4. Click the first field value for AnimalID. AnimalID is now the current field.

5. Position the pointer on the right border of the first value in the AnimalID column until the pointer changes to ↔, click and drag to the left until the column is slightly wider than its field name, and then release the mouse button.

6. Drag the scroll box on the vertical scroll bar down to the bottom of the report to check its entire layout.

   The Report tool displays the number "75" at the bottom left of the report, showing the total number of records in the report and the table on which it is based—the Visit table. The Report tool also displays the page number at the bottom right, but the text "Page 1 of 1" appears cut off through the vertical dashed line. This will cause a problem when you print the report, so you need to move this text to the left.

7. Click anywhere on the words **Page 1 of 1**. An orange outline appears around the text, indicating it is selected. See Figure 1-26.

Figure 1-26   Report page number selected

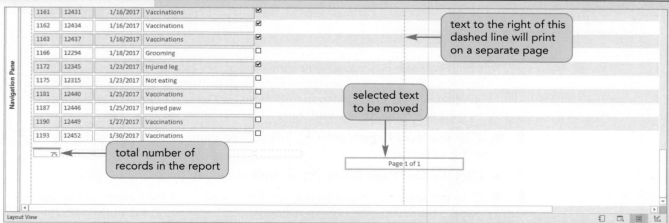

text to the right of this dashed line will print on a separate page

selected text to be moved

total number of records in the report

Page 1 of 1

With the text selected, you can use the keyboard arrow keys to move it.

**TIP**

You can also use the mouse to drag the selected page number, but the arrow key is more precise.

8. Press the ← key repeatedly until the selected page number is to the left of the vertical dashed line (roughly 35 times). The page number text is now completely within the page area and will print on the same page as the rest of the report.

9. Drag the vertical scroll box up to redisplay the top of the report.

The report is displayed in Layout view, which doesn't show how many pages there are in the report. To see this, you need to switch to Print Preview.

### To view the report in Print Preview:

1. On the Design tab, in the Views group, click the **View button arrow**, and then click **Print Preview**. The first page of the report is displayed in Print Preview. See Figure 1-27.

**Figure 1-27**   **First page of the report in Print Preview**

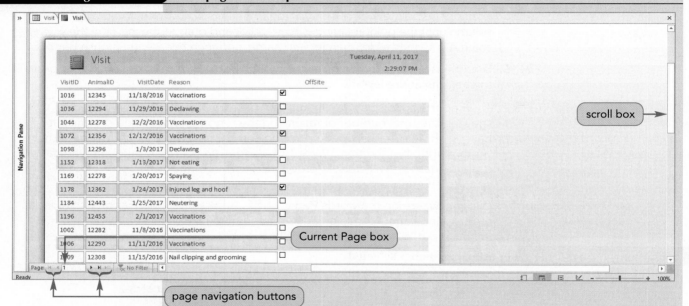

**Print Preview** shows exactly how the report will look when printed. Notice that Print Preview provides page navigation buttons at the bottom of the window, similar to the navigation buttons you've used to move through records in a table, query, and form.

2. Click the **Next Page** button. The second page of the report is displayed in Print Preview.

3. Click the **Last Page** button to move to the last page of the report.

4. Drag the scroll box in the vertical scroll bar down until the bottom of the report page is displayed. The notation "Page 3 of 3" appears at the bottom of the page, indicating that you are on page 3 out of a total of 3 pages in the report.

**Trouble?** Depending on the printer you are using, your report might have more or fewer pages, and some of the pages might be blank. If so, don't worry. Different printers format reports in different ways, sometimes affecting the total number of pages and the number of records printed per page.

**5.** Click the **First Page** button ◀ to return to the first page of the report, and then drag the scroll box in the vertical scroll bar up to display the top of the report.

Next you'll save the report as VisitDetails, and then print it.

**6.** On the Quick Access Toolbar, click the **Save** button 🖫. The Save As dialog box opens.

**7.** In the Report Name box, click at the end of the selected word "Visit," type **Details**, and then press the **Enter** key. The dialog box closes and the report is saved as VisitDetails in the Riverview database. The tab containing the report now displays the name "VisitDetails."

## Printing a Report

After creating a report, you might need to print it to distribute it to others who need to view the report's contents. You can print a report without changing any print settings, or display the Print dialog box and select options for printing.

**REFERENCE**

### Printing a Report

- Open the report in any view, or select the report in the Navigation Pane.
- Click the File tab to display Backstage view, click Print, and then click Quick Print to print the report with the default print settings.

*or*

- Open the report in any view, or select the report in the Navigation Pane.
- Click the File tab, click Print, and then click Print (or, if the report is displayed in Print Preview, click the Print button in the Print group on the Print Preview tab). The Print dialog box opens, in which you can select the options you want for printing the report.

Kimberly asks you to print the entire report with the default settings, so you'll use the Quick Print option in Backstage view.

**Note:** To complete the following steps, your computer must be connected to a printer. Check with your instructor first to see if you should print the report.

### To print the report and then close it:

**1.** On the ribbon, click the **File** tab to open Backstage view.

**2.** In the navigation bar, click **Print** to display the Print screen, and then click **Quick Print**. The report prints with the default print settings, and you return to the report in Print Preview.

**Trouble?** If your report did not print, make sure that your computer is connected to a printer, and that the printer is turned on and ready to print. Then repeat Steps 1 and 2.

**3.** Click the **Close 'VisitDetails'** button ✖ on the object tab to close the report.

**4.** Click the **Close 'Visit'** button ✖ on the object tab to close the Visit table.

**Trouble?** If you are asked to save changes to the layout of the table, click the Yes button.

You can also use the Print dialog box to print other database objects, such as table and query datasheets. Most often, these objects are used for viewing and entering data, and reports are used for printing the data in a database.

# Viewing Objects in the Navigation Pane

The Riverview database now contains four objects—the Visit table, the VisitList query, the VisitData form, and the VisitDetails report. When you work with the database file—such as closing it, opening it, or distributing it to others—the file includes all the objects you created and saved in the database. You can view and work with these objects in the Navigation Pane.

**To view the objects in the Riverview database:**

▶ **1.** On the Navigation Pane, click the **Shutter Bar Open/Close Button** ⏩ to open the pane. See Figure 1-28.

| Figure 1-28 | First page of the report in Print Preview |

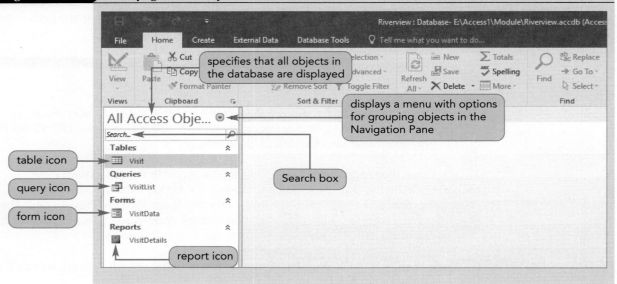

The Navigation Pane currently displays the default category, **All Access Objects**, which lists all the database objects in the pane. Each object type (Tables, Queries, Forms, and Reports) appears in its own group. Each database object (the Visit table, the VisitList query, the VisitData form, and the VisitDetails report) has a unique icon to its left to indicate the type of object. This makes it easy for you to identify the objects and choose which one you want to open and work with.

The arrow on the All Access Objects bar displays a menu with options for various ways to group and display objects in the Navigation Pane. The Search box enables you to enter text for Access to find; for example, you could search for all objects that contain the word "Visit" in their names. Note that Access searches for objects only in the categories and groups currently displayed in the Navigation Pane.

As you continue to build the Riverview database and add more objects to it in later modules, you'll use the options in the Navigation Pane to manage those objects.

# Using Microsoft Access Help

Access includes a Help system you can use to search for information about specific program features. You start Help by clicking the Microsoft Access Help button in the top right of the Access window, or by pressing the F1 key.

You'll use Help now to learn more about the Navigation Pane.

### To search for information about the Navigation Pane in Help:

1. Click the **Microsoft Access Help** button ? on the title bar. The Access 2016 Help window opens, as shown earlier in the Session 1.2 Visual Overview.

2. Click in the **Search** box, type **Navigation Pane**, and then press the **Enter** key. The Access 2016 Help window displays a list of topics related to the Navigation Pane.

3. Click the topic **Manage Access database objects in the Navigation Pane**. The Access Help window displays the article you selected. See Figure 1-29.

| Figure 1-29 | Article displayed in the Access Help window |

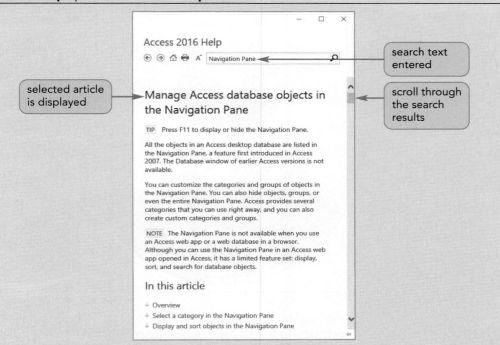

selected article is displayed

search text entered

scroll through the search results

Access 2016 Help

Navigation Pane

**Manage Access database objects in the Navigation Pane**

TIP    Press F11 to display or hide the Navigation Pane.

All the objects in an Access desktop database are listed in the Navigation Pane, a feature first introduced in Access 2007. The Database window of earlier Access versions is not available.

You can customize the categories and groups of objects in the Navigation Pane. You can also hide objects, groups, or even the entire Navigation Pane. Access provides several categories that you can use right away, and you can also create custom categories and groups.

NOTE    The Navigation Pane is not available when you use an Access web app or a web database in a browser. Although you can use the Navigation Pane in an Access web app opened in Access, it has a limited feature set: display, sort, and search for database objects.

In this article

↓ Overview
↓ Select a category in the Navigation Pane
↓ Display and sort objects in the Navigation Pane

**Trouble?** If the article on managing database objects is not listed in your Help window, choose another article related to the Navigation Pane to read.

4. Scroll through the article to read detailed information about working with the Navigation Pane.

5. When finished, click the **Close** button ✕ on the Access 2016 Help window to close it.

The Access Help system is an important reference tool for you to use if you need additional information about databases in general, details about specific Access features, or support with problems you might encounter.

## Managing a Database

One of the main tasks involved in working with database software is managing your databases and the data they contain. Some of the activities involved in database management include compacting and repairing a database and backing up and restoring a database. By managing your databases, you can ensure that they operate in the most efficient way, that the data they contain is secure, and that you can work with the data effectively.

## Compacting and Repairing a Database

Whenever you open an Access database and work in it, the size of the database increases. Further, when you delete records or when you delete or replace database objects—such as queries, forms, and reports—the storage space that had been occupied by the deleted or replaced records or objects does not automatically become available for other records or objects. To make the space available, and also to increase the speed of data retrieval, you must compact the database. **Compacting** a database rearranges the data and objects in a database to decrease its file size, thereby making more storage space available and enhancing the performance of the database. Figure 1-30 illustrates the compacting process.

| Figure 1-30 | Compacting a database |

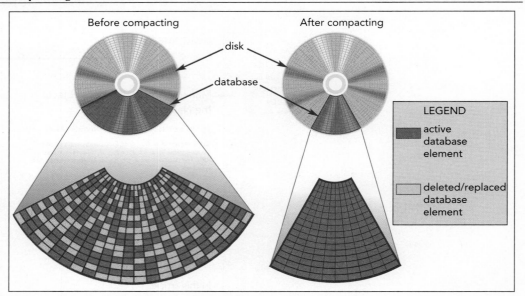

When you compact a database, Access repairs the database at the same time, if necessary. In some cases, Access detects that a database is damaged when you try to open it and gives you the option to compact and repair it at that time. For example, the data in your database might become damaged, or corrupted, if you exit the Access program suddenly by turning off your computer. If you think your database might be damaged because it is behaving unpredictably, you can use the Compact & Repair Database option to fix it.

Access also allows you to set an option to compact and repair a database file automatically every time you close it. The Compact on Close option is available in the Current Database section of the Access Options dialog box, which you open from

Backstage view by clicking the Options command in the navigation bar. By default, the Compact on Close option is turned off.

Next, you'll compact the Riverview database manually using the Compact & Repair Database option. This will make the database smaller and allow you to work with it more efficiently. After compacting the database, you'll close it.

### To compact and repair the Riverview database:

▶ **1.** On the ribbon, click the **File** tab to open the Info screen in Backstage view.

▶ **2.** Click the **Compact & Repair Database** button. Although nothing visible happens on the screen, the Riverview database is compacted, making it smaller, and repairs it at the same time. The Home tab is again the active tab on the ribbon.

▶ **3.** Click the **File** tab to return to Backstage view, and then click **Close** in the navigation bar. The Riverview database closes.

## Backing Up and Restoring a Database

**Backing up** a database is the process of making a copy of the database file to protect your database against loss or damage. The Back Up Database command enables you to back up your database file from within the Access program, while you are working on your database. To use this option, click the File tab to display the Info screen in Backstage view, click Save As in the navigation bar, click Back Up Database in the Advanced section of the Save Database As pane, and then click the Save As button. In the Save As dialog box that opens, a default filename is provided for the backup copy that consists of the same filename as the database you are backing up (for example, "Riverview"), and an underscore character, plus the current date. This filenaming system makes it easy for you to keep track of your database backups and when they were created. To restore a backup database file, you simply copy the backup from the location where it is stored to your hard drive, or whatever device you use to work in Access, and start working with the restored database file. (You will not actually back up the Riverview database in this module unless directed by your instructor to do so.)

**INSIGHT**

### Planning and Performing Database Backups

Experienced database users make it a habit to back up a database before they work with it for the first time, keeping the original data intact. They also make frequent backups while continuing to work with a database; these backups are generally on flash drives, recordable CDs or DVDs, external or network hard drives, or cloud-based storage (such as OneDrive). Also, it is recommended to store the backup copy in a different location from the original. For example, if the original database is stored on a flash drive, you should not store the backup copy on the same flash drive. If you lose the drive or the drive is damaged, you would lose both the original database and its backup copy.

If the original database file and the backup copy have the same name, restoring the backup copy might replace the original. If you want to save the original file, rename it before you restore the backup copy. To ensure that the restored database has the most current data, you should update the restored database with any changes made to the original between the time you created the backup copy and the time the original database became damaged or lost.

By properly planning for and performing backups, you can avoid losing data and prevent the time-consuming effort required to rebuild a lost or damaged database.

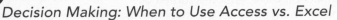

## Decision Making: When to Use Access vs. Excel

Using a spreadsheet application like Microsoft Excel to manage lists or tables of information works well when the data is simple, such as a list of contacts or tasks. As soon as the data becomes complex enough to separate into tables that need to be related, you start to see the limitations of using a spreadsheet application. The strength of a database application such as Access is in its ability to easily relate one table of information to another. Consider a table of contacts that includes home addresses, with a separate row for each person living at the same address. When an address changes, it's too easy to make a mistake and not update the home address for each person who lives there. To ensure you have the most accurate data at all times, it's important to have only one instance of each piece of data. By creating separate tables that are related and keeping only one instance of each piece of data, you'll ensure the integrity of the data. Trying to accomplish this in Excel is a complex process, whereas Access is specifically designed for this functionality.

Another limitation of using Excel instead of Access to manage data has to do with the volume of data. Although a spreadsheet can hold thousands of records, a database can hold millions. A spreadsheet containing thousands of pieces of information is cumbersome to use. Think of large-scale commercial applications such as enrollment at a college or tracking customers for a large company. It's hard to imagine managing such information in an Excel spreadsheet. Instead, you'd use a database. Finally, with an Access database, multiple users can access the information it contains at the same time. Although an Excel spreadsheet can be shared, there can be problems when users try to open and edit the same spreadsheet at the same time.

When you're trying to decide whether to use Excel or Access, ask yourself the following questions.

1. Do you need to store data in separate tables that are related to each other?
2. Do you have a very large amount of data to store?
3. Will more than one person need to access the data at the same time?

If you answer "yes" to any of these questions, an Access database is most likely the appropriate application to use.

In the following modules, you'll help Kimberly complete and maintain the Riverview database, and you'll use it to meet the specific information needs of the employees of the care center.

## Session 1.2 Quick Check

1. To copy the records from a table in one database to another table in a different database, the two tables must have the same _____.

2. A(n) _____ is a question you ask about the data stored in a database.

3. The quickest way to create a form is to use the _____.

4. Which view enables you to see the total number of pages in a report and navigate through the report pages?

5. In the Navigation Pane, each database object has a unique _____ to its left that identifies the object's type.

6. _____ a database rearranges the data and objects in a database to decrease its file size and enhance the speed and performance of the database.

7. _____ a database is the process of making a copy of the database file to protect the database against loss or damage.

## Review Assignments

**PRACTICE**

**Data File needed for the Review Assignments: Company.accdb**

For Riverview Veterinary Care Center, Kimberly asks you to create a new database to contain information about the vendors that the care center works with to obtain supplies, equipment, and resale items, and the vendors who service and maintain the equipment. Complete the following steps:

1. Create a new, blank database named **Vendor** and save it in the folder where you are storing your files, as specified by your instructor.
2. In Datasheet view for the Table1 table, rename the default ID primary key field to **SupplierID**. Change the data type of the SupplierID field to Short Text.
3. Add the following 10 fields to the new table in the order shown; all of them are Short Text fields *except* InitialContact, which is a Date/Time field: **Company**, **Category**, **Address**, **City**, **State**, **Zip**, **Phone**, **ContactFirst**, **ContactLast**, and **InitialContact**. Resize the columns as necessary so that the complete field names are displayed. Save the table as **Supplier**.
4. Enter the records shown in Figure 1-31 in the Supplier table. For the first record, be sure to enter your first name in the ContactFirst field and your last name in the ContactLast field.
   **Note:** When entering field values that are shown on multiple lines in the figure, do not try to enter the values on multiple lines. The values are shown on multiple lines in the figure for page spacing purposes only.

**Figure 1-31**    **Supplier table records**

| SupplierID | Company | Category | Address | City | State | Zip | Phone | ContactFirst | ContactLast | InitialContact |
|---|---|---|---|---|---|---|---|---|---|---|
| YUM345 | Yummy Dog Food | Resale | 345 Riverside Dr | Charlotte | NC | 28201 | 704-205-8725 | *Student First* | *Student Last* | 2/1/2017 |
| FTS123 | Flea & Tick Supplies | Resale | 123 Overlook Ln | Atlanta | GA | 30301 | 404-341-2981 | Robert | Jackson | 3/6/2017 |
| PMC019 | Pet Medical | Equipment | 19 Waverly Ct | Blacksburg | VA | 24061 | 540-702-0098 | Julie | Baxter | 2/21/2017 |
| APL619 | A+ Labs | Equipment | 619 West Dr | Omaha | NE | 68022 | 531-219-7206 | Jacques | Dupont | 4/10/2017 |
| CWI444 | Cat World Inc. | Supplies | 444 Boxcar Way | San Diego | CA | 92110 | 619-477-9482 | Amelia | Kline | 5/1/2017 |

5. Kimberly created a database named Company that contains a Business table with supplier data. The Supplier table you created has the same design as the Business table. Copy all the records from the **Business** table in the **Company** database (located in the Access1 > Review folder provided with your Data Files) and then paste them at the end of the Supplier table in the Vendor database.
6. Resize all datasheet columns to their best fit, and then save the Supplier table.
7. Close the Supplier table, and then use the Navigation Pane to reopen it. Note that the records are displayed in primary key order by the values in the SupplierID field.
8. Use the Simple Query Wizard to create a query that includes the Company, Category, ContactFirst, ContactLast, and Phone fields (in that order) from the Supplier table. Name the query **SupplierList**, and then close the query.
9. Use the Form tool to create a form for the Supplier table. Save the form as **SupplierInfo**, and then close it.

10. Use the Report tool to create a report based on the Supplier table. In Layout view, resize all fields except the Company field, so that each field is slightly wider than the longest entry (either the field name itself or an entry in the field). Display the report in Print Preview and verify that all the fields fit across one page in the report. Save the report as **SupplierDetails**, and then close it.

11. Close the Supplier table, and then compact and repair the Vendor database.

12. Close the Vendor database.

## Case Problem 1

APPLY

**Data File needed for this Case Problem: BeautyToGo.accdb**

*Beauty To Go* Sue Miller, an owner of a nail and hair salon in Orlando, Florida, regularly checks in on her grandmother, who resides in a retirement community. On some of her visits, Sue does her grandmother's hair and nails. Her grandmother recently asked if Sue would also be willing to do the hair and nails of some of her friends in her retirement community and other surrounding communities. She said that these friends would happily pay for her services. Sue thinks this is an excellent way to expand her current business and serve the needs of the retirement community at the same time. In discussing the opportunity with some of the members of the retirement community, she found that the ladies would very much like to pay Sue in advance for her services and have them scheduled on a regular basis; however, the frequency and types of the services vary from person to person. Sue decides to come up with different options that would serve the needs of the ladies in the retirement community. Sue wants to use Access to maintain information about the customers and the types of options offered. She needs your help in creating this database. Complete the following:

1. Create a new, blank database named **Beauty** and save it in the folder where you are storing your files, as specified by your instructor.

2. In Datasheet view for the Table1 table, rename the default primary key ID field to **OptionID**. Change the data type of the OptionID field to Short Text.

3. Add the following three fields to the new table in the order shown: **OptionDescription** (a Short Text field), **OptionCost** (a Currency field), and **FeeWaived** (a Yes/No field). Save the table as **Option**.

4. Enter the records shown in Figure 1-32 in the Option table. *Hint*: When entering the OptionCost field values, you do not have to type the dollar signs, commas, or decimal places; they will be entered automatically.

**Figure 1-32** Option table records

when entering currency values, you do not have to type the dollar signs, commas, or decimal places

| OptionID | OptionDescription | OptionCost | FeeWaived |
|---|---|---|---|
| 136 | Wash/cut bi-weekly for 6 months | $500.00 | Yes |
| 101 | Manicure weekly for 1 month | $125.00 | No |
| 124 | Manicure/pedicure weekly for 3 months | $700.00 | Yes |
| 142 | Wash/cut/color monthly for 6 months | $600.00 | Yes |
| 117 | Pedicure bi-weekly for 3 months | $190.00 | No |

5. Sue created a database named BeautyToGo that contains a MoreOptions table with plan data. The Option table you created has the same design as the MoreOptions table. Copy all the records from the **MoreOptions** table in the **BeautyToGo** database (located in the Access1 > Case1 folder provided with your Data Files), and then paste them at the end of the Option table in the Beauty database.

6. Resize all datasheet columns to their best fit, and then save the Option table.

7. Close the Option table, and then use the Navigation Pane to reopen it. Note that the records are displayed in primary key order by the values in the OptionID field.

8. Use the Simple Query Wizard to create a query that includes the OptionID, OptionDescription, and OptionCost fields from the Option table. In the second Simple Query Wizard dialog box, select the Detail option if necessary. (This option appears because the query includes a Currency field.) Save the query as **OptionData**, and then close the query.

9. Use the Form tool to create a form for the Option table. Save the form as **OptionInfo**, and then close it.

10. Use the Report tool to create a report based on the Option table. In Layout view, resize the OptionID field so it is slightly wider than the longest entry, which is the field name in this case. Resize the OptionDescription field so there are no entries with multiple lines. Also, resize the box containing the total amount that appears below the OptionCost column by clicking the box and then dragging its bottom border down so that the amount is fully displayed. (The Report Tool calculated this total automatically.) Display the report in Print Preview; then verify that all the fields are within the page area and all field values are fully displayed. Save the report as **OptionList**, print the report (only if asked by your instructor to do so), and then close it.

11. Close the Option table, and then compact and repair the Beauty database.

12. Close the Beauty database.

## Case Problem 2

APPLY

Data File needed for this Case Problem: **ProgPros.accdb**

**Programming Pros**   While in college obtaining his bachelor's degree in Raleigh, North Carolina, Brent Hovis majored in computer science and learned programming. Brent found that many of his fellow classmates found it difficult to write code, and he was constantly assisting them with helpful tips and techniques. Prior to graduating, Brent began tutoring freshman and sophomore students in programming to make some extra money. As his reputation grew, high school students began contacting him for help with their programming classes. When Brent entered graduate school, he started Programming Pros, a company offering expanded tutoring service for high school and college students through group, private, and semi-private tutoring sessions. As demand for the company's services grew, Brent hired many of his fellow classmates to assist him. Brent wants to use Access to maintain information about the tutors who work for him, the students who sign up for tutoring, and the contracts they sign. He needs your help in creating this database. Complete the following steps:

1. Create a new, blank database named **Programming** and save it in the folder where you are storing your files, as specified by your instructor.

2. In Datasheet view for the Table1 table, rename the default primary key ID field to **TutorID**. Change the data type of the TutorID field to Short Text.

3. Add the following five fields to the new table in the order shown; all of them are Short Text fields *except* HireDate, which is a Date/Time field: **FirstName**, **LastName**, **Major**, **YearInSchool**, **School**, and **HireDate**. Resize the columns, if necessary, so that the complete field names are displayed. Save the table as **Tutor**.

4. Enter the records shown in Figure 1-33 in the Tutor table. For the first record, be sure to enter your first name in the FirstName field and your last name in the LastName field.

**Figure 1-33**   Tutor table records

| TutorID | FirstName | LastName | Major | YearInSchool | School | HireDate |
|---|---|---|---|---|---|---|
| 1060 | *Student First* | *Student Last* | Computer Science | Senior | Ellings College | 2/14/2017 |
| 1010 | Cathy | Cowler | Computer Engineering | Graduate | Eikenville College | 2/1/2017 |
| 1051 | Donald | Gallager | Computer Science | Graduate | Hogan University | 1/18/2017 |
| 1031 | Nichole | Schneider | Computer Science | Junior | Switzer University | 2/28/2017 |
| 1018 | Fredrik | Karlsson | Mechatronics | Junior | Smith Technical College | 2/6/2017 |

5. Brent created a database named ProgPros that contains a MoreTutors table with tutor data. The Tutor table you created has the same design as the MoreTutors table. Copy all the records from the **MoreTutors** table in the **ProgPros** database (located in the Access1 > Case2 folder provided with your Data Files), and then paste them at the end of the Tutor table in the Programming database.

6. Resize all datasheet columns to their best fit, and then save the Tutor table.

7. Close the Tutor table, and then use the Navigation Pane to reopen it. Note that the records are displayed in primary key order by the values in the TutorID field.

8. Use the Simple Query Wizard to create a query that includes the FirstName, LastName, and HireDate fields from the Tutor table. Save the query as **StartDate**, and then close the query.

9. Use the Form tool to create a form for the Tutor table. Save the form as **TutorInfo**, and then close it.

10. Use the Report tool to create a report based on the Tutor table. In Layout view, resize the TutorID, FirstName, LastName, Major, YearInSchool, School, and HireDate fields so they are slightly wider than the longest entry (either the field name itself or an entry in the field). All seven fields should fit within the page area after you resize the fields. At the bottom of the report, move the text "Page 1 of 1" to the left so it is within the page area. Display the report in Print Preview; then verify that the fields and page number fit within the page area and that all field values are fully displayed. Save the report as **TutorList**, print the report (only if asked by your instructor to do so), and then close it.

11. Close the Tutor table, and then compact and repair the Programming database.

12. Close the Programming database.

## Case Problem 3

Data File needed for this Case Problem: Diane.accdb

**Diane's Community Center**  Diane Coleman is a successful businesswoman in Dallas, Georgia, but things were not always that way. Diane experienced trying times and fortunately had people in the community come into her life to assist her and her children when times were difficult. Diane now wants to give back to her community and support those in need, just as she was supported many years ago, by creating a community center in Dallas where those in need can come in for goods and services. Diane plans to open a thrift store as well to sell donated items to support the center. Diane has been contacted by many people in the community wishing to donate materials to the center as well as items to be sold at the thrift store. Diane has asked you to create an Access database to manage information about the center's patrons and donations. Complete the following steps:

1. Create a new, blank database named **Center** and save it in the folder where you are storing your files, as specified by your instructor.

2. In Datasheet view for the Table1 table, rename the default primary key ID field to **PatronID**. Change the data type of the PatronID field to Short Text.

3. Add the following five Short Text fields to the new table in the order shown: **Title**, **FirstName**, **LastName**, **Phone**, and **Email**. Save the table as **Patron**.

4. Enter the records shown in Figure 1-34 in the Patron table. For the first record, be sure to enter your title in the Title field, your first name in the FirstName field, and your last name in the LastName field.

**Figure 1-34**  Patron table records

| PatronID | Title | FirstName | LastName | Phone | Email |
| --- | --- | --- | --- | --- | --- |
| 3001 | Student Title | Student First | Student Last | 404-987-1234 | student@example.com |
| 3030 | Mr. | David | Hampton | 404-824-3381 | thehamptons@example.net |
| 3006 | Dr. | Elbert | Schneider | 678-492-9101 | countrydoc@example.com |
| 3041 | Mr. | Frank | Miller | 404-824-3431 | frankmiller12@example.net |
| 3019 | Mrs. | Jane | Michaels | 706-489-3310 | jjmichaels@example.com |

5. Diane created a database named Diane that contains a MorePatrons table with data about additional patrons. The Patron table you created has the same design as the MorePatrons table. Copy all the records from the **MorePatrons** table in the **Diane** database (located in the Access1 > Case3 folder provided with your Data Files), and then paste them at the end of the Patron table in the Center database.

6. Resize all datasheet columns to their best fit, and then save the Patron table.

7. Close the Patron table, and then use the Navigation Pane to reopen it. Note that the records are displayed in primary key order by the values in the PatronID field.

✛ **Explore** 8. Use the Simple Query Wizard to create a query that includes all the fields in the Patron table *except* the Title field. (*Hint*: Use the  >>  and  <  buttons to select the necessary fields.) Save the query using the name **PatronContactList**.

✛ **Explore** 9. The query results are displayed in order by the PatronID field values. You can specify a different order by sorting the query. Display the Home tab. Then, click the insertion point anywhere in the LastName column to make it the current field. In the Sort & Filter group on the Home tab, click the Ascending button. The records are now listed in order by the values in the LastName field. Save and close the query.

✛ **Explore** 10. Use the Form tool to create a form for the Patron table. In the new form, navigate to record 13 (the record with PatronID 3028), and then print the form *for the current record only*. (*Hint*: You must use the Print dialog box in order to print only the current record. Go to Backstage view, click Print in the navigation bar, and then click Print to open the Print dialog box. Click the Selected Record(s) option button, and then click the OK button to print the current record.) Save the form as **PatronInfo**, and then close it.

11. Use the Report tool to create a report based on the Patron table. In Layout view, resize each field so it is slightly wider than the longest entry (either the field name itself or an entry in the field). All six fields should fit within the page area after resizing. At the bottom of the report, move the text "Page 1 of 1" to the left so it is within the page area. Display the report in Print Preview, then verify that the fields and page number fit within the page area and that all field values are fully displayed. Save the report as **PatronList**. Print the report (only if asked by your instructor to do so), and then close it.

12. Close the Patron table, and then compact and repair the Center database.

13. Close the Center database.

## Case Problem 4

Data File needed for this Case Problem: HikeApp.accdb

**Hike Appalachia**   Molly and Bailey Johnson grew up in the Blue Ridge Mountains of North Carolina. Their parents were avid outdoors people and loved to take the family on long hikes and teach the girls about the great outdoors. During middle school and high school, their friends would ask them to guide them in the surrounding area because it could be quite dangerous. One summer, the girls had an idea to expand their hiking clientele beyond their friends and help earn money for college; this was the start of their business, which they named Hike Appalachia. The girls advertised in local and regional outdoor magazines and were flooded with requests from people all around the region. They would like you to build an Access database to manage information about the hikers they guide, the tours they provide, and tour reservations. Complete the following:

1. Create a new, blank database named **Appalachia** and save it in the folder where you are storing your files, as specified by your instructor.

2. In Datasheet view for the Table1 table, rename the default primary key ID field to **HikerID**. Change the data type of the HikerID field to Short Text.

3. Add the following seven Short Text fields to the new table in the order shown: **HikerFirst**, **HikerLast**, **Address**, **City**, **State**, **Zip**, and **Phone**. Save the table as **Hiker**.

*CHALLENGE*

4. Enter the records shown in Figure 1-35 in the Hiker table. For the first record, be sure to enter your first name in the HikerFirst field and your last name in the HikerLast field.

| Figure 1-35 | Hiker table records |
| --- | --- |

| HikerID | HikerFirst | HikerLast | Address | City | State | Zip | Phone |
| --- | --- | --- | --- | --- | --- | --- | --- |
| 501 | *Student First* | *Student Last* | 123 Jackson St | Boone | NC | 28607 | 828-497-9128 |
| 547 | Heather | Smith | 412 Sentry Ln | Gastonia | NC | 28052 | 704-998-0987 |
| 521 | Zack | Hoskins | 2 Hope Rd | Atlanta | GA | 30301 | 404-998-2381 |
| 535 | Elmer | Jackson | 99 River Rd | Blacksburg | SC | 29702 | 864-921-2384 |
| 509 | Sarah | Peeler | 32 Mountain Ln | Ridgeview | WV | 25169 | 703-456-9381 |

5. Molly and Bailey created a database named HikeApp that contains a MoreHikers table with data about hikers. The Hiker table you created has the same design as the MoreHikers table. Copy all the records from the **MoreHikers** table in the **HikeApp** database (located in the Access1 > Case4 folder provided with your Data Files), and then paste them at the end of the Hiker table in the Appalachia database.

6. Resize all datasheet columns to their best fit, and then save the Hiker table.

7. Close the Hiker table, and then use the Navigation Pane to reopen it. Note that the records are displayed in primary key order.

8. Use the Simple Query Wizard to create a query that includes the following fields from the Hiker table, in the order shown: HikerID, HikerLast, HikerFirst, State, and Phone. Name the query **HikerData**.

🜨 **Explore** 9. The query results are displayed in order by the HikerID field values. You can specify a different order by sorting the query. Display the Home tab. Then, click the insertion point anywhere in the State column to make it the current field. In the Sort & Filter group on the Home tab, click the Ascending button. The records are now listed in order by the values in the State field. Save and close the query.

🜨 **Explore** 10. Use the Form tool to create a form for the Hiker table. In the new form, navigate to record 10 (the record with HikerID 527), and then print the form *for the current record only*. (*Hint*: You must use the Print dialog box in order to print only the current record. Go to Backstage view, click Print in the navigation bar, and then click Print to open the Print dialog box. Click the Selected Record(s) option button, and then click the OK button to print the current record.) Save the form as **HikerInfo**, and then close it.

11. Use the Report tool to create a report based on the Hiker table. In Layout view, resize each field so it is slightly wider than the longest entry (either the field name itself or an entry in the field). At the bottom of the report, move the text "Page 1 of 1" to the left so it is within the page area on the report's first page. All fields should fit on one page. Save the report as **HikerList**.

12. Print the report (only if asked by your instructor to do so), and then close it.

a. Close the Hiker table, and then compact and repair the Appalachia database.

b. Close the Appalachia database.

ACCESS

# Building a Database and Defining Table Relationships

*Creating the Billing, Owner, and Animal Tables*

## OBJECTIVES

**Session 2.1**
- Learn the guidelines for designing databases and setting field properties
- Create a table in Design view
- Define fields, set field properties, and specify a table's primary key
- Modify the structure of a table
- Change the order of fields in Design view
- Add new fields in Design view
- Change the Format property for a field in Datasheet view
- Modify field properties in Design view

**Session 2.2**
- Import data from Excel
- Import an existing table structure
- Add fields to a table with the Data Type gallery
- Delete and rename fields
- Change the data type for a field in Design view
- Set the Default Value property for a field
- Import a text file
- Define a relationship between two tables

## Case | *Riverview Veterinary Care Center*

The Riverview database currently contains one table, the Visit table. Kimberly Johnson also wants to track information about the clinic's animals, their owners, and the invoices sent to them for services provided by Riverview Veterinary Care Center. This information includes such items as each owner's name and address, animal information, and the amount and billing date for each invoice.

In this module, you'll create three new tables in the Riverview database—named Billing, Owner, and Animal—to contain the additional data Kimberly wants to track. You will use two different methods for creating the tables, and learn how to modify the fields. After adding records to the tables, you will define the necessary relationships between the tables in the Riverview database to relate the tables, enabling Kimberly and her staff to work with the data more efficiently.

## STARTING DATA FILES

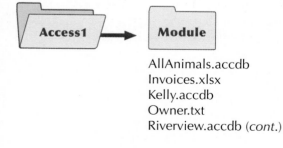

**Access1** → **Module**

AllAnimals.accdb
Invoices.xlsx
Kelly.accdb
Owner.txt
Riverview.accdb (*cont.*)

**Review**

Supplies.xlsx
Vendor.accdb (*cont.*)

**Case1**

Beauty.accdb (*cont.*)
Customers.txt

**Case2**

Agreements.xlsx
Client.accdb
Programming.accdb (*cont.*)
Students.txt

**Case3**

Auctions.txt
Center.accdb (*cont.*)
Donations.xlsx

**Case4**

Appalachia.accdb (*cont.*)
Bookings.txt
Travel.accdb

# Session 2.1 Visual Overview:

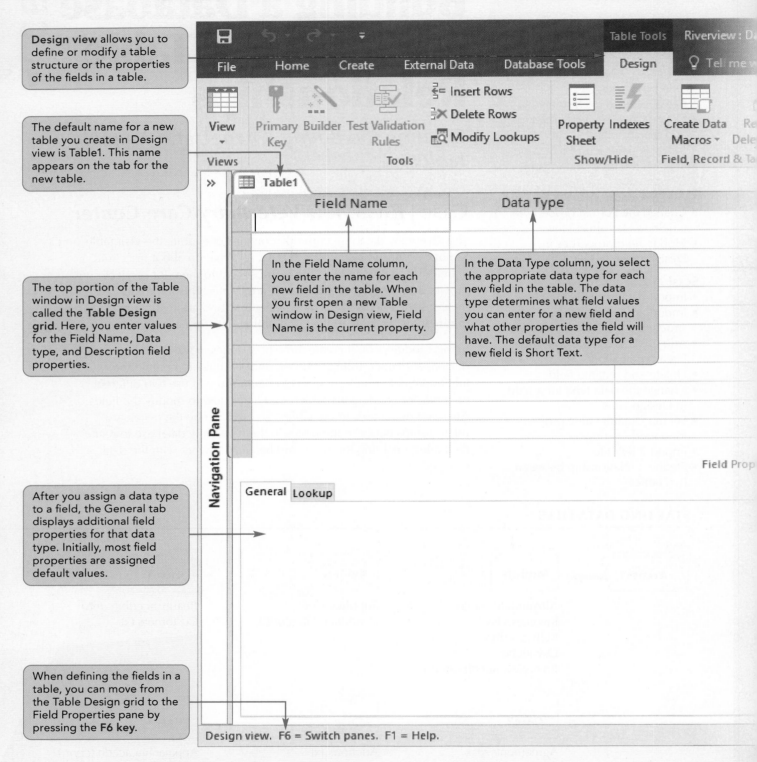

Design view allows you to define or modify a table structure or the properties of the fields in a table.

The default name for a new table you create in Design view is Table1. This name appears on the tab for the new table.

The top portion of the Table window in Design view is called the **Table Design grid**. Here, you enter values for the Field Name, Data type, and Description field properties.

In the Field Name column, you enter the name for each new field in the table. When you first open a new Table window in Design view, Field Name is the current property.

In the Data Type column, you select the appropriate data type for each new field in the table. The data type determines what field values you can enter for a new field and what other properties the field will have. The default data type for a new field is Short Text.

After you assign a data type to a field, the General tab displays additional field properties for that data type. Initially, most field properties are assigned default values.

When defining the fields in a table, you can move from the Table Design grid to the Field Properties pane by pressing the **F6 key**.

Design view. F6 = Switch panes. F1 = Help.

# Table Window in Design View

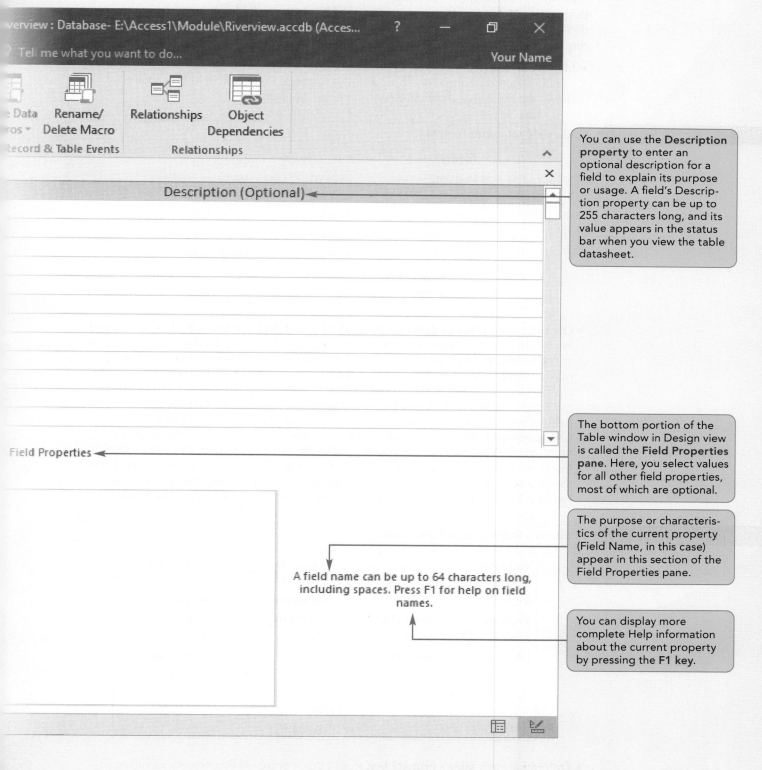

verview : Database- E:\Access1\Module\Riverview.accdb (Acces...    ?    —    □    ✕

Tell me what you want to do...    Your Name

Data    Rename/    Relationships    Object
os ▾    Delete Macro         Dependencies
Record & Table Events         Relationships

Description (Optional)

You can use the **Description property** to enter an optional description for a field to explain its purpose or usage. A field's Description property can be up to 255 characters long, and its value appears in the status bar when you view the table datasheet.

Field Properties

The bottom portion of the Table window in Design view is called the **Field Properties pane**. Here, you select values for all other field properties, most of which are optional.

The purpose or characteristics of the current property (Field Name, in this case) appear in this section of the Field Properties pane.

A field name can be up to 64 characters long, including spaces. Press F1 for help on field names.

You can display more complete Help information about the current property by pressing the **F1 key**.

# Guidelines for Designing Databases

A database management system can be a useful tool, but only if you first carefully design the database so that it meets the needs of its users. In database design, you determine the fields, tables, and relationships needed to satisfy the data and processing requirements. When you design a database, you should follow these guidelines:

- **Identify all the fields needed to produce the required information.** For example, Kimberly needs information about animals, owners, visits, and invoices. Figure 2-1 shows the fields that satisfy these information requirements.

| Figure 2-1 | Kimberly's data requirements |
| --- | --- |

| | | |
| --- | --- | --- |
| VisitID | AnimalBreed | Zip |
| VisitDate | OwnerID | Email |
| Reason | FirstName | InvoiceNum |
| OffSite | LastName | InvoiceDate |
| AnimalID | Phone | InvoiceAmt |
| AnimalName | Address | InvoiceItem |
| AnimalBirthDate | City | InvoicePaid |
| AnimalType | State | |

- **Organize each piece of data into its smallest useful part.** For example, Kimberly could store each owner's complete name in one field called Name instead of using two fields called FirstName and LastName, as shown in Figure 2-1. However, doing so would make it more difficult to work with the data. If Kimberly wanted to view the records in alphabetical order by last name, she wouldn't be able to do so with field values such as "Reggie Baxter" and "Aaron Jackson" stored in a Name field. She could do so with field values such as "Baxter" and "Jackson" stored separately in a LastName field.
- **Group related fields into tables.** For example, Kimberly grouped the fields related to visits into the Visit table, which you created in the previous module. The fields related to invoices are grouped into the Billing table, the fields related to owners are grouped into the Owner table, and the fields related to animals are grouped into the Animal table. Figure 2-2 shows the fields grouped into all four tables for the Riverview database.

| Figure 2-2 | Kimberly's fields grouped into tables |
| --- | --- |

| Visit table | Billing table | Owner table | Animal table |
| --- | --- | --- | --- |
| VisitID | InvoiceNum | OwnerID | AnimalID |
| AnimalID | VisitID | FirstName | OwnerID |
| VisitDate | InvoiceDate | LastName | AnimalName |
| Reason | InvoiceAmt | Phone | AnimalBirthDate |
| OffSite | InvoiceItem | Address | AnimalType |
| | InvoicePaid | City | AnimalBreed |
| | | State | |
| | | Zip | |
| | | Email | |

- **Determine each table's primary key.** Recall that a primary key uniquely identifies each record in a table. For some tables, one of the fields, such as a credit card number, naturally serves the function of a primary key. For other tables, two or more fields might be needed to function as the primary key. In these cases, the primary key is called a **composite key**. For example, a school grade table would use a combination of student number, term, and course code to serve as the primary key. For a third category of tables, no single field or combination of fields can uniquely identify a record in a table. In these cases, you need to add a field whose sole purpose is to serve as the table's primary key. For Kimberly's tables, VisitID is the primary key for the Visit table, InvoiceNum is the primary key for the Billing table, OwnerID is the primary key for the Owner table, and AnimalID is the primary key for the Animal table.

- **Include a common field in related tables.** You use the common field to connect one table logically with another table. For example, Kimberly's Visit and Animal tables include the AnimalID field as a common field. Recall that when you include the primary key from one table as a field in a second table to form a relationship, the field in the second table is called a foreign key; therefore, the AnimalID field is a foreign key in the Visit table. With this common field, Kimberly can find all visits to the clinic made by a particular animal; she can use the AnimalID value for an animal and search the Visit table for all records with that AnimalID value. Likewise, she can determine which animal made a particular visit by searching the Animal table to find the one record with the same AnimalID value as the corresponding value in the Visit table. Similarly, the VisitID field is a common field, serving as the primary key in the Visit table and a foreign key in the Billing table. Since animals have owners responsible for their bills, there must be a relationship between the animals and owners for the clinic to contact; therefore, the OwnerID field is a foreign key in the Animal table.
- **Avoid data redundancy.** When you store the same data in more than one place, **data redundancy** occurs. With the exception of common fields to connect tables, you should avoid data redundancy because it wastes storage space and can cause inconsistencies. An inconsistency would exist, for example, if you type a field value one way in one table and a different way in the same table or in a second table. Figure 2-3, which contains portions of potential data stored in the Animal and Visit tables, shows an example of incorrect database design that has data redundancy in the Visit table. In Figure 2-3, the AnimalName field in the Visit table is redundant, and one value for this field was entered incorrectly, in three different ways.

**Figure 2-3**    Incorrect database design with data redundancy

| AnimalID | AnimalName | AnimalBirthDate | AnimalType |
|----------|------------|-----------------|------------|
| 12286 | Lady | 8/12/2015 | Dog |
| 12304 | Tweets | 11/12/2010 | Bird |
| 12332 | Smittie | 5/19/2014 | Cat |
| 12345 | Herford5 | 4/28/2015 | Cattle |
| 12359 | Merino4 | 8/2/2014 | Sheep |

data redundancy

| VisitID | AnimalID | AnimalName | VisitDate | OffSite |
|---------|----------|------------|-----------|---------|
| 1202 | 12500 | Bonkers | 12/11/2016 | No |
| 1250 | 12332 | Smitty | 12/19/2016 | No |
| 1276 | 12492 | Bessie | 1/10/2017 | Yes |
| 1308 | 12332 | Smity | 1/23/2017 | No |
| 1325 | 12612 | Tweets | 2/6/2017 | No |
| 1342 | 12595 | Angus | 2/27/2017 | Yes |
| 1367 | 12332 | Smittee | 3/7/2017 | No |

Inconsistent data

- **Determine the properties of each field.** You need to identify the **properties**, or characteristics, of each field so that the DBMS knows how to store, display, and process the field values. These properties include the field's name, data type, maximum number of characters or digits, description, valid values, and other field characteristics. You will learn more about field properties later in this module.

The Billing, Owner, and Animal tables you need to create will contain the fields shown in Figure 2-2. Before creating these new tables in the Riverview database, you first need to learn some guidelines for setting field properties.

# Guidelines for Setting Field Properties

As just noted, the last step of database design is to determine which values to assign to the properties, such as the name and data type, of each field. When you select or enter a value for a property, you **set** the property. Access has rules for naming fields and objects, assigning data types, and setting other field properties.

## Naming Fields and Objects

You must name each field, table, and other object in an Access database. Access stores these items in the database, using the names you supply. It's best to choose a field or object name that describes the purpose or contents of the field or object so that later you can easily remember what the name represents. For example, the four tables in the Riverview database are named Visit, Billing, Owner, and Animal because these names suggest their contents. Note that a table or query name must be unique within a database. A field name must be unique within a table, but it can be used again in another table.

## Assigning Field Data Types

Each field must have a data type, which is either assigned automatically by Access or specifically by the table designer. The data type determines what field values you can enter for the field and what other properties the field will have. For example, the Billing table will include an InvoiceDate field, which will store date values, so you will assign the Date/Time data type to this field. Then Access will allow you to enter and manipulate only dates or times as values in the InvoiceDate field.

Figure 2-4 lists the most commonly used data types in Access, describes the field values allowed for each data type, explains when you should use each data type, and indicates the field size of each data type. You can find more complete information about all available data types in Access Help.

| Figure 2-4 | **Common data types** |
|---|---|

| Data Type | Description | Field Size |
|---|---|---|
| Short Text | Allows field values containing letters, digits, spaces, and special characters. Use for names, addresses, descriptions, and fields containing digits that are *not used in calculations*. | 0 to 255 characters; default is 255 |
| Long Text | Allows field values containing letters, digits, spaces, and special characters. Use for long comments and explanations. | 1 to 65,535 characters; exact size is determined by entry |
| Number | Allows positive and negative numbers as field values. A number can contain digits, a decimal point, commas, a plus sign, and a minus sign. Use for fields that will be used in calculations, except those involving money. | 1 to 15 digits |
| Date/Time | Allows field values containing valid dates and times from January 1, 100 to December 31, 9999. Dates can be entered in month/day/year format, several other date formats, or a variety of time formats, such as 10:35 PM. You can perform calculations on dates and times, and you can sort them. For example, you can determine the number of days between two dates. | 8 bytes |
| Currency | Allows field values similar to those for the Number data type, but is used for storing monetary values. Unlike calculations with Number data type decimal values, calculations performed with the Currency data type are not subject to round-off error. | Accurate to 15 digits on the left side of the decimal point and to 4 digits on the right side |
| AutoNumber | Consists of integer values created automatically by Access each time you create a new record. You can specify sequential numbering or random numbering, which guarantees a unique field value, so that such a field can serve as a table's primary key. | 9 digits |
| Yes/No | Limits field values to yes and no, on and off, or true and false. Use for fields that indicate the presence or absence of a condition, such as whether an order has been filled or whether an invoice has been paid. | 1 character |
| Hyperlink | Consists of text used as a hyperlink address, which can have up to four parts: the text that appears in a field or control; the path to a file or page; a location within the file or page; and text displayed as a ScreenTip. | Up to 65,535 characters total for the four parts of the hyperlink |

## Setting Field Sizes

The **Field Size property** defines a field value's maximum storage size for Short Text, Number, and AutoNumber fields only. The other data types have no Field Size property because their storage size is either a fixed, predetermined amount or is determined automatically by the field value itself, as shown in Figure 2-4. A Short Text field has a default field size of 255 characters; you can also set its field size by entering a number from 0 to 255. For example, the FirstName and LastName fields in the Owner table will be Short Text fields with sizes of 20 characters and 25 characters, respectively. These field sizes will accommodate the values that will be entered in each of these fields.

## Decision Making: Specifying the Field Size Property for Number Fields

When you use the Number data type to define a field, you need to decide what the Field Size setting should be for the field. You should set the Field Size property based on the largest value that you expect to store in that field. Access processes smaller data sizes faster, using less memory, so you can optimize your database's performance and its storage space by selecting the correct field size for each field. Field Size property settings for Number fields are as follows:

- **Byte**: Stores whole numbers (numbers with no fractions) from 0 to 255 in one byte
- **Integer**: Stores whole numbers from −32,768 to 32,767 in two bytes
- **Long Integer** (default): Stores whole numbers from −2,147,483,648 to 2,147,483,647 in four bytes
- **Single**: Stores positive and negative numbers to precisely seven decimal places in four bytes
- **Double**: Stores positive and negative numbers to precisely 15 decimal places in eight bytes
- **Replication ID**: Establishes a unique identifier for replication of tables, records, and other objects in databases created using Access 2003 and earlier versions in 16 bytes
- **Decimal**: Stores positive and negative numbers to precisely 28 decimal places in 12 bytes

Choosing an appropriate field size is important to optimize efficiency. For example, it would be wasteful to use the Long Integer field size for a Number field that will store only whole numbers ranging from 0 to 255 because the Long Integer field size uses four bytes of storage space. A better choice would be the Byte field size, which uses one byte of storage space to store the same values. By first gathering and analyzing information about the number values that will be stored in a Number field, you can make the best decision for the field's Field Size property and ensure the most efficient user experience for the database.

## Setting the Caption Property for Fields

The **Caption property** for a field specifies how the field name is displayed in database objects, including table and query datasheets, forms, and reports. If you don't set the Caption property, Access displays the field name as the column heading or label for a field. For example, field names such as InvoiceAmt and InvoiceDate in the Billing table can be difficult to read. Setting the Caption property for these fields to "Invoice Amt" and "Invoice Date" would make it easier for users to read the field names and work with the database.

## Setting the Caption Property vs. Naming Fields

Although Access allows you to include spaces in field names, this practice is not recommended because the spaces cause problems when you try to perform more complex tasks with the data in your database. Setting the Caption property allows you to follow best practices for naming fields, such as not including spaces in field names, while still providing users with more readable field names in datasheets, forms, and reports.

In the previous module, you created the Riverview database file and, within that file, you created the Visit table working in Datasheet view. According to her plan for the Riverview database, Kimberly also wants to track information about the invoices the care center sends to the owners of the animals. Next, you'll create the Billing table for Kimberly—this time, working in Design view.

# Creating a Table in Design View

Creating a table in Design view involves entering the field names and defining the properties for the fields, specifying a primary key for the table, and then saving the table structure. Kimberly documented the design for the new Billing table by listing each field's name and data type; each field's size and description (if applicable); and any other properties to be set for each field. See Figure 2-5.

| Figure 2-5 | Design for the Billing table |
| --- | --- |

| Field Name | Data Type | Field Size | Description | Other |
| --- | --- | --- | --- | --- |
| InvoiceNum | Short Text | 5 | Primary key | Caption = Invoice Num |
| VisitID | Short Text | 4 | Foreign key | Caption = Visit ID |
| InvoiceAmt | Currency | | | Format = Currency |
| | | | | Decimal Places = 2 |
| | | | | Caption = Invoice Amt |
| InvoiceDate | Date/Time | | | Format = mm/dd/yyyy |
| | | | | Caption = Invoice Date |
| InvoicePaid | Yes/No | | | Caption = Invoice Paid |

You'll use Kimberly's design as a guide for creating the Billing table in the Riverview database.

### To begin creating the Billing table:

1. Start Access and open the **Riverview** database you created in the previous module.

   **Trouble?** If the security warning is displayed below the ribbon, click the **Enable Content** button.

2. If the Navigation Pane is open, click the **Shutter Bar Open/Close Button** ⟪ to close it.

3. On the ribbon, click the **Create** tab.

4. In the Tables group, click the **Table Design** button. A new table named Table1 opens in Design view. Refer to the Session 2.1 Visual Overview for a complete description of the Table window in Design view.

## Defining Fields

When you first create a table in Design view, the insertion point is located in the first row's Field Name box, ready for you to begin defining the first field in the table. You enter values for the Field Name, Data Type, and Description field properties, and then select values for all other field properties in the Field Properties pane. These other properties will appear when you move to the first row's Data Type box.

### REFERENCE

*Defining a Field in Design View*

- In the Field Name box, type the name for the field, and then press the Tab key.
- Accept the default Short Text data type, or click the arrow and select a different data type for the field. Press the Tab key.
- Enter an optional description for the field, if necessary.
- Use the Field Properties pane to type or select other field properties, as appropriate.

The first field you need to define is the InvoiceNum field. This field will be the primary key for the Billing table. Each invoice at Riverview Veterinary Care Center is assigned a specific five-digit number. Although the InvoiceNum field will contain these number values, the numbers will never be used in calculations; therefore, you'll assign the Short Text data type to this field. Any time a field contains number values that will not be used in calculations—such as phone numbers, zip codes, and so on—you should use the Short Text data type instead of the Number data type.

### To define the InvoiceNum field:

**TIP**

You can also press the Enter key to move from one property to the next in the Table Design grid.

1. Type **InvoiceNum** in the first row's Field Name box, and then press the **Tab** key to advance to the Data Type box. The default data type, Short Text, is selected in the Data Type box, which now also contains an arrow, and the field properties for a Short Text field appear in the Field Properties pane. See Figure 2-6.

**Figure 2-6**    **Table window after entering the first field name**

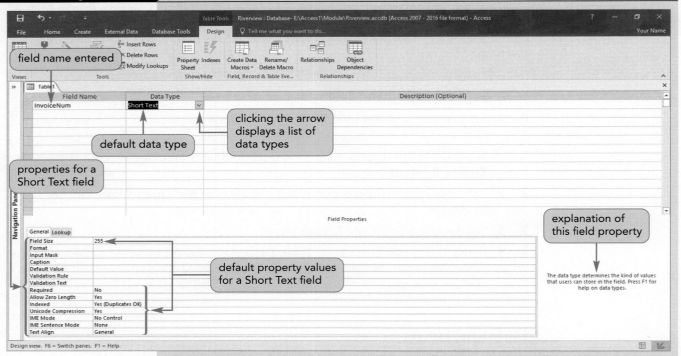

Notice that the right side of the Field Properties pane now provides an explanation for the current property, Data Type.

**Trouble?** If you make a typing error, you can correct it by clicking to position the insertion point, and then using either the Backspace key to delete characters to the left of the insertion point or the Delete key to delete characters to the right of the insertion point. Then type the correct text.

Because the InvoiceNum field values will not be used in calculations, you will accept the default Short Text data type for the field.

2. Press the **Tab** key to accept Short Text as the data type and to advance to the Description (Optional) box.

**3.** Next you'll enter the Description property value as "Primary key." The value you enter for the Description property will appear in the status bar when you view the table datasheet. Note that specifying "Primary key" for the Description property does *not* establish the current field as the primary key; you use a button on the ribbon to specify the primary key in Design view, which you will do later in this session.

**4.** Type **Primary key** in the Description (Optional) box.

Notice the Field Size property for the field. The default setting of 255 for Short Text fields is displayed. You need to change this number to 5 because all invoice numbers at Riverview Veterinary Care Center contain only five digits.

**5.** Double-click the number **255** in the Field Size property box to select it, and then type **5**.

Finally, you need to set the Caption property for the field so that its name appears with a space, as "Invoice Num."

**6.** Click the **Caption** property box, and then type **Invoice Num**. The definition of the first field is complete. See Figure 2-7.

| Figure 2-7 | InvoiceNum field defined |
| --- | --- |

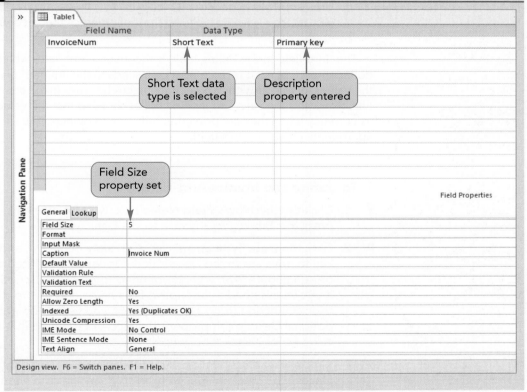

Kimberly's Billing table design (Figure 2-5) shows VisitID as the second field. Because Kimberly and other staff members need to relate information about invoices to the visit data in the Visit table, the Billing table must include the VisitID field, which is the Visit table's primary key. Recall that when you include the primary key from one table as a field in a second table to connect the two tables, the field is a foreign key in the second table. The field must be defined in the same way in both tables—that is, the field properties, including field size and data type, must match exactly.

Next, you will define VisitID as a Short Text field with a field size of 4. Later in this session, you'll change the Field Size property for the VisitID field in the Visit table to 4 so that the field definition is the same in both tables.

## To define the VisitID field:

**1.** In the Table Design grid, click the second row's **Field Name** box, type **VisitID**, and then press the **Tab** key to advance to the Data Type box.

**2.** Press the **Tab** key to accept Short Text as the field's data type. Because the VisitID field is a foreign key to the Visit table, you'll enter "Foreign key" in the Description (Optional) box to help users of the database understand the purpose of this field.

**3.** Type **Foreign key** in the Description (Optional) box. Next, you'll change the Field Size property.

**4.** Press the **F6** key to move to the Field Properties pane. The current entry for the Field Size property, 255, is selected.

**5.** Type **4** to set the Field Size property. Finally, you need to set the Caption property for this field.

**6.** Press the **Tab** key three times to position the insertion point in the Caption box, and then type **Visit ID** (be sure to include a space between the two words). You have completed the definition of the second field.

The third field in the Billing table is the InvoiceAmt field, which will display the dollar amount of each invoice the clinic sends to the animals' owners. Kimberly wants the values to appear with two decimal places because invoice amounts include cents. She also wants the values to include dollar signs, so that the values will be formatted as currency when they are printed in bills sent to owners. The Currency data type is the appropriate choice for this field.

## To define the InvoiceAmt field:

**1.** Click the third row's **Field Name** box, type **InvoiceAmt** in the box, and then press the **Tab** key to advance to the Data Type box.

**2.** Click the **Data Type** arrow, click **Currency** in the list, and then press the **Tab** key to advance to the Description (Optional) box. According to Kimberly's design (Figure 2-5), you do not need to enter a description for this field. If you've assigned a descriptive field name and the field does not fulfill a special function (such as primary key), you usually do not enter a value for the optional Description property. InvoiceAmt is a field that does not require a value for its Description property.

Kimberly wants the InvoiceAmt field values to be displayed with two decimal places. The **Decimal Places property** specifies the number of decimal places that are displayed to the right of the decimal point.

**TIP**

You can display the arrow and the list simultaneously by clicking the right side of a box.

3. In the Field Properties pane, click the **Decimal Places** box to position the insertion point there. An arrow appears on the right side of the Decimal Places box, which you can click to display a list of options.

4. Click the **Decimal Places** arrow, and then click **2** in the list to specify two decimal places for the InvoiceAmt field values.

5. Press the **Tab** key twice to position the insertion point in the Caption box, and then type **Invoice Amt**. The definition of the third field is now complete. Notice that the Format property is set to "Currency," which formats the values with dollar signs. See Figure 2-8.

**Figure 2-8**    **Table window after defining the first three fields**

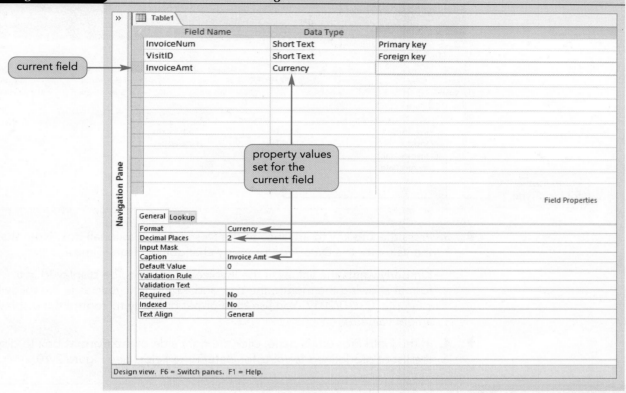

The fourth field in the Billing table is the InvoiceDate field. This field will contain the dates on which invoices are generated for the animals in the care center. You'll define the InvoiceDate field using the Date/Time data type. Also, according to Kimberly's design (Figure 2-5), the date values should be displayed in the format mm/dd/yyyy, which is a two-digit month, a two-digit day, and a four-digit year.

## To define the InvoiceDate field:

1. Click the fourth row's **Field Name** box, type **InvoiceDate**, and then press the **Tab** key to advance to the Data Type box.

   You can select a value from the Data Type list as you did for the InvoiceAmt field. Alternately, you can type the property value in the box or type just the first character of the property value.

2. Type **d**. Access completes the entry for the fourth row's Data Type box to "date/Time," with the letters "ate/Time" selected. See Figure 2-9.

| Figure 2-9 | Selecting a value for the Data Type property |
| --- | --- |

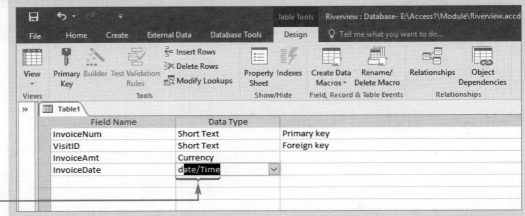

completed entry for Data Type

3. Press the **Tab** key to advance to the Description (Optional) box. Note that the value for the Data Type property changes to "Date/Time."

   Kimberly wants the values in the InvoiceDate field to be displayed in a format showing the month, the day, and a four-digit year, as in the following example: 03/10/2017. You use the Format property to control the display of a field value.

4. In the Field Properties pane, click the right side of the **Format** box to display the list of predefined formats for Date/Time fields. See Figure 2-10.

| Figure 2-10 | Displaying available formats for Date/Time fields |
| --- | --- |

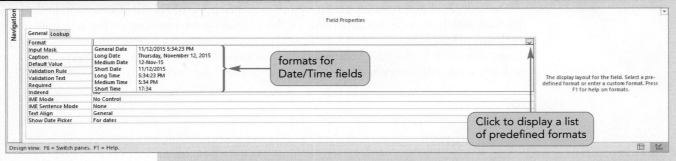

**Trouble?** If you see an arrow instead of a list of predefined formats, click the arrow to display the list.

As noted in the right side of the Field Properties pane, you can either choose a predefined format or enter a custom format. Even though the Short Date format seems to match the format Kimberly wants, it displays only one digit for months that contain only one digit. For example, it would display the month of March with only the digit "3"—as in 3/10/2017—instead of displaying the month with two digits, as in 03/10/2017.

Because none of the predefined formats matches the exact layout Kimberly wants for the InvoiceDate values, you need to create a custom date format. Figure 2-11 shows some of the symbols available for custom date and time formats.

**Figure 2-11**    **Symbols for some custom date formats**

| Symbol | Description |
| --- | --- |
| / | date separator |
| d | day of the month in one or two numeric digits, as needed (1 to 31) |
| dd | day of the month in two numeric digits (01 to 31) |
| ddd | first three letters of the weekday (Sun to Sat) |
| dddd | full name of the weekday (Sunday to Saturday) |
| w | day of the week (1 to 7) |
| ww | week of the year (1 to 53) |
| m | month of the year in one or two numeric digits, as needed (1 to 12) |
| mm | month of the year in two numeric digits (01 to 12) |
| mmm | first three letters of the month (Jan to Dec) |
| mmmm | full name of the month (January to December) |
| yy | last two digits of the year (01 to 99) |
| yyyy | full year (0100 to 9999) |

Kimberly wants the dates to be displayed with a two-digit month (mm), a two-digit day (dd), and a four-digit year (yyyy).

5. Click the **Format** arrow to close the list of predefined formats, and then type **mm/dd/yyyy** in the Format box.

6. Press the **Tab** key twice to position the insertion point in the Caption box, and then type **Invoice Date**. See Figure 2-12.

Figure 2-12 Specifying the custom date format

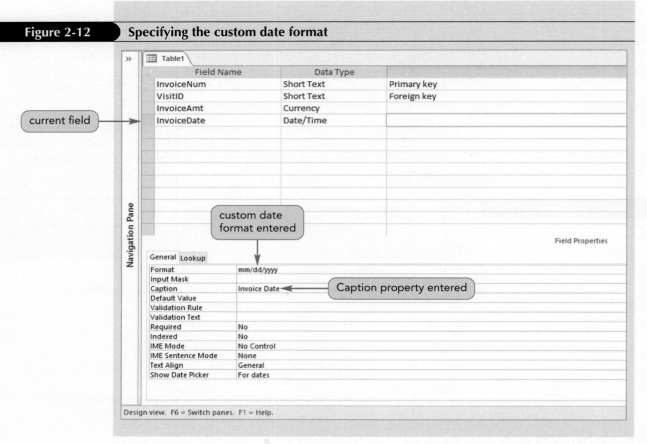

The fifth and final field to be defined in the Billing table is InvoicePaid. This field will be a Yes/No field to indicate the payment status of each invoice record stored in the Billing table. Recall that the Yes/No data type is used to define fields that store true/false, yes/no, and on/off field values. When you create a Yes/No field in a table, the default Format property is set to Yes/No.

## To define the InvoicePaid field:

1. Click the fifth row's **Field Name** box, type **InvoicePaid**, and then press the **Tab** key to advance to the Data Type box.

2. Type **y**. Access completes the data type as "yes/No".

3. Press the **Tab** key to select the Yes/No data type and move to the Description (Optional) box. In the Field Properties pane, note that the default format of "Yes/No" is selected, so you do not have to change this property.

4. In the Field Properties pane, click the **Caption** box, and then type **Invoice Paid**.

You've finished defining the fields for the Billing table. Next, you need to specify the primary key for the table.

## Specifying the Primary Key

As you learned earlier, the primary key for a table uniquely identifies each record in the table.

### Specifying a Primary Key in Design View

- Display the table in Design view.
- Click in the row for the field you've chosen to be the primary key to make it the active field. If the primary key will consist of two or more fields, click the row selector for the first field, press and hold the Ctrl key, and then click the row selector for each additional primary key field.
- In the Tools group on the Table Tools Design tab, click the Primary Key button.

According to Kimberly's design, you need to specify InvoiceNum as the primary key for the Billing table. You can do so while the table is in Design view.

**TIP**

This button is a toggle; you can click it to remove the key symbol.

### To specify InvoiceNum as the primary key:

1. Click in the row for the InvoiceNum field to make it the current field.

2. On the Table Tools Design tab, in the Tools group, click the **Primary Key** button. The Primary Key button in the Tools group is now selected, and a key symbol appears in the row selector for the first row, indicating that the InvoiceNum field is the table's primary key. See Figure 2-13.

**Figure 2-13**    **InvoiceNum field selected as the primary key**

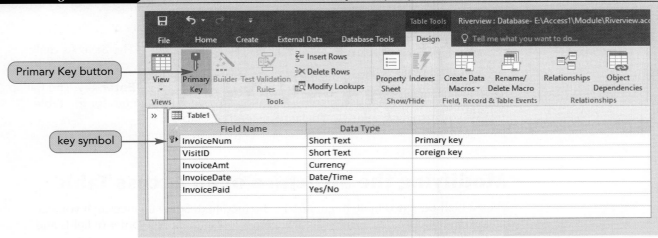

*Understanding the Importance of the Primary Key*

Although Access does not require a table to have a primary key, including a primary key offers several advantages:

- A primary key uniquely identifies each record in a table.
- Access does not allow duplicate values in the primary key field. For example, if a record already exists in the Visit table with a VisitID value of 1550, Access prevents you from adding another record with this same value in the VisitID field. Preventing duplicate values ensures the uniqueness of the primary key field.
- When a primary key has been specified, Access forces you to enter a value for the primary key field in every record in the table. This is known as **entity integrity**. If you do not enter a value for a field, you have actually given the field a **null value**. You cannot give a null value to the primary key field because entity integrity prevents Access from accepting and processing that record.
- You can enter records in any order, but Access displays them by default in order of the primary key's field values. If you enter records in no specific order, you are ensured that you will later be able to work with them in a more meaningful, primary key sequence.
- Access responds faster to your requests for specific records based on the primary key.

## Saving the Table Structure

The last step in creating a table is to name the table and save the table's structure. When you save a table structure, the table is stored in the database file (in this case, the Riverview database file). Once the table is saved, you can enter data into it. According to Kimberly's plan, you need to save the table you've defined as "Billing."

**To name and save the Billing table:**

▶ 1. On the Quick Access Toolbar, click the **Save** button 🔲. The Save As dialog box opens.

▶ 2. Type **Billing** in the Table Name box, and then press the **Enter** key. The Billing table is saved in the Riverview database. Notice that the tab for the table now displays the name "Billing" instead of "Table1."

# Modifying the Structure of an Access Table

Even a well-designed table might need to be modified. Some changes that you can make to a table's structure in Design view include changing the order of fields and adding new fields.

After meeting with her assistant, Kelly Flannagan, and reviewing the structure of the Billing table, Kimberly has changes she wants you to make to the table. First, she wants the InvoiceAmt field to be moved so that it appears right before the InvoicePaid field. Then, she wants you to add a new Short Text field named InvoiceItem to the table to include information about what the invoice is for, such as office visits, lab work, and so on. Kimberly would like the InvoiceItem field to be inserted between the InvoiceAmt and InvoicePaid fields.

## Moving a Field in Design View

To move a field, you use the mouse to drag it to a new location in the Table Design grid. Although you can move a field in Datasheet view by dragging its column heading to a new location, doing so rearranges only the *display* of the table's fields; the table structure is not changed. To move a field permanently, you must move the field in Design view.

Next, you'll move the InvoiceAmt field so that it is before the InvoicePaid field in the Billing table.

### To move the InvoiceAmt field:

1. Position the pointer on the row selector for the InvoiceAmt field until the pointer changes to ➡.

2. Click the **row selector** to select the entire InvoiceAmt row.

3. Place the pointer on the row selector for the InvoiceAmt field until the pointer changes to ⬚, press and hold the mouse button and then drag to the row selector for the InvoicePaid field. Notice that as you drag, the pointer changes to ⬚. See Figure 2-14.

**Figure 2-14** — **Moving the InvoiceAmt field in the table structure**

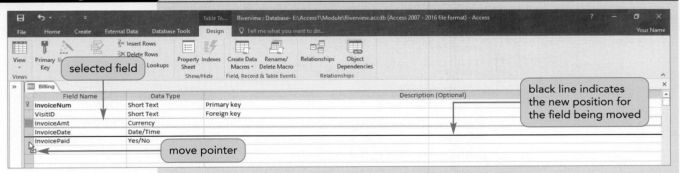

4. Release the mouse button. The InvoiceAmt field now appears between the InvoiceDate and InvoicePaid fields in the table structure.

   **Trouble?** If the InvoiceAmt field did not move, repeat Steps 1 through 4, making sure you hold down the mouse button during the drag operation.

## Adding a Field in Design View

To add a new field between existing fields, you must insert a row. You begin by selecting the row below where you want the new field to be inserted.

**REFERENCE**

### Adding a Field Between Two Existing Fields

- In the Table window in Design view, select the row below where you want the new field to be inserted.
- In the Tools group on the Table Tools Design tab, click the Insert Rows button.
- Define the new field by entering the field name, data type, optional description, and any property specifications.

Next, you need to add the InvoiceItem field to the Billing table structure between the InvoiceAmt and InvoicePaid fields.

### To add the InvoiceItem field to the Billing table:

1. Click the **InvoicePaid Field Name** box. You need to establish this field as the current field so that the row for the new record will be inserted above this field.

2. On the Table Tools Design tab, in the Tools group, click the **Insert Rows** button. A new, blank row is added between the InvoiceAmt and InvoicePaid fields. The insertion point is positioned in the Field Name box for the new row, ready for you to type the name for the new field. See Figure 2-15.

---

**Figure 2-15**   Table structure after inserting a row

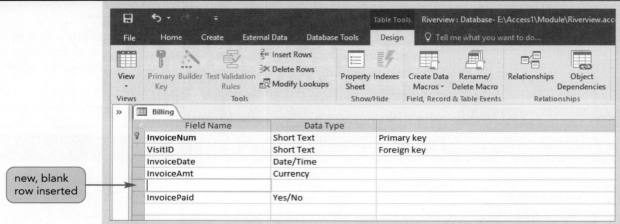

new, blank row inserted

**Trouble?** If you selected the InvoicePaid field's row selector and then inserted the new row, you need to click the new row's Field Name box to position the insertion point in it.

You'll define the InvoiceItem field in the new row of the Billing table. This field will be a Short Text field with a field size of 40, and you need to set the Caption property to include a space between the words in the field name.

3. Type **InvoiceItem**, press the **Tab** key to move to the Data Type property, and then press the **Tab** key again to accept the default Short Text data type.

4. Press the **F6** key to select the default field size in the Field Size box, and then type **40**.

5. Press the **Tab** key three times to position the insertion point in the Caption box, and then type **Invoice Item**. The definition of the new field is complete. See Figure 2-16.

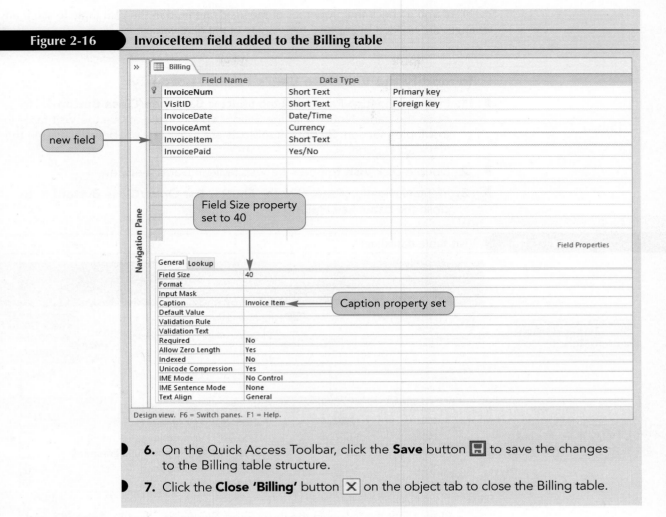

Figure 2-16    InvoiceItem field added to the Billing table

new field

Field Size property set to 40

Caption property set

Field Properties

Design view.  F6 = Switch panes.  F1 = Help.

6. On the Quick Access Toolbar, click the **Save** button 🖫 to save the changes to the Billing table structure.

7. Click the **Close 'Billing'** button ✕ on the object tab to close the Billing table.

# Modifying Field Properties

With the Billing table design complete, you can now go back and modify the properties of the fields in the Visit table you created in the previous module, as necessary. You can make some changes to properties in Datasheet view; for others, you'll work in Design view.

## Changing the Format Property in Datasheet View

The Formatting group on the Table Tools Fields tab in Datasheet view allows you to modify some formatting for certain field types. When you format a field, you change the way data is displayed, but not the actual values stored in the table.

Next, you'll check the properties of the VisitDate field in the Visit table to see if any changes are needed to improve the display of the date values.

## To modify the VisitDate field's Format property:

1. In the Navigation Pane, click the **Shutter Bar Open/Close Button** ≫ to open the pane. Notice that the Billing table is listed above the Visit table in the Tables section. By default, objects are listed in alphabetical order in the Navigation pane.

2. Double-click **Visit** to open the Visit table in Datasheet view.

3. In the Navigation Pane, click the **Shutter Bar Open/Close Button** ≪ to close the pane. See Figure 2-17.

**Figure 2-17**     **Visit table datasheet**

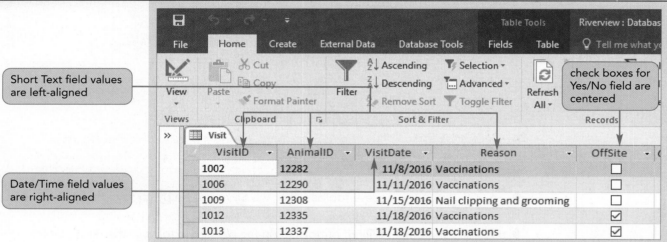

Notice that the values in the three Short Text fields—VisitID, AnimalID, and Reason—appear left-aligned within their boxes, and the values in the Date/Time field (VisitDate) appear right-aligned. In Access, values for Short Text fields are left-aligned, and values for Number, Date/Time, and Currency fields are right-aligned. The Offsite field is a Yes/No field, so its values appear in check boxes that are centered within the column.

4. On the ribbon, click the **Table Tools Fields** tab.

5. Click the **first field value** in the VisitDate column. The Data Type option shows that this field is a Date/Time field.

   By default, Access assigns the General Date format to Date/Time fields. Note the Format box in the Formatting group, which you use to set the Format property (similar to how you set the Format property in the Field Properties pane in Design view.) Even though the Format box is empty, the VisitDate field has the General Date format applied to it. The General Date format includes settings for date or time values, or a combination of date and time values. However, Kimberly wants only date values to be displayed in the VisitDate field, so she asks you to specify the Short Date format for the field.

6. In the Formatting group, click the **Format** arrow, and then click **Short Date**. See Figure 2-18.

**Figure 2-18** | **VisitDate field after modifying the format**

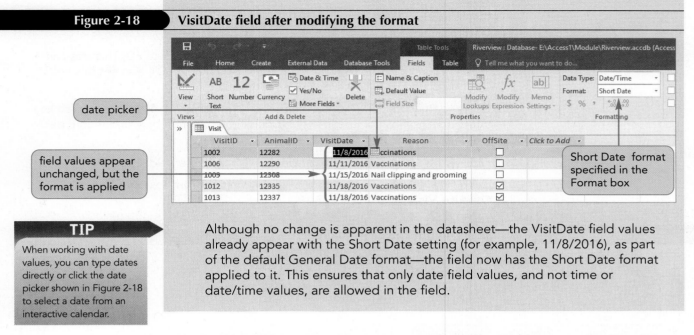

date picker

field values appear unchanged, but the format is applied

Short Date format specified in the Format box

Although no change is apparent in the datasheet—the VisitDate field values already appear with the Short Date setting (for example, 11/8/2016), as part of the default General Date format—the field now has the Short Date format applied to it. This ensures that only date field values, and not time or date/time values, are allowed in the field.

## Changing Properties in Design View

Recall that each of the Short Text fields in the Visit table—VisitID, AnimalID, and Reason—still has the default field size of 255, which is too large for the data contained in these fields. Also, the VisitID and AnimalID fields need descriptions to identify them as the primary and foreign keys, respectively, in the table. Finally, each of these fields needs a caption either to include a space between the words in the field name or to make the name more descriptive. You can make all of these property changes more easily in Design view.

### To modify the Field Size, Description, and Caption field properties:

1. On the Table Tools Fields tab, in the Views group, click the **View** button. The table is displayed in Design view with the VisitID field selected. You need to enter a Description property value for this field, the primary key in the table, and change its Field Size property to 4 because each visit number at Riverview Veterinary Care Center consists of four digits.

2. Press the **Tab** key twice to position the insertion point in the Description (Optional) box, and then type **Primary key**.

3. Press the **F6** key to move to and select the default setting of 255 in the Field Size box in the Fields Properties pane, and then type **4**. Next you need to set the Caption property for this field.

4. Press the **Tab** key three times to position the insertion point in the Caption box, and then type **Visit ID**.

Next you need to enter a Description property value for the AnimalID field, a foreign key in the table, and set its Field Size property to 5 because each AnimalID number at Riverview Veterinary Care Center consists of five digits. You also need to set this field's Caption property.

**5.** Click the **VisitDate** Field Name box, click the **Caption** box, and then type **Date of Visit**.

For the Reason field, you will set the Field Size property to 60. This size can accommodate the longer values in the Reason field. You'll also set this field's Caption property to provide a more descriptive name.

**6.** Click the **Reason** Field Name box, press the **F6** key, type **60**, press the **Tab** key three times to position the insertion point in the Caption box, and then type **Reason/Diagnosis**.

Finally, you'll set the Caption property for the OffSite field.

**7.** Click the **OffSite** Field Name box, click the **Caption** box, and then type **Off-Site Visit?**. See Figure 2-19.

**Figure 2-19** **Visit table after modifying field properties**

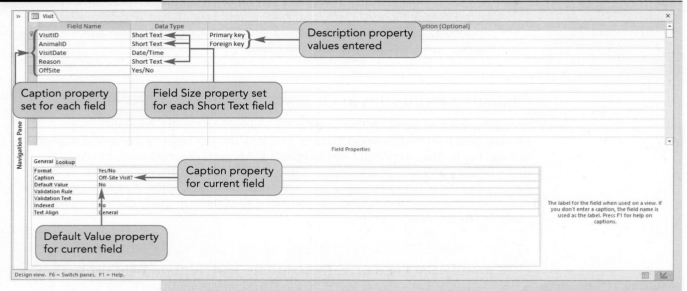

Notice that the OffSite field's Default Value property is automatically set to "No," which means the check box for this field will be empty for each new record. This is the default for this property for any Yes/No field. You can set the Default Value property for other types of fields to make data entry easier. You'll learn more about setting this property in the next session.

The changes to the Visit table's properties are now complete, so you can save the table and view the results of your changes in Datasheet view.

**To save and view the modified Visit table:**

**1.** On the Quick Access Toolbar, click the **Save** button 🖫 to save the modified table. A dialog box opens informing you that some data may be lost because you decreased the field sizes. Because all of the values in the VisitID, AnimalID, and Reason fields contain the same number of or fewer characters than the new Field Size properties you set for each field, you can ignore this message.

**2.** Click the **Yes** button.

**3.** On the Table Tools Design tab, in the Views group, click the **View** button to display the Visit table in Datasheet view. Notice that each column (field) heading now displays the text you specified in the Caption property for that field. However, now the Off-Site Visit? field caption doesn't fully display.

**4.** Place the pointer on the column border to the right of the Off-Site Visit? field name until the pointer changes to ↔, and then double-click the column border to fully display this field name. See Figure 2-20.

**Figure 2-20**    **Modified Visit table in Datasheet view**

column headings display Caption property values

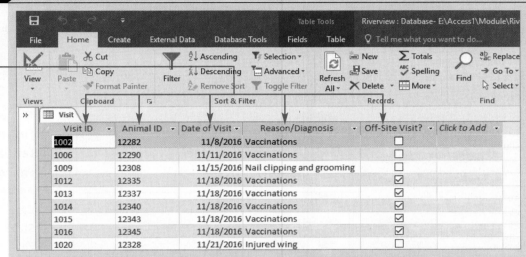

**5.** Click the **Close 'Visit'** button ☒ on the object tab to close the Visit table, and click **Yes** to save the changes to the Visit table.

**6.** If you are not continuing to Session 2.2, click the **File** tab, and then click **Close** in the navigation bar of Backstage view to close the Riverview database.

You have created the Billing table and made modifications to its design. In the next session, you'll add records to the Billing table and create the Animal and Owner tables in the Riverview database.

## Session 2.1 Quick Check

REVIEW

**1.** What guidelines should you follow when designing a database?

**2.** What is the purpose of the Data Type property for a field?

**3.** The _____ property specifies how a field's name is displayed in database objects, including table and query datasheets, forms, and reports.

**4.** For which three types of fields can you assign a field size?

**5.** The default Field Size property setting for a Short Text field is _____.

**6.** In Design view, which key do you press to move from the Table Design grid to the Field Properties pane?

**7.** List three reasons why you should specify a primary key for an Access table.

# Session 2.2 Visual Overview:

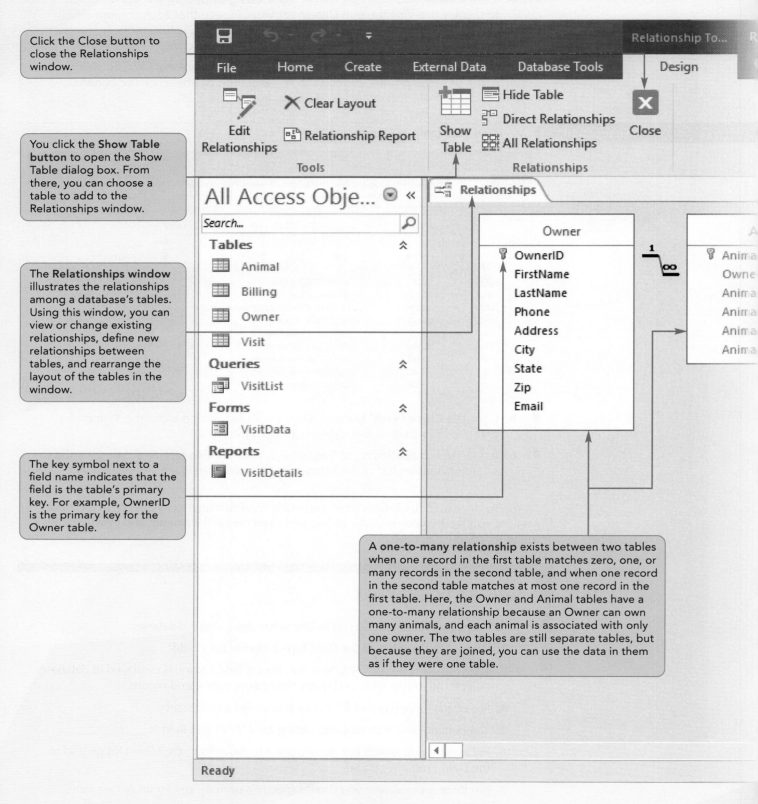

Click the Close button to close the Relationships window.

You click the **Show Table button** to open the Show Table dialog box. From there, you can choose a table to add to the Relationships window.

The **Relationships window** illustrates the relationships among a database's tables. Using this window, you can view or change existing relationships, define new relationships between tables, and rearrange the layout of the tables in the window.

The key symbol next to a field name indicates that the field is the table's primary key. For example, OwnerID is the primary key for the Owner table.

A **one-to-many relationship** exists between two tables when one record in the first table matches zero, one, or many records in the second table, and when one record in the second table matches at most one record in the first table. Here, the Owner and Animal tables have a one-to-many relationship because an Owner can own many animals, and each animal is associated with only one owner. The two tables are still separate tables, but because they are joined, you can use the data in them as if they were one table.

# Modified Visit table in Datasheet view

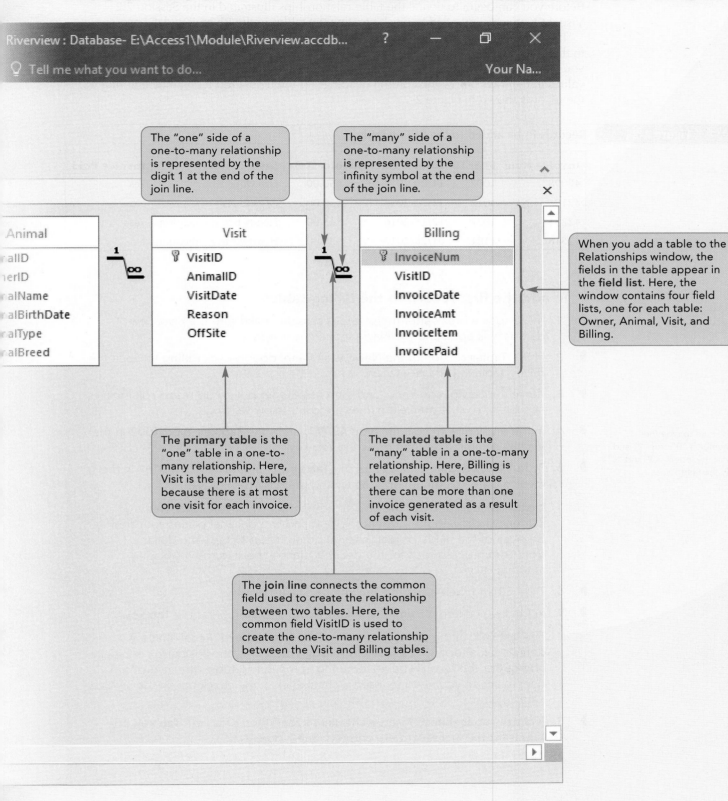

Riverview : Database- E:\Access1\Module\Riverview.accdb...    ?    —    ⬜    ✕

Tell me what you want to do...    Your Na...

The "one" side of a one-to-many relationship is represented by the digit 1 at the end of the join line.

The "many" side of a one-to-many relationship is represented by the infinity symbol at the end of the join line.

**Animal**
- allD
- ...erID
- ...alName
- ...alBirthDate
- ...alType
- ...alBreed

**Visit**
- VisitID
- AnimalID
- VisitDate
- Reason
- OffSite

**Billing**
- InvoiceNum
- VisitID
- InvoiceDate
- InvoiceAmt
- InvoiceItem
- InvoicePaid

When you add a table to the Relationships window, the fields in the table appear in the **field list**. Here, the window contains four field lists, one for each table: Owner, Animal, Visit, and Billing.

The **primary table** is the "one" table in a one-to-many relationship. Here, Visit is the primary table because there is at most one visit for each invoice.

The **related table** is the "many" table in a one-to-many relationship. Here, Billing is the related table because there can be more than one invoice generated as a result of each visit.

The **join line** connects the common field used to create the relationship between two tables. Here, the common field VisitID is used to create the one-to-many relationship between the Visit and Billing tables.

# Adding Records to a New Table

Before you can begin to define the table relationships illustrated in the Session 2.2 Visual Overview, you need to finish creating the tables in the Riverview database.

The Billing table design is complete. Now, Kimberly would like you to add records to the table so it will contain the invoice data for Riverview Veterinary Care Center. As you learned earlier, you add records to a table in Datasheet view by typing the field values in the rows below the column headings for the fields. You'll begin by entering the records shown in Figure 2-21.

| Figure 2-21 | Records to be added to the Billing table |
| --- | --- |

| Invoice Num | Visit ID | Invoice Date | Invoice Amt | Invoice Item | Invoice Paid |
| --- | --- | --- | --- | --- | --- |
| 42098 | 1002 | 11/09/2016 | $50.00 | Lab work | Yes |
| 42125 | 1012 | 11/21/2016 | $50.00 | Off-site visit | No |
| 42271 | 1077 | 12/15/2016 | $45.00 | Flea & tick medications | Yes |
| 42518 | 1181 | 01/26/2017 | $35.00 | Heartworm medication | No |

## To add the first record to the Billing table:

1. If you took a break after the previous session, make sure the Riverview database is open and the Navigation Pane is open.

2. In the Tables section of the Navigation Pane, double-click **Billing** to open the Billing table in Datasheet view.

3. Close the Navigation Pane, and then use the ✛ pointer to resize columns, as necessary, so that the field names are completely visible.

> Be sure to type the numbers "0" and "1" and *not* the letters "O" and "I" in the field values.

4. In the Invoice Num column, type **42098**, press the **Tab** key, type **1002** in the Visit ID column, and then press the **Tab** key.

5. Type **11/9/2016** and then press the **Tab** key. The date "11/09/2016" in the Invoice Date column reflects the custom date format you set.

   Next you need to enter the invoice amount for the first record. This is a Currency field with the Currency format and two decimal places specified. Because of the field's properties, you do not need to type the dollar sign, comma, or zeroes for the decimal places; these items will display automatically.

6. Type **50** and then press the **Tab** key. The value displays as "$50.00."

7. In the Invoice Item column, type **Lab work**, and then press the **Tab** key.

   The last field in the table, InvoicePaid, is a Yes/No field. Recall that the default value for any Yes/No field is "No"; therefore, the check box is initially empty. For the record you are entering in the Billing table, the invoice has been paid, so you need to insert a checkmark in the check box in the Invoice Paid column.

8. Press the **spacebar** to insert a checkmark, and then press the **Tab** key. The values for the first record are entered. See Figure 2-22.

Figure 2-22    **First record entered in the Billing table**

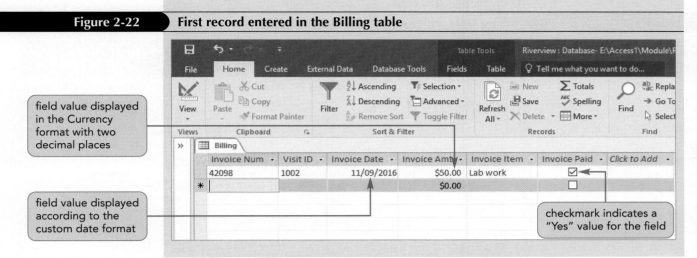

field value displayed in the Currency format with two decimal places

field value displayed according to the custom date format

checkmark indicates a "Yes" value for the field

Now you can add the remaining three records. As you do, you'll learn a keyboard shortcut for inserting the value from the same field in the previous record. A **keyboard shortcut** is a key or combination of keys you press to complete an action more efficiently.

**To add the next three records to the Billing table:**

1. Refer to Figure 2-21 and enter the values in the second record's Invoice Num, Visit ID, and Invoice Date columns.

   Notice that the value in the second record's Invoice Amt column is $50.00. This value is the exact same value as in the first record. You can quickly insert the value from the same column in the previous record using the Ctrl + ' (apostrophe) keyboard shortcut. To use this shortcut, you press and hold the Ctrl key, press the ' key once, and then release both keys. (The plus sign in the keyboard shortcut indicates you're pressing two keys at once; you do not press the + key.)

2. With the insertion point in the Invoice Amt column, press the **Ctrl + ' keys**. The value "$50.00" is inserted in the Invoice Amt column for the second record.

3. Press the **Tab** key to move to the Invoice Item column, and then type **Off-site visit**.

4. Press the **Tab** key to move to the Invoice Paid column, and then press the **Tab** key to leave the Invoice Paid check box unchecked to indicate the invoice has not been paid. The second record is entered in the Billing table.

5. Refer to Figure 2-21 to enter the values for the third and fourth records. Your table should look like the one in Figure 2-23.

| Figure 2-23 | Billing table with four records entered |

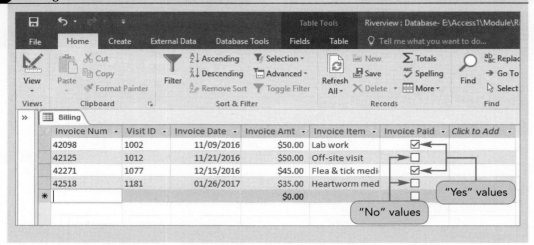

To finish entering records in the Billing table, you'll use a method that allows you to import the data.

# Importing Data from an Excel Worksheet

Often, the data you want to add to an Access table exists in another file, such as a Word document or an Excel workbook. You can bring the data from other files into Access in different ways. For example, you can copy and paste the data from an open file, or you can **import** the data, which is a process that allows you to copy the data from a source without having to open the source file.

Kimberly had been using Excel to track invoice data for Riverview Veterinary Care Center and already created a worksheet, named "Invoices," containing this data. You'll import this Excel worksheet into your Billing table to complete the entry of data in the table. To use the import method, the columns in the Excel worksheet must match the names and data types of the fields in the Access table.

The Invoices worksheet contains the following columns: InvoiceNum, VisitID, InvoiceDate, InvoiceAmt, InvoiceItem, and InvoicePaid. These column headings match the field names in the Billing table exactly, so you can import the data. Before you import data into a table, you need to close the table.

> **TIP**
>
> Caption property values set for fields are not considered in the import process. Therefore make sure that the field names match the Excel worksheet column headings. If there are differences, change the column headings in the Excel worksheet to match the Access table field names.

## To import the Invoices worksheet into the Billing table:

1. Click the **Close 'Billing'** button ⊠ on the object tab to close the Billing table, and then click the **Yes** button in the dialog box asking if you want to save the changes to the table layout.

2. On the ribbon, click the **External Data** tab.

3. In the Import & Link group, click the **Excel** button. The Get External Data - Excel Spreadsheet dialog box opens. See Figure 2-24.

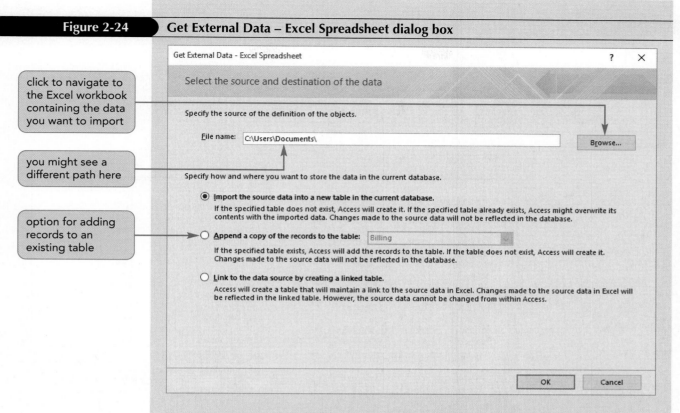

**Figure 2-24**    **Get External Data – Excel Spreadsheet dialog box**

click to navigate to the Excel workbook containing the data you want to import

you might see a different path here

option for adding records to an existing table

Get External Data - Excel Spreadsheet

Select the source and destination of the data

Specify the source of the definition of the objects.

File name:    C:\Users\Documents\                                                Browse...

Specify how and where you want to store the data in the current database.

○ Import the source data into a new table in the current database.
  If the specified table does not exist, Access will create it. If the specified table already exists, Access might overwrite its contents with the imported data. Changes made to the source data will not be reflected in the database.

○ Append a copy of the records to the table:    Billing
  If the specified table exists, Access will add the records to the table. If the table does not exist, Access will create it. Changes made to the source data will not be reflected in the database.

○ Link to the data source by creating a linked table.
  Access will create a table that will maintain a link to the source data in Excel. Changes made to the source data in Excel will be reflected in the linked table. However, the source data cannot be changed from within Access.

OK    Cancel

The dialog box provides options for importing the entire worksheet as a new table in the current database, adding the data from the worksheet to an existing table, or linking the data in the worksheet to the table. You need to add, or append, the worksheet data to the Billing table.

▶ **4.** Click the **Browse** button. The File Open dialog box opens. The Excel workbook file is named "Invoices" and is located in the Access1 > Module folder provided with your Data Files.

▶ **5.** Navigate to the **Access1 > Module** folder, where your Data Files are stored, and then double-click the **Invoices** Excel file. You return to the dialog box.

▶ **6.** Click the **Append a copy of the records to the table** option button. The box to the right of this option becomes active and displays the Billing table name, because it is the first table listed in the Navigation Pane.

▶ **7.** Click the **OK** button. The first Import Spreadsheet Wizard dialog box opens. The dialog box confirms that the first row of the worksheet you are importing contains column headings. The bottom section of the dialog box displays some of the data contained in the worksheet. See Figure 2-25.

**Figure 2-25** **First Import Spreadsheet Wizard dialog box**

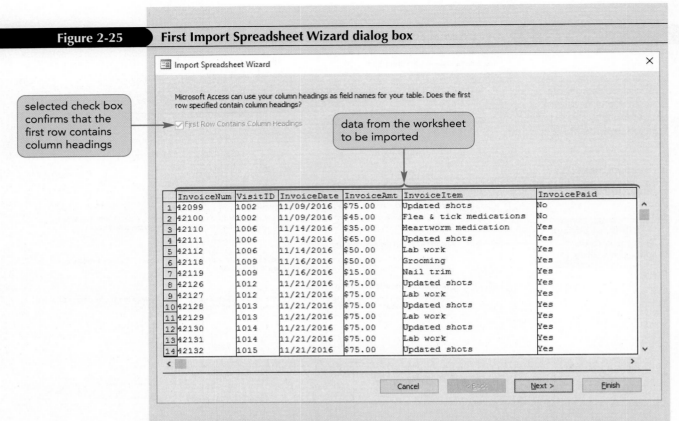

selected check box confirms that the first row contains column headings

data from the worksheet to be imported

8. Click the **Next** button. The second, and final, Import Spreadsheet Wizard dialog box opens. Notice that the Import to Table box shows that the data from the spreadsheet will be imported into the Billing table.

9. Click the **Finish** button. A dialog box opens asking if you want to save the import steps. If you needed to repeat this same import procedure many times, it would be a good idea to save the steps for the procedure. However, you don't need to save these steps because you'll be importing the data only one time. Once the data is in the Billing table, Kimberly will no longer use Excel to track invoice data.

10. Click the **Close** button in the dialog box to close it without saving the steps.

The data from the Invoices worksheet has been added to the Billing table. Next, you'll open the table to view the new records.

### To open the Billing table and view the imported data:

1. Open the Navigation Pane, and then double-click **Billing** in the Tables section to open the table in Datasheet view.

2. Resize the Invoice Item column to its best fit, scrolling the worksheet and resizing, as necessary.

▶ **3.** Press the **Ctrl + Home** keys to scroll to the top of the datasheet. Notice that the table now contains a total of 204 records—the four records you entered plus 200 records imported from the Invoices worksheet. The records are displayed in primary key order by the values in the Invoice Num column. See Figure 2-26.

| Figure 2-26 | Billing table after importing data from Excel |

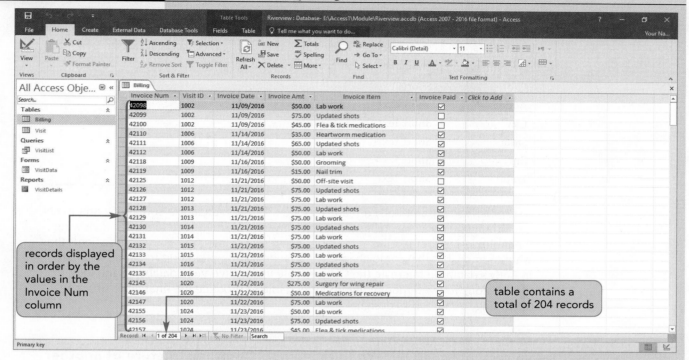

▶ **4.** Save and close the Billing table, and then close the Navigation Pane.

Two of the tables—Visit and Billing—are now complete. According to Kimberly's plan for the Riverview database, you still need to create the Owner and Animal tables. You'll use a different method to create these tables.

# Creating a Table by Importing an Existing Table or Table Structure

If another Access database contains a table—or even just the design, or structure, of a table—that you want to include in your database, you can import the table and any records it contains or import only the table structure into your database. To create the new Owner and Animal tables per Kimberly's plan shown in Figure 2-2, you will import a table structure from a different Access database to create the Owner table and an existing table structure and records from another database to create the Animal table.

## Importing an Existing Table Structure

Kimberly documented the design for the new Owner table by listing each field's name and data type, as well as any applicable field size, description, and caption property values, as shown in Figure 2-27. Note that each field in the Owner table will be a Short Text field, and the OwnerID field will be the table's primary key.

**Figure 2-27** **Design for the Owner table**

| Field Name | Data Type | Field Size | Description | Caption |
|---|---|---|---|---|
| OwnerID | Short Text | 4 | Primary key | Owner ID |
| FirstName | Short Text | 20 | | First Name |
| LastName | Short Text | 25 | | Last Name |
| Phone | Short Text | 14 | | |
| Address | Short Text | 35 | | |
| City | Short Text | 25 | | |
| State | Short Text | 2 | | |
| Zip | Short Text | 10 | | |
| Email | Short Text | 50 | | |

Kimberly's assistant Kelly already created an Access database containing an Owner table design, however, she hasn't entered any records into the table. After reviewing the table design, both Kelly and Kimberly agree that it contains some of the fields they want to track, but that some changes are needed. You will import the table structure in Kelly's database to create the Owner table in the Riverview database, and later in this session, you will modify the imported table to produce the final table structure according to Kimberly's design.

### To create the Owner table by importing the structure of another table:

1. Make sure the External Data tab is the active tab on the ribbon.

2. In the Import & Link group, click the **Access** button. The Get External Data - Access Database dialog box opens. This dialog box is similar to the one you used earlier when importing the Excel spreadsheet.

3. Click the **Browse** button. The File Open dialog box opens. The Access database file from which you need to import the table structure is named "Kelly" and is located in the Access1 > Module folder provided with your Data Files.

4. Navigate to the **Access1 > Module** folder, where your Data Files are stored, and then double-click the **Kelly** database file. You return to the dialog box.

5. Make sure the **Import tables, queries, forms, reports, macros, and modules into the current database** option button is selected, and then click the **OK** button. The Import Objects dialog box opens. The dialog box contains tabs for importing all the different types of Access database objects—tables, queries, forms, and so on. The Tables tab is the current tab.

6. Click the **Options** button in the dialog box to see all the options for importing tables. See Figure 2-28.

Figure 2-28 **Import Objects dialog box**

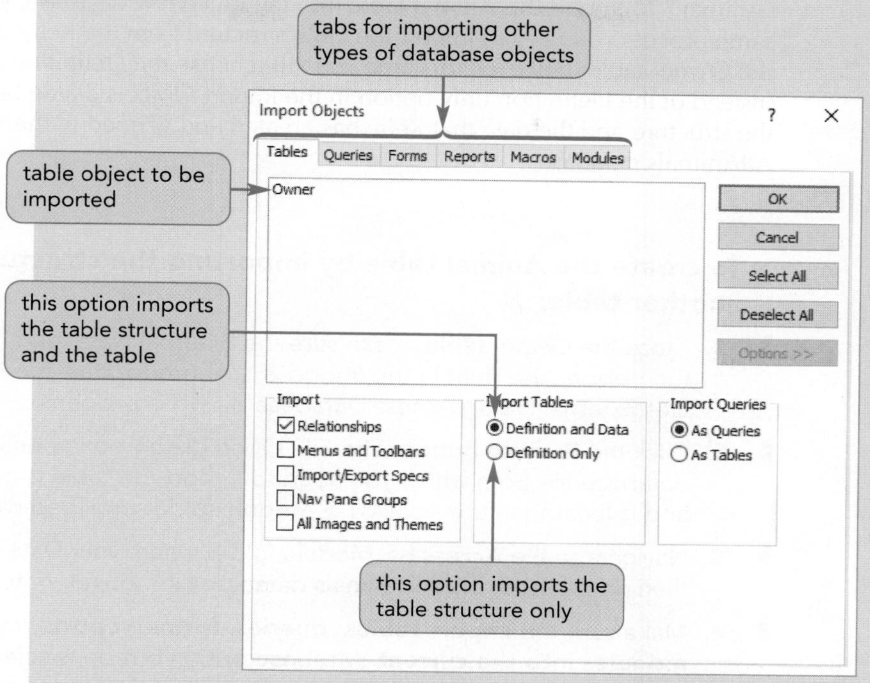

tabs for importing other types of database objects

table object to be imported

this option imports the table structure and the table

this option imports the table structure only

7. On the Tables tab, click **Owner** to select this table.

8. In the Import Tables section of the dialog box, click the **Definition Only** option button, and then click the **OK** button. Access creates the Owner table in the Riverview database using the structure of the Owner table in the Kelly database, and opens a dialog box asking if you want to save the import steps.

9. Click the **Close** button to close the dialog box without saving the import steps.

10. Open the Navigation Pane, double-click **Owner** in the Tables section to open the table, and then close the Navigation Pane. The Owner table opens in Datasheet view. The table contains no records. See Figure 2-29.

**Figure 2-29** **Imported Owner table in Datasheet view**

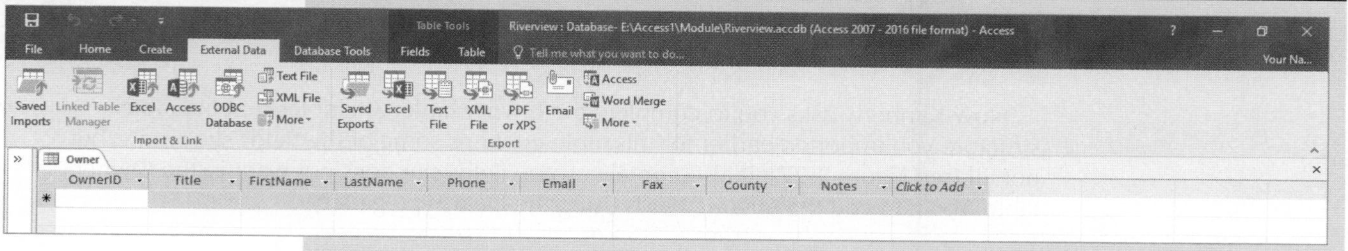

Before you add records to the Owner table and fine-tune its design, you need to first add the Animal table to the Riverview database. You will do this by importing a table and its data from another database.

## Importing an Existing Table

Kelly has already created a database called "AllAnimals" that contains a table called "Animal." To import this Animal table into the Riverview database, you will follow the same process you used to import the table structure from the Kelly database to create the Owner table; however, this time you will choose the Definition and Data option, instead of the Definition only option in the Import Objects dialog box. This will import the structure and the data that Kelly has created and verified in the Animal table in the AllAnimals database.

### To create the Animal table by importing the structure and data of another table:

▶ 1. Close the Owner table, make sure the External Data tab is the active tab on the ribbon, and then in the Import & Link group, click the **Access** button. The Get External Data - Access Database dialog box opens.

▶ 2. Click the **Browse** button. The File Open dialog box opens. The Access database file from which you need to import the table is named "AllAnimals" and is located in the Access1 > Module folder provided with your Data Files.

▶ 3. Navigate to the **Access1 > Module** folder, where your Data Files are stored, and then double-click the **AllAnimals** database file. You return to the dialog box.

▶ 4. Make sure the **Import tables, queries, forms, reports, macros, and modules into the current database** option button is selected, and then click the **OK** button to open the Import Objects dialog box opens. The Tables tab is the current tab.

▶ 5. Click **Animal** to select this table, click the **Options** button to display the options for importing tables, and then, in the Import Tables section, make sure the **Definition and Data** option button is selected.

▶ 6. Click the **OK** button, and then click the **Close** button to close the dialog box without saving the import steps. Access creates the Animal table in the Riverview database using the records and structure of the Animal table in the AllAnimals database.

▶ 7. Open the Navigation Pane, double-click **Animal** in the Tables section to open the table, and then close the Navigation Pane. The Animal table opens in Datasheet view. Kimberly reviews the new Animal table and is satisfied with its structure and the records it contains, so you can close this table.

▶ 8. Close the Animal table.

Now Kimberly asks you to complete the Owner table. She notes that the table structure you imported earlier for this table contains some of the fields she wants, but not all (see Figure 2-27); it also contains some fields she does not want in the Owner table. You can add the missing fields using the Data Type gallery.

# Adding Fields to a Table Using the Data Type Gallery

The **Data Type gallery**, available from the More Fields button located on the Add & Delete group on the Table Tools Fields tab, allows you to add a group of related fields to a table at the same time, rather than adding each field to the table individually.

The group of fields you add is called a **Quick Start selection**. For example, the **Address Quick Start selection** adds a collection of fields related to an address, such as Address, City, State, and so on, to the table at one time. When you use a Quick Start selection, the fields added already have properties set. However, you need to review and possibly modify the properties to ensure the fields match your design needs for the database.

Next, you'll use the Data Type gallery to add the missing fields to the Owner table.

### To add fields to the Owner table using the Data Type gallery:

1. Open the **Owner** table, and then on the ribbon, click the **Table Tools Fields** tab. Before inserting fields from the Data Type gallery, you need to place the insertion point in the field to the right of where you want to insert the new fields. According to Kimberly's design, the Address field should come after the Phone field, so you need to make the next field, Email, the active field.

Make sure the correct field is active before adding new fields.

2. Click the **first row** in the Email field to make it the active field.

3. In the Add & Delete group, click the **More Fields** button. The Data Type gallery opens and displays options for different types of fields you can add to your table.

4. Scroll down the gallery until the Quick Start section is visible. See Figure 2-30.

**Figure 2-30**    **Owner table with the Data Type gallery displayed**

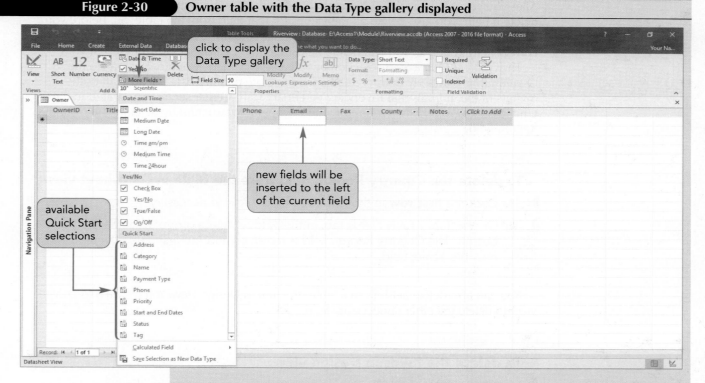

The Quick Start section provides options that will add multiple, related fields to the table at one time. The new fields will be inserted to the left of the current field.

5. In the Quick Start section, click **Address**. Five fields are added to the table: Address, City, State Province, ZIP Postal, and Country Region. See Figure 2-31.

| Figure 2-31 | Owner table after adding fields from the Data Type gallery |
| --- | --- |

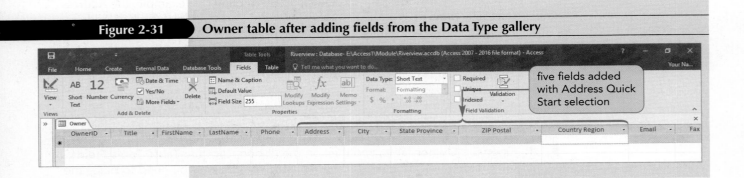

## Modifying the Structure of an Imported Table

Refer back to Kimberly's design for the Owner table (Figure 2-27). To finalize the table design, you need to modify the imported table by deleting fields, renaming fields, and changing field data types. You'll begin by deleting fields.

### Deleting Fields from a Table Structure

After you've created a table, you might need to delete one or more fields. When you delete a field, you also delete all the values for that field from the table. So, before you delete a field, you should make sure that you want to do so and that you choose the correct field to delete. You can delete fields in either Datasheet view or Design view.

The Address Quick Start selection added a field named "Country Region" to the Owner table. Kimberly doesn't need a field to store country data because all of the owners of the animals that Riverview Veterinary Care Center serves are located in the United States. You'll begin to modify the Owner table structure by deleting the Country Region field.

**To delete the Country Region field from the table in Datasheet view:**

▶ **1.** Click the **first row** in the Country Region field (if necessary).

▶ **2.** On the Table Tools Fields tab, in the Add & Delete group, click the **Delete** button. The Country Region field is removed and the first field, OwnerID, is now the active field.

You can also delete fields from a table structure in Design view. You'll switch to Design view to delete the other unnecessary fields.

**To delete the fields in Design view:**

▶ **1.** On the Table Tools Fields tab, in the Views group, click the **View** button. The Owner table opens in Design view. See Figure 2-32.

**Figure 2-32**    Owner table in Design view

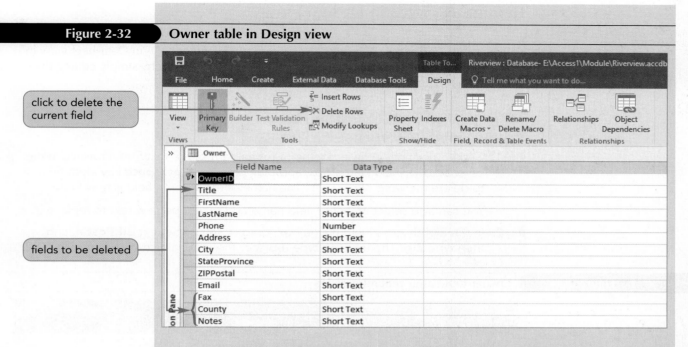

click to delete the current field

fields to be deleted

2. Click the **Title** Field Name box to make it the current field.

3. On the Table Tools Design tab, in the Tools group, click the **Delete Rows** button. The Title field is removed from the Owner table structure. You'll delete the Fax, County, and Notes fields next. Instead of deleting these fields individually, you'll select and delete them at the same time.

4. On the row selector for the **Fax** field, press and hold the mouse button and then drag the mouse to select the **County** and **Notes** fields.

5. Release the mouse button. The rows for the three fields are outlined in red, indicating all three fields are selected.

6. In the Tools group, click the **Delete Rows** button. See Figure 2-33.

**Figure 2-33**    Owner table after deleting fields

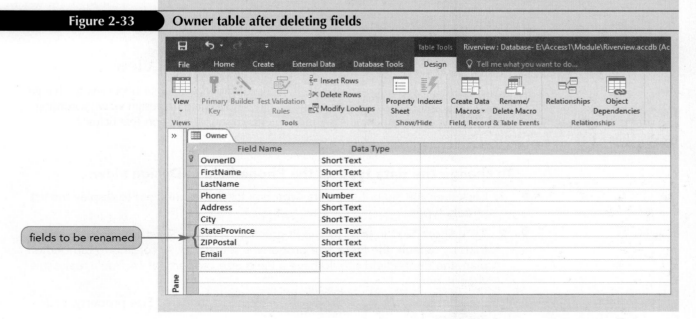

fields to be renamed

## Renaming Fields in Design View

To match Kimberly's design for the Owner table, you need to rename some of the fields. You already have renamed the default primary key field (ID) in Datasheet view in the previous module. You can also rename fields in Design view by simply editing the names in the Table Design grid.

### To rename the fields in Design view:

▶ 1. Click to position the insertion point to the right of the text StateProvince in the seventh row's Field Name box, and then press the **Backspace** key eight times to delete the word "Province." The name of the seventh field is now State.

You can also select an entire field name and then type new text to replace it.

▶ 2. In the eighth row's Field Name box, drag to select the text **ZIPPostal**, and then type **Zip**. The text you type replaces the original text. See Figure 2-34.

| Figure 2-34 | Owner table after renaming fields |
| --- | --- |

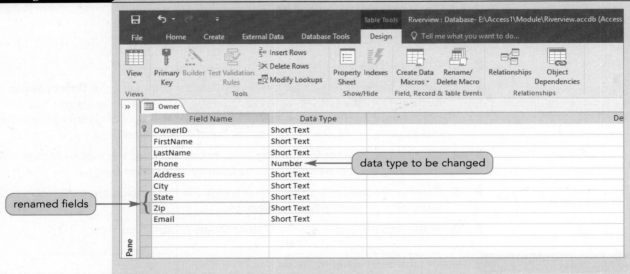

## Changing the Data Type for a Field in Design View

In the table structure you imported earlier, you used an option in Datasheet view to change a field's data type. You can also change the data type for a field in Design view. According to Kimberly's plan, all of the fields in the Owner table should be Short Text fields.

### To change the data type of the Phone field in Design view:

▶ 1. Click the right side of the Data Type box for the Phone field to display the list of data types.

▶ 2. Click **Short Text** in the list. The Phone field is now a Short Text field. Note that, by default, the Field Size property is set to 255. According to Kimberly's plan, the Phone field should have a Field Size property of 14. You'll make this change next.

▶ 3. Press the **F6** key to move to and select the default Field Size property, and then type **14**.

Each of the remaining fields you added using the Address Quick Start selection—Address, City, State, and Zip—also has the default field size of 255. You need to change the Field Size property for these fields to match Kimberly's design. You'll also delete any Caption property values for these fields because the field names match how Kimberly wants them displayed, so captions are unnecessary.

### To change the Field Size and Caption properties for the fields:

1. Click the **Address Field Name** box to make it the current field.

2. Press the **F6** key to move to and select the default Field Size property, and then type **35**. Note that the Caption property setting for this field is the same as the field name. This field doesn't need a caption, so you can delete this value.

3. Press the **Tab** key three times to select Address in the Caption box, and then press the **Delete** key. The Caption property value is removed.

4. Repeat Steps 1 through 3 for the City field to change the Field Size property to **25** and delete its Caption property value.

5. Change the Field Size property for the State field to **2**, and then delete its Caption property value.

6. Change the Field Size property for the Zip field to **10**, and then delete its Caption property value.

7. On the Quick Access Toolbar, click the **Save** button 🖫 to save your changes to the Owner table.

Finally, Kimberly would like you to set the Description property for the OwnerID field and the Caption property for the OwnerID, FirstName, and LastName fields. You'll make these changes now.

### To enter the Description and Caption property values:

1. Click the **Description (Optional)** box for the OwnerID field, and then type **Primary key**.

2. In the Field Properties pane, click the **Caption** box.

   After you leave the Description (Optional) box, the Property Update Options button 📝 appears below this box for the OwnerID field. When you change a field's property in Design view, you can use this button to update the corresponding property on forms and reports that include the modified field. For example, if the Riverview database included a form that contained the OwnerID field, you could choose to propagate, or update, the modified Description property in the form by clicking the Property Update Options button, and then choosing the option to make the update everywhere the field is used. The ScreenTip on the Property Update Options button and the options it lists vary depending on the task; in this case, if you click the button, the option is "Update Status Bar Text everywhere OwnerID is used." Because the Riverview database does not include any forms or reports that are based on the Owner table, you do not need to update the properties, so you can ignore the button for now. In most cases, however, it is a good idea to perform the update.

3. In the Caption box for the OwnerID field, type **Owner ID**.

4. Click the **FirstName** Field Name box to make it the current field, click the **Caption** box, and then type **First Name**.

5. Click the **LastName** Field Name box to make it the current field, click the **Caption** box, and then type **Last Name**. See Figure 2-35.

**Figure 2-35**    **Owner table after entering descriptions and captions**

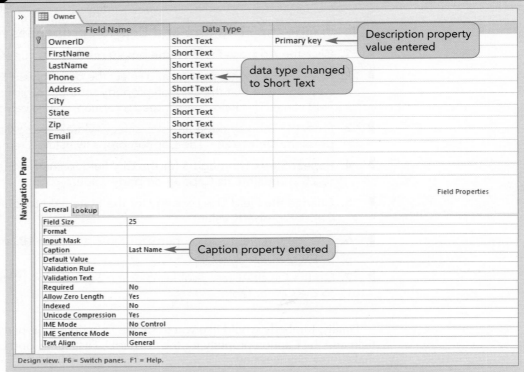

6. On the Quick Access Toolbar, click the **Save** button to save your changes to the Owner table.

7. On the Table Tools Design tab, in the Views group, click the **View** button to display the table in Datasheet view.

8. Resize each column to its best fit, and then click in the first row for the **Owner ID** column. See Figure 2-36.

**Figure 2-36**    **Modified Owner table in Datasheet view**

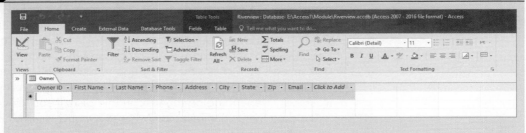

Kimberly feels that data entry would be made easier if the State field value of "WY" was automatically filled in for each new record added to the table, because all of the owners live in Wyoming. You can accomplish this by setting the Default Value property for the field.

# Setting the Default Value Property for a Field

The **Default Value property** for a field specifies what value will appear, by default, for the field in each new record you add to a table.

Because all of the owners at Riverview Veterinary Care Center live in Wyoming, you'll specify a default value of "WY" for the State field in the Owner table. With this setting, each new record in the Owner table will have the correct State field value entered automatically.

### To set the Default Value property for the State field:

1. On the Home tab, in the Views group, click the **View** button to display the Owner table in Design view.

2. Click the **State** Field Name box to make it the current field.

3. In the Field Properties pane, click the **Default Value** box, type **WY**, and then press the **Tab** key. See Figure 2-37.

| Figure 2-37 | Specifying the Default Value property for the State field |

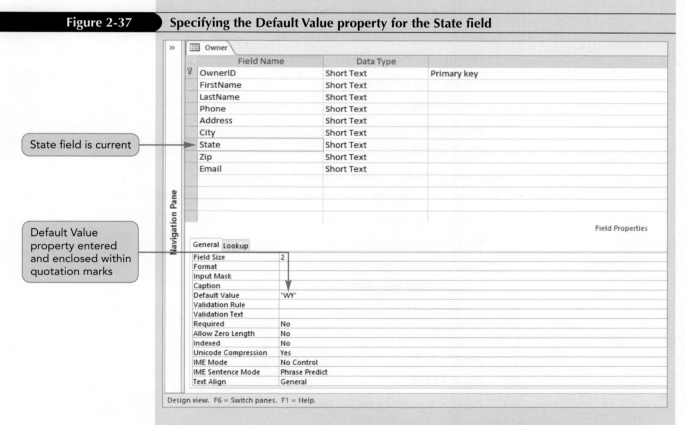

Note that a text entry in the Default Value property must be enclosed within quotation marks. If you do not type the quotation marks, Access adds them for you. However, for some entries, you would receive an error message indicating invalid syntax if you omitted the quotation marks. In such cases, you have to enter the quotation marks yourself.

4. On the Quick Access Toolbar, click the **Save** button 🖫 to save your changes to the Owner table.

5. Display the table in Datasheet view. Note that the State field for the first row now displays the default value "WY" as specified by the Default Value property. Each new record entered in the table will automatically have this State field value entered.

With the Owner table design set, you can now enter records in it. You'll begin by entering two records, and then you'll use a different method to add the remaining records.

**Note:** Be sure to enter your last name and first name where indicated.

### To add two records to the Owner table:

1. Enter the following values in the columns in the first record; note that you can press **Tab** to move past the default State field value:

   Owner ID = **2310**

   First Name = **[student's first name]**

   Last Name = **[student's last name]**

   Phone = **307-824-1245**

   Address = **12 Elm Ln**

   City = **Cody**

   State = **WY**

   Zip = **82414**

   Email = **student@example.com**

2. Enter the following values in the columns in the second record:

   Owner ID = **2314**

   First Name = **Sally**

   Last Name = **Cruz**

   Phone = **307-406-4321**

   Address = **199 18th Ave**

   City = **Ralston**

   State = **WY**

   Zip = **82440**

   Email = **scruz@example.com**

3. Resize columns to their best fit, as necessary, and then save and close the Owner table.

Before Kimberly decided to store data using Access, Kelly managed the owner data for the care center in a different system. She exported that data into a text file and now asks you to import it into the new Owner table. You can import the data contained in this text file to add the remaining records to the Owner table.

# Adding Data to a Table by Importing a Text File

There are many ways to import data into an Access database. So far, you've learned how to add data to an Access table by importing an Excel spreadsheet, and you've created a new table by importing the structure of an existing table. You can also import data contained in text files.

To complete the entry of records in the Owner table, you'll import the data contained in Kelly's text file. The file is named "Owner" and is located in the Access1 > Module folder provided with your Data Files.

### To import the data contained in the Owner text file:

▶ **1.** On the ribbon, click the **External Data** tab.

▶ **2.** In the Import & Link group, click the **Text File** button. The Get External Data - Text File dialog box opens. This dialog box is similar to the one you used earlier when importing the Excel spreadsheet and the Access table structure.

▶ **3.** Click the **Browse** button. The File Open dialog box opens.

▶ **4.** Navigate to the **Access1 > Module** folder, where your Data Files are stored, and then double-click the **Owner** file. You return to the dialog box.

▶ **5.** Click the **Append a copy of the records to the table** option button. The box to the right of this option becomes active. Next, you need to select the table to which you want to add the data.

▶ **6.** Click the arrow on the box, and then click **Owner**.

▶ **7.** Click the **OK** button. The first Import Text Wizard dialog box opens. The dialog box indicates that the data to be imported is in a delimited format. A **delimited text file** is one in which fields of data are separated by a character such as a comma or a tab. In this case, the dialog box shows that data is separated by the comma character in the text file.

▶ **8.** Make sure the **Delimited** option button is selected in the dialog box, and then click the **Next** button. The second Import Text Wizard dialog box opens. See Figure 2-38.

**Figure 2-38** Second Import Wizard dialog box

fields in the text file are separated by commas

preview of the data being imported

This dialog box asks you to confirm the delimiter character that separates the fields in the text file you're importing. Access detects that the comma character is used in the Owner text file and selects this option. The bottom area of the dialog box provides a preview of the data you're importing.

9. Make sure the **Comma** option button is selected, and then click the **Next** button. The third and final Import Text Wizard dialog box opens. Notice that the Import to Table box shows that the data will be imported into the Owner table.

10. Click the **Finish** button, and then click the **Close** button in the dialog box that opens to close it without saving the import steps.

Kimberly asks you to open the Owner table in Datasheet view so she can see the results of importing the text file.

### To view the Owner table datasheet:

1. Open the Navigation Pane, and then double-click **Owner** to open the Owner table in Datasheet view. The Owner table contains a total of 25 records.

2. Close the Navigation Pane, and then resize columns to their best fit, scrolling the table datasheet as necessary, so that all field values are displayed. When finished, scroll back to display the first fields in the table, and then click the first row's **Owner ID** field, if necessary. See Figure 2-39.

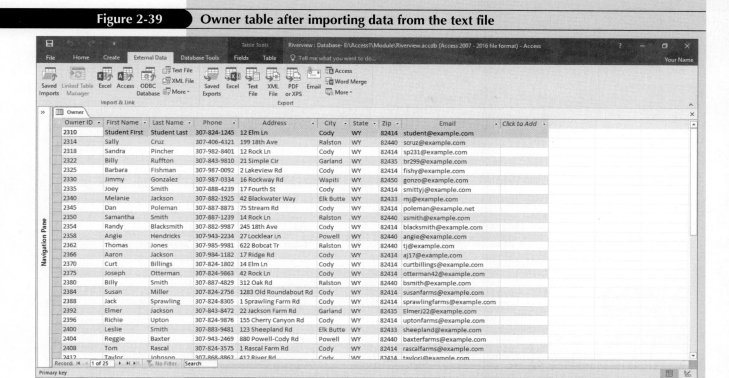

**Figure 2-39**    **Owner table after importing data from the text file**

> **3.** Save and close the Owner table, and then open the Navigation Pane.

The Riverview database now contains four tables—Visit, Billing, Owner, and Animal—and the tables contain all the necessary records. Your final task is to complete the database design by defining the necessary relationship between its tables.

# Defining Table Relationships

One of the most powerful features of a relational database management system is its ability to define relationships between tables. You use a common field to relate one table to another. The process of relating tables is often called performing a **join**. When you join tables that have a common field, you can extract data from them as if they were one larger table. For example, you can join the Animal and Visit tables by using the AnimalID field in both tables as the common field. Then you can use a query, form, or report to extract selected data from each table, even though the data is contained in two separate tables, as shown in Figure 2-40. The AnimalVisits query shown in Figure 2-40 includes the AnimalID, AnimalName, AnimalType, and AnimalBreed fields from the Animal table, and the VisitDate and Reason fields from the Visit table. The joining of records is based on the common field of AnimalID. The Animal and Visit tables have a type of relationship called a one-to-many relationship.

| Figure 2-40 | One-to-many relationship and sample query |
| --- | --- |

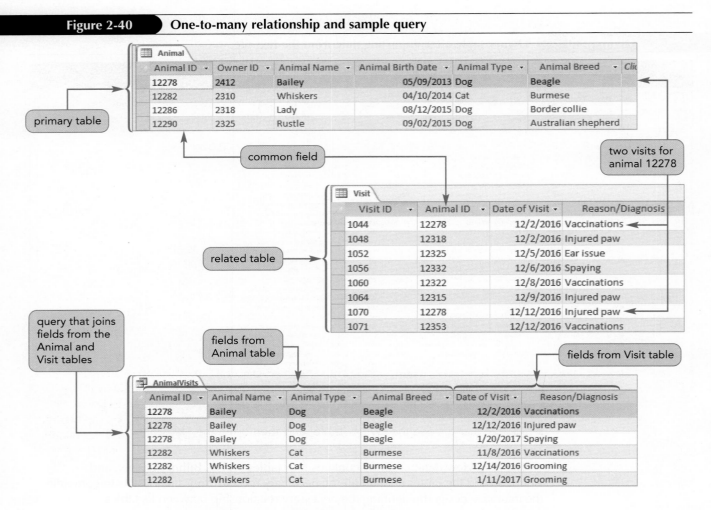

## One-to-Many Relationships

As shown earlier in the Session 2.2 Visual Overview, a one-to-many relationship exists between two tables when one record in the first table matches zero, one, or many records in the second table, and when one record in the second table matches at most one record in the first table. For example, as shown in Figure 2-40, Animal 12278 has two visits in the Visit table. Other animals have one or more visits. Every visit has a single matching animal.

In Access, the two tables that form a relationship are referred to as the primary table and the related table. The primary table is the "one" table in a one-to-many relationship; in Figure 2-40, the Animal table is the primary table because there is only one animal for each visit. The related table is the "many" table; in Figure 2-40, the Visit table is the related table because an animal can have zero, one, or many visits.

Because related data is stored in two tables, inconsistencies between the tables can occur. Referring to Figure 2-40, consider the following three scenarios:

- Kimberly adds a record to the Visit table for a new animal, Fluffy (a Siberian cat), using Animal ID 12500. She did not first add the new animal's information to the animal table, so this visit does not have a matching record in the animal table. The data is inconsistent, and the visit record is considered to be an **orphaned record**.
- In another situation, Kimberly changes the AnimalID in the Animal table for Bailey the beagle from 12278 to 12510. Because there is no longer an animal with the AnimalID 12278 in the Animal table, this change creates two orphaned records in the Visit table, and the database is inconsistent.

- In a third scenario, Kimberly deletes the record for Bailey the beagle, Animal 12278, from the Animal table because this animal and its owner have moved and so the animal no longer receives care from Riverview. The database is again inconsistent; two records for Animal 12278 in the Visit table have no matching record in the Animal table.

You can avoid these types of problems and avoid having inconsistent data in your database by specifying referential integrity between tables when you define their relationships.

## Referential Integrity

**Referential integrity** is a set of rules that Access enforces to maintain consistency between related tables when you update data in a database. Specifically, the referential integrity rules are as follows:

- When you add a record to a related table, a matching record must already exist in the primary table, thereby preventing the possibility of orphaned records.
- If you attempt to change the value of the primary key in the primary table, Access prevents this change if matching records exist in a related table. However, if you choose the **Cascade Update Related Fields option**, Access permits the change in value to the primary key and changes the appropriate foreign key values in the related table, thereby eliminating the possibility of inconsistent data.
- When you attempt to delete a record in the primary table, Access prevents the deletion if matching records exist in a related table. However, if you choose the **Cascade Delete Related Records option**, Access deletes the record in the primary table and also deletes all records in related tables that have matching foreign key values. However, you should rarely select the Cascade Delete Related Records option because doing so might cause you to inadvertently delete records you did not intend to delete. It is best to use other methods for deleting records that give you more control over the deletion process.

## Defining a Relationship Between Two Tables

At the Riverview Veterinary Care Center, the owners own animals, the animals visit the clinic, and the owner receives the bill for the visits. It is important to understand these relationships in order to determine which owner to send the bill to for the visit each animal makes. Understanding these relationships also allows you to establish relationships between the tables of records in the Riverview database. When two tables have a common field, you can define a relationship between them in the Relationships window, as shown in the Session 2.2 Visual Overview.

Next, you need to define a series of relationships in the Riverview database. First, you will define a one-to-many relationship between the Owner and Animal tables, with Owner as the primary table and Animal as the related table and with OwnerID as the common field (primary key in the Owner table and a foreign key in the Animal table). Second, you will define a one-to-many relationship between the Animal and Visit tables, with Animal as the primary table and Visit as the related table and with AnimalID as the common field (the primary key in the Animal table and a foreign key in the Visit table). Finally, you will define a one-to-many relationship between the Visit and Billing tables, with Visit as the primary table and Billing as the related table and with VisitID as the common field (the primary key in the Visit table and a foreign key in the Billing table).

**To define the one-to-many relationship between the Owner and Animal tables:**

▶ **1.** On the ribbon, click the **Database Tools** tab.

▶ **2.** In the Relationships group, click the **Relationships** button to display the Relationship window and open the Show Table dialog box. See Figure 2-41.

| Figure 2-41 | Show Table dialog box |
| --- | --- |

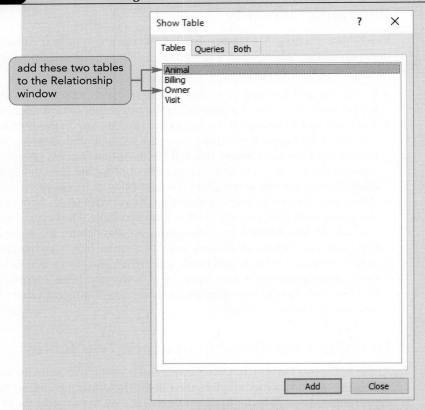

You must add each table participating in a relationship to the Relationships window. Because the Owner table is the primary table in the relationship, you'll add it first.

**TIP**

You can also double-click a table in the Show Table dialog box to add it to the Relationships window.

▶ **3.** Click **Owner**, and then click the **Add** button. The Owner table's field list is added to the Relationships window.

▶ **4.** Click **Animal**, and then click the **Add** button. The Animal table's field list is added to the Relationships window.

▶ **5.** Click the **Close** button in the Show Table dialog box to close it.

So that you can view all the fields and complete field names, you'll resize the Owner table field list.

▶ **6.** Position the mouse pointer on the bottom border of the Owner table field list until it changes to ↕, and then drag the bottom of the Owner table field list to lengthen it until the vertical scroll bar disappears and all the fields are visible.

To form the relationship between the two tables, you drag the common field of OwnerID from the primary table to the related table. Then Access opens the Edit Relationships dialog box, in which you select the relationship options for the two tables.

7. Click **OwnerID** in the Owner field list, and then drag it to **OwnerID** in the Animal field list. When you release the mouse button, the Edit Relationships dialog box opens. See Figure 2-42.

| Figure 2-42 | Edit Relationships dialog box |

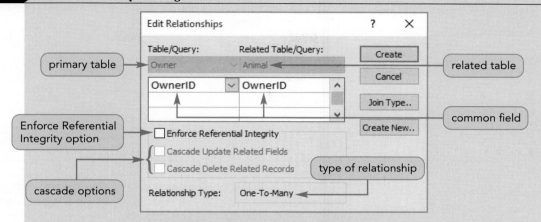

The primary table, related table, common field, and relationship type (One-To-Many) appear in the dialog box. Note that Access correctly identifies the "One" side of the relationship and places the primary table Owner in the Table/Query section of the dialog box; similarly, Access correctly identifies the "Many" side of the relationship and places the related table Animal in the Related Table/Query section of the dialog box.

8. Click the **Enforce Referential Integrity** check box. After you click the Enforce Referential Integrity check box, the two cascade options become available. If you select the Cascade Update Related Fields option, Access will update the appropriate foreign key values in the related table when you change a primary key value in the primary table. You will *not* select the Cascade Delete Related Records option because doing so could cause you to delete records that you do not want to delete; this option is rarely selected.

9. Click the **Cascade Update Related Fields** check box.

10. Click the **Create** button to define the one-to-many relationship between the two tables and to close the dialog box. The completed relationship appears in the Relationships window, with the join line connecting the common field of OwnerID in each table. See Figure 2-43.

**Figure 2-43** Defined relationship in the Relationship window

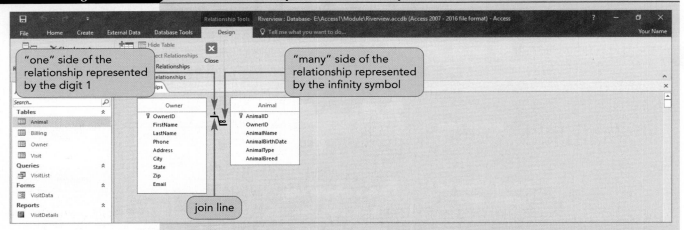

**Trouble?** If a dialog box opens indicating a problem that prevents you from creating the relationship, you most likely made a typing error when entering the two records in the Owner table. If so, click the OK button in the dialog box and then click the Cancel button in the Edit Relationships dialog box. Refer back to the earlier steps instructing you to enter the two records in the Owner table and carefully compare your entries with those shown in the text, especially the OwnerID field values. Make any necessary corrections to the data in the Owner table, and then repeat Steps 7 through 10. If you still receive an error message, ask your instructor for assistance.

The next step is to define the one-to-many relationship between the Animal and Visit tables. In this relationship, Animal is the primary ("one") table because there is at most one animal for each visit. Visit is the related ("many") table because there are zero, one, or many visits that are generated for each animal. Similarly, you need to define the one-to-many relationship between the Visit and Billing tables. In this relationship, Visit is the primary ("one") table because there is at most one visit for each invoice. Billing is the related ("many") table because there are zero, one, or many invoices that are generated for each animal visit. For example, some visits require lab work, which is invoiced separately.

**To define the relationship between the Animal and Visit tables and to define the relationship between the Visit and billing tables:**

1. On the Relationship Tools Design tab, in the Relationships group, click the **Show Table** button to open the Show Table dialog box.

**TIP**

You can also use the mouse to drag a table from the Navigation Pane to add it to the Relationships window.

2. Click **Visit** on the Tables tab, click the **Add** button, and then click the **Close** button to close the Show Table dialog box. The Visit table's field list appears in the Relationships window to the right of the Animal table's field list.

Because the Animal table is the primary table in this relationship, you need to drag the AnimalID field from the Animal field list to the Visit field list.

3. Drag the **AnimalID** field in the Animal field list to the **AnimalID** field in the Visit field list. When you release the mouse button, the Edit Relationships dialog box opens.

4. Click the **Enforce Referential Integrity** check box, click the **Cascade Update Related Fields** check box, and then click the **Create** button. The Edit Relationships dialog box closes and the completed relationship appears in the Relationships window.

Finally, you will define the relationship between the Visit and Billing tables.

5. On the Relationship Tools Design tab, in the Relationships group, click the **Show Table** button to open the Show Table dialog box.

6. Click **Billing** on the Tables tab, click the **Add** button, and then click the **Close** button to close the Show Table dialog box. The Billing table's field list appears in the Relationships window to the right of the Visit table's field list.

7. Click and drag the **VisitID** field in the Visit field list to the **VisitID** field in the Billing field list. The Edit Relationships dialog box opens.

8. In the Edit Relationships dialog box, click the **Enforce Referential Integrity** check box, click the **Cascade Update Related Fields** check box, and then click the **Create** button to define the one-to-many relationship between the two tables and to close the dialog box. The completed relationships for the Riverview database appear in the Relationships window. See Figure 2-44.

| Figure 2-44 | All three relationships now defined |

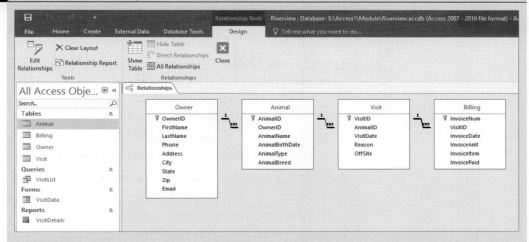

9. On the Quick Access Toolbar, click the **Save** button 🖫 to save the layout in the Relationships window.

10. On the Relationship Tools Design tab, in the Relationships group, click the **Close** button to close the Relationships window.

11. Compact and repair the Riverview database, and then close the database.

## Problem Solving: Creating a Larger Database

The Riverview database is a relatively small database containing only a few tables, and the data and the reports you will generate from it will be fairly simple. A larger database would most likely have many more tables and different types of relationships that can be quite complex. When creating a large database, follow this standard process:

- Consult people who will be using the data to gain an understanding of how it will be used. Gather sample reports and representative data if possible.
- Plan the tables, fields, data types, other properties, and the relationships between the tables.
- Create the tables and define the relationships between them.
- Populate the tables with sample data.
- Design some queries, forms, and reports that will be needed, and then test them.
- Modify the database structure, if necessary, based on the results of your tests.
- Enter the actual data into the database tables.

Testing is critical at every stage of creating a database. Once the database is finalized and implemented, it's not actually finished. The design of a database evolves as new functionality is required and as the data that is gathered changes.

## Session 2.2 Quick Check

1. What is the keyboard shortcut for inserting the value from the same field in the previous record into the current record?

2. _____ data is a process that allows you to copy the data from a source without having to open the source file.

3. The _____ gallery allows you to add a group of related fields to a table at the same time, rather than adding each field to the table individually.

4. What is the effect of deleting a field from a table structure?

5. A(n) _____ text file is one in which fields of data are separated by a character such as a comma or a tab.

6. The _____ is the "one" table in a one-to-many relationship, and the _____ is the "many" table in the relationship.

7. _____ is a set of rules that Access enforces to maintain consistency between related tables when you update data in a database.

## Review Assignments

**PRACTICE**

**Data File needed for the Review Assignments: Vendor.accdb** (*cont. from Module 1*) **and Supplies.xlsx**

In addition to tracking information about the vendors Riverview Veterinary Care Center works with, Kimberly also wants to track information about their products and services. First, Kimberly asks you to modify the necessary properties in the existing Supplier table in the Vendor database; then she wants you to create a new table in the Vendor database to contain product data. Complete the following:

1. Open the **Vendor** database you created in the previous module.
2. Open the **Supplier** table in Design view, and set the field properties as shown in Figure 2-45.

**Figure 2-45    Field properties for the Supplier table**

| Field Name | Data Type | Description | Field Size | Other |
|---|---|---|---|---|
| SupplierID | Short Text | Primary key | 6 | Caption = Supplier ID |
| Company | Short Text | | 50 | |
| Category | Short Text | | 15 | |
| Address | Short Text | | 35 | |
| City | Short Text | | 25 | |
| State | Short Text | | 2 | |
| Zip | Short Text | | 10 | |
| Phone | Short Text | | 14 | Caption = Contact Phone |
| ContactFirst | Short Text | | 20 | Caption = Contact First Name |
| ContactLast | Short Text | | 25 | Caption = Contact Last Name |
| InitialContact | Date/Time | | | Format = Short Date |
| | | | | Caption = Initial Contact |

3. Save the Supplier table. Click the **Yes** button when a message appears, indicating some data might be lost. Switch to Datasheet view and resize columns, as necessary, to their best fit. Then save and close the Supplier table.
4. Create a new table in Design view, using the table design shown in Figure 2-46.

**Figure 2-46    Design for the Product table**

| Field Name | Data Type | Description | Field Size | Other |
|---|---|---|---|---|
| ProductID | Short Text | Primary key | 5 | Caption = Product ID |
| SupplierID | Short Text | Foreign key | 6 | Caption = Supplier ID |
| ProductName | Short Text | | 75 | Caption = Product Name |
| Price | Currency | | | Format = Standard |
| | | | | Decimal Places = 2 |
| TempControl | Yes/No | | | Caption = Temp Controlled? |
| Sterile | Yes/No | | | Caption = Sterile? |
| Units | Number | | Integer | Decimal Places = 0 |
| | | | | Caption = Units/Case |
| | | | | Default Value = [no entry] |

5. Specify ProductID as the primary key, and then save the table as **Product**.

6. Modify the table structure by adding a new field between the Price and TempControl fields. Name the new field **Weight** (data type: **Number**; field size: **Single**; Decimal Places: **2**; Caption: **Weight in Lbs**; Default Value: [no entry]). Then move the **Units** field so that it is positioned between the Price and Weight fields.

7. Enter the records shown in Figure 2-47 in the Product table. Resize all datasheet columns to their best fit. When finished, save and close the Product table.

**Figure 2-47**    **Records for the Product table**

| Product ID | Supplier ID | Product Name | Price | Units/Case | Weight in Lbs | Temp Controlled? | Sterile? |
|---|---|---|---|---|---|---|---|
| PT100 | KLS321 | Paper tape roll | 20.00 | 12 | 3 | No | No |
| TC050 | QLS002 | Thermometer covers | 27.00 | 50 | 1 | No | Yes |

8. Use the Import Spreadsheet Wizard to add data to the Product table. The data you need to import is contained in the Supplies workbook, which is an Excel file located in the Access1 > Review folder provided with your Data Files.

   a. Specify the Supplies workbook as the source of the data.

   b. Select the option for appending the data.

   c. Select Product as the table.

   d. In the Import Spreadsheet Wizard dialog boxes, make sure Access confirms that the first row contains column headings, and import to the Product table. Do not save the import steps.

9. Open the **Product** table in Datasheet view, and resize columns to their best fit, as necessary. Then save and close the Product table.

10. Define a one-to-many relationship between the primary Supplier table and the related Product table. Resize the table field lists so that all field names are visible. Select the referential integrity option and the cascade updates option for the relationship.

11. Save the changes to the Relationships window and close it, compact and repair the Vendor database, and then close the database.

## Case Problem 1

**Data Files needed for this Case Problem: Beauty.accdb *(cont. from Module 1)* and Customers.txt**

***Beauty To Go***   Sue Miller wants to use the Beauty database to track information about customers who subscribe to her business, which provides a variety of salon services on a subscription basis, and the plans in which customers are enrolled. She asks you to help maintain this database. Complete the following:

1. Open the **Beauty** database you created in the previous module, open the **Option** table in Design view, and then change the following field properties:

   a. OptionID: Enter **Primary key** for the description, change the field size to **3**, and enter **Option ID** for the caption.

   b. OptionDescription: Change the field size to **45** and enter **Option Description** for the caption.

   c. OptionCost: Change the format to **Standard**, specify **0** decimal places, enter **Option Cost** for the caption, no default value.

   d. FeeWaived: Enter **Fee Waived** for the caption.

2. Save and close the Option table. Click the Yes button when a message appears, indicating some data might be lost.

3. Create a new table in Design view, using the table design shown in Figure 2-48.

| Figure 2-48 | Design for the Member table |
| --- | --- |

| Field Name | Data Type | Description | Field Size | Other |
| --- | --- | --- | --- | --- |
| MemberID | Short Text | Primary key | 4 | Caption = Member ID |
| OptionID | Short Text | Foreign key | 3 | Caption = Option ID |
| FirstName | Short Text | | 20 | Caption = First Name |
| LastName | Short Text | | 25 | Caption = Last Name |
| Phone | Short Text | | 14 | |
| OptionEnd | Date/Time | Date Option Ends | | Format = Short Date |
| | | | | Caption = Option Ends |

4. Specify **MemberID** as the primary key, and then save the table as **Member**.

5. Use the Address Quick Start selection in the Data Type gallery to add five fields between the LastName and Phone fields.

6. Switch to Design view, and then make the following changes to the Member table design:

   a. Address field: Change the name of this field to **Street**, change the field size to **40**, and delete the entry for the caption.

   b. City field: Change the field size to **25**, and delete the entry for the caption.

   c. StateProvince field: Change the name of this field to **State**, change the field size to **2**, delete the entry for the caption, and enter **FL** for the default value.

   d. ZIPPostal field: Change the name of this field to **Zip**, change the field size to **10**, and delete the entry for the caption.

   e. Delete the **CountryRegion** field from the Member table structure.

   f. Between the Phone and OptionEnd fields, add a new field named **OptionBegin** (data type: **Date/Time**; format: **Short Date**; Caption: **Option Begins**).

7. Enter the records shown in Figure 2-49 in the Member table. Resize all datasheet columns to their best fit. When finished, save and close the Member table. Be sure to enter your first and last name in the appropriate fields in the first record.

| Figure 2-49 | Records for the Member table |
| --- | --- |

| Member ID | Option ID | First Name | Last Name | Street | City | State | Zip | Phone | Option Begins | Option Ends |
| --- | --- | --- | --- | --- | --- | --- | --- | --- | --- | --- |
| 2103 | 123 | *Student First* | *Student Last* | 22 Oak St | Orlando | FL | 32801 | 407-832-3944 | 2/1/17 | 3/1/17 |
| 2118 | 120 | Susan | Reyes | 3 Balboa St | Orlando | FL | 32804 | 407-216-0091 | 11/2/16 | 2/2/17 |

8. Use the Import Text File Wizard to add data to the Member table. The data you need to import is contained in the Customers text file, which is located in the Access1 > Case1 folder provided with your Data Files.

   a. Specify the Customers text file as the source of the data.

   b. Select the option for appending the data.

   c. Select Member as the table.

   d. In the Import Text File Wizard dialog boxes, choose the options to import delimited data, to use a comma delimiter, and to import the data into the Member table. Do not save the import steps.

9. Open the **Member** table in Datasheet view and resize columns to their best fit, as necessary. Then save and close the Member table.

10. Define a one-to-many relationship between the primary Option table and the related Member table. Resize the Member table field list so that all field names are visible. Select the referential integrity option and the cascade updates option for this relationship.

11. Save the changes to the Relationships window and close it, compact and repair the Beauty database, and then close the database.

## Case Problem 2

**Data Files needed for this Case Problem: Programming.accdb** *(cont. from Module 1)*, **Client.accdb, Students.txt, and Agreements.xlsx**

***Programming Pros***  Brent Hovis plans to use the Programming database to maintain information about the students, tutors, and contracts for his tutoring services company. Brent asks you to help him build the database by updating one table and creating two new tables in the database. Complete the following:

1. Open the **Programming** database you created in the previous module, open the **Tutor** table in Design view, and then set the field properties as shown in Figure 2-50.

| Figure 2-50 | Field properties for the Tutor table |
| --- | --- |

| Field Name | Data Type | Description | Field Size | Other |
| --- | --- | --- | --- | --- |
| TutorID | Short Text | Primary key | 4 | Caption = Tutor ID |
| FirstName | Short Text | | 20 | Caption = First Name |
| LastName | Short Text | | 25 | Caption = Last Name |
| Major | Short Text | | 25 | |
| YearInSchool | Short Text | | 12 | Caption = Year In School |
| School | Short Text | | 30 | |
| HireDate | Date/Time | | | Format = Short Date |
| | | | | Caption = Hire Date |

2. Add a new field as the last field in the Tutor table with the field name **Groups**, the **Yes/No** data type, and the caption **Groups Only**.

3. Save the Tutor table. Click the **Yes** button when a message appears, indicating some data might be lost.

4. In the table datasheet, specify that the following tutors conduct group tutoring sessions only: Carey Billings, Fredrik Karlsson, Ellen Desoto, and Donald Gallager. Close the Tutor table.

5. Brent created a table named Student in the Client database that is located in the Access1 > Case2 folder provided with your Data Files. Import the structure of the Student table in the Client database into a new table named Student in the Programming database. Do not save the import steps.

6. Open the **Student** table in Datasheet view, and then add the following two fields to the end of the table: **BirthDate** (Date/Time field) and **Gender** (Short Text field).

7. Use the Phone Quick Start selection in the Data Type gallery to add four fields related to phone numbers between the Zip and BirthDate fields. (*Hint:* Be sure to make the BirthDate field the active field before adding the new fields.)

8. Display the Student table in Design view, delete the BusinessPhone and FaxNumber fields, and then save and close the Student table.

9. Reopen the Student table and modify its design so that it matches the design in Figure 2-51, *including the revised field names and data types.*

**Figure 2-51**    **Field properties for the Student table**

| Field Name | Data Type | Description | Field Size | Other |
|---|---|---|---|---|
| StudentID | Short Text | Primary key | 7 | Caption = Student ID |
| LastName | Short Text | | 25 | Caption = Last Name |
| FirstName | Short Text | | 20 | Caption = First Name |
| Address | Short Text | | 35 | |
| City | Short Text | | 25 | |
| State | Short Text | | 2 | Default Value = NC |
| Zip | Short Text | | 10 | |
| HomePhone | Short Text | | 14 | Caption = Home Phone |
| CellPhone | Short Text | | 14 | Caption = Cell Phone |
| BirthDate | Date/Time | | | Format = Short Date |
| | | | | Caption = Birth Date |
| Gender | Short Text | | 1 | |

10. Move the LastName field so it follows the FirstName field.
11. Save your changes to the table design, and then add the records shown in Figure 2-52 to the Student table.

**Figure 2-52**    **Records for the Student table**

| Student ID | First Name | Last Name | Address | City | State | Zip | Home Phone | Cell Phone | Date of Birth | Gender |
|---|---|---|---|---|---|---|---|---|---|---|
| LOP4015 | Henry | Lopez | 19 8th St | Raleigh | NC | 27601 | 919-264-9981 | 919-665-8110 | 2/19/1998 | M |
| PER4055 | Rosalyn | Perez | 421 Pine Ln | Cary | NC | 27511 | 984-662-4761 | 919-678-0012 | 4/12/1996 | F |

12. Resize the fields to their best fit, and then save and close the Student table.
13. Use the Import Text File Wizard to add data to the Student table. The data you need to import is contained in the Students text file, which is located in the Access1 > Case2 folder provided with your Data Files.
    a. Specify the Students text file as the source of the data.
    b. Select the option for appending the data.
    c. Select Student as the table.
    d. In the Import Text File Wizard dialog boxes, choose the options to import delimited data, to use a comma delimiter, and to import the data into the Student table. Do not save the import steps.
14. Open the **Student** table in Datasheet view, resize columns in the datasheet to their best fit (as necessary), and then save and close the table.
15. Create a new table in Design view, using the table design shown in Figure 2-53.

**Figure 2-53**    **Design for the Contract table**

| Field Name | Data Type | Description | Field Size | Other |
|---|---|---|---|---|
| ContractID | Short Text | Primary key | 4 | Caption = Contract ID |
| StudentID | Short Text | Foreign key | 7 | Caption = Student ID |
| TutorID | Short Text | Foreign key | 4 | Caption = Tutor ID |
| SessionType | Short Text | | 15 | Caption = Session Type |
| Length | Number | | Integer | Decimal Places = 0 |
| | | | | Caption = Length (Hrs) |
| | | | | Default Value = [no entry] |
| NumSessions | Number | | Integer | Decimal Places = 0 |
| | | | | Caption = Number of Sessions |
| | | | | Default Value = [no entry] |
| Cost | Currency | | | Format = Currency |
| | | | | Decimal Places = 0 |
| | | | | Default Value = [no entry] |
| Assessment | Yes/No | Pre-assessment exam complete | | Caption = Assessment Complete |

16. Specify ContractID as the primary key, and then save the table using the name **Contract**.
17. Add a new field to the Contract table, between the TutorID and SessionType fields, with the field name **ContractDate**, the **Date/Time** data type, the description **Date contract is signed**, the **Short Date** format, and the caption **Contract Date**. Save and close the Contract table.
18. Use the Import Spreadsheet Wizard to add data to the Contract table. The data you need to import is contained in the Agreements workbook, which is an Excel file located in the Access1 > Case2 folder provided with your Data Files.
    a. Specify the Agreements workbook as the source of the data.
    b. Select the option for appending the data to the table.
    c. Select Contract as the table.
    d. In the Import Spreadsheet Wizard dialog boxes, choose the Agreements worksheet, make sure Access confirms that the first row contains column headings, and import to the Contract table. Do not save the import steps.
19. Open the **Contract** table, and add the records shown in Figure 2-54. (*Hint:* Use the New (blank) record button in the navigation buttons to add a new record.)

**Figure 2-54**    **Records for the Contract table**

| Contract ID | Student ID | Tutor ID | Contract Date | Session Type | Length (Hrs) | Number of Sessions | Cost | Assessment Complete |
|---|---|---|---|---|---|---|---|---|
| 6215 | PER4055 | 1018 | 7/6/2017 | Group | 2 | 5 | $400 | Yes |
| 6350 | LOP4015 | 1010 | 10/12/2017 | Private | 3 | 4 | $720 | Yes |

20. Resize columns in the datasheet to their best fit (as necessary), and then save and close the Contract table.
21. Define the one-to-many relationships between the database tables as follows: between the primary Student table and the related Contract table, and between the primary Tutor table and the related Contract table. Resize the table field lists so that all field names are visible. Select the referential integrity option and the cascade updates option for each relationship.
22. Save the changes to the Relationships window and close it, compact and repair the Programming database, and then close the database.

## Case Problem 3

Data Files needed for this Case Problem: Center.accdb *(cont. from Module 1)*, Donations.xlsx, and Auctions.txt

***Diane's Community Center***    Diane Coleman wants to use the Center database to maintain information about the patrons and donations for her not-for-profit community center. Diane asks you to help her maintain the database by updating one table and creating two new ones. Complete the following:

1. Open the **Center** database you created in the previous module, open the **Patron** table in Design view, and then change the following field properties:
   a. PatronID: Enter **Primary key** for the description, change the field size to **5**, and enter **Patron ID** for the caption.
   b. Title: Change the field size to **4**.
   c. FirstName: Change the field size to **20**, and enter **First Name** for the caption.
   d. LastName: Change the field size to **25**, and enter **Last Name** for the caption.
   e. Phone: Change the field size to **14**.
   f. Email: Change field size to **35**.
2. Save and close the Patron table. Click the Yes button when a message appears, indicating some data might be lost.

⊕ **Explore** 3. Use the Import Spreadsheet Wizard to create a table in the Center database. As the source of the data, specify the Donations workbook, which is located in the Access1 > Case3 folder provided with your Data Files. Select the option to import the source data into a new table in the database.

⊕ **Explore** 4. Complete the Import Spreadsheet Wizard dialog boxes as follows:
   a. Select Donation as the worksheet you want to import.
   b. Specify that the first row contains column headings.
   c. Accept the field options suggested by the wizard, and do not skip any fields.
   d. Choose DonationID as your own primary key.
   e. Import the data to a table named **Donation**, and do not save the import steps.

⊕ **Explore** 5. Open the Donation table in Datasheet view. Left-justify the DonationDescription field by clicking the column heading, and then on the Home tab, clicking the Align Left button in the Text Formatting group.

6. Open the Donation table in Design view, and then modify the table so it matches the design shown in Figure 2-55, including changes to data types, field name, and field position. For the Short Text fields, delete any formats specified in the Format property boxes.

CHALLENGE

**Figure 2-55** Design for the Donation table

| Field Name | Data Type | Description | Field Size | Other |
|---|---|---|---|---|
| DonationID | Short Text | Primary key | 4 | Caption = Donation ID |
| PatronID | Short Text | Foreign key | 5 | Caption = Patron ID |
| DonationDate | Date/Time | | | Format = mm/dd/yyyy |
| | | | | Caption = Donation Date |
| Description | Short Text | | 30 | |
| DonationValue | Currency | Dollar amount or estimated value | | Format = Currency |
| | | | | Decimal Places = 2 |
| | | | | Caption = Donation Value |
| | | | | Default Value = [no entry] |
| CashDonation | Yes/No | | | Caption = Cash Donation? |
| AuctionItem | Yes/No | | | Caption = Possible Auction Item? |

7. Save your changes to the table design, click Yes for the message about lost data, and then switch to Datasheet view.
8. Resize the columns in the Donation datasheet to their best fit.
⊕ **Explore** 9. Diane decides that the values in the Donation Value column would look better without the two decimal places. Make this field the current field in the datasheet. Then, on the Table Tools Fields tab, in the Formatting group, use the Decrease Decimals button to remove the two decimal places and the period from these values. Switch back to Design view, and note that the Decimal Places property for the DonationValue field is now set to 0.
10. Save and close the Donation table.
11. Use Design view to create a table using the table design shown in Figure 2-56.

**Figure 2-56** Design for the Auction table

| Field Name | Data Type | Description | Field Size | Other |
|---|---|---|---|---|
| AuctionID | Short Text | Primary key | 3 | Caption = Auction ID |
| AuctionDate | Date/Time | | | Format = mm/dd/yyyy |
| | | | | Caption = Date of Auction |
| DonationID | Short Text | | 4 | Caption = Donation ID |
| MinPrice | Currency | | | Format = Currency |
| | | | | Decimal Places = 0 |
| | | | | Caption = Minimum Sale Price |
| ItemSold | Yes/No | | | Caption = Item Sold at Auction? |

12. Specify **AuctionID** as the primary key, save the table as **Auction**, and then close the table.
13. Use the Import Text File Wizard to add data to the Auction table. The data you need to import is contained in the Auctions text file, which is located in the Access1 > Case3 folder provided with your Data Files.
   a. Specify the Auctions text file as the source of the data.
   b. Select the option for appending the data.
   c. Select Auction as the table.
   d. In the Import Text File Wizard dialog boxes, choose the options to import delimited data, to use a comma delimiter, and to import the data into the Auction table. Do not save the import steps.

14. Open the Auction table in Datasheet view, and resize all columns to their best fit.

15. Display the Auction table in Design view. Move the DonationID field to make it the second field in the table, and enter the description **Foreign key** for the DonationID field. Save the modified Auction table design.

16. Switch to Datasheet view, and then add the records shown in Figure 2-57 to the Auction table. (*Hint:* Use the New (blank) record button in the navigation buttons to add a new record.) Close the table when finished.

**Figure 2-57**    **Records for the Auction table**

| AuctionID | DonationID | AuctionDate | MinPrice | ItemSold |
|-----------|------------|-------------|----------|----------|
| 205 | 5132 | 8/12/2017 | 200 | No |
| 235 | 5217 | 10/14/2017 | 150 | No |

17. Define the one-to-many relationships between the database tables as follows: between the primary Patron table and the related Donation table, and between the primary Donation table and the related Auction table. Resize any field lists so that all field names are visible. Select the referential integrity option and the cascade updates option for each relationship.

18. Save the changes to the Relationships window and close it, compact and repair the Center database, and then close the database.

## Case Problem 4

**CHALLENGE**

Data Files needed for this Case Problem: Appalachia.accdb *(cont. from Module 1)*, Travel.accdb, and Bookings.txt

*Hike Appalachia*    Molly and Bailey Johnson use the Appalachia database to track the data about the hikers and tours offered through their business. They ask you to help them maintain this database. Complete the following:

1. Open the **Appalachia** database you created in the previous module, open the **Hiker** table in Design view, and then change the following field properties:
   a. HikerID: Enter **Primary key** for the description, change the field size to **3**, and enter **Hiker ID** for the caption.
   b. HikerFirst: Change the field size to **20**, and enter **Hiker First Name** for the caption.
   c. HikerLast: Change the field size to **25**, and enter **Hiker Last Name** for the caption.
   d. Address: Change the field size to **35**.
   e. City: Change the field size to **25**.
   f. State: Change the field size to **2**.
   g. Zip: Change the field size to **10**.
   h. Phone: Change the field size to **14**.

2. Save the Hiker table, click the Yes button when a message appears, indicating some data might be lost, resize the Hiker First Name and Hiker Last Name columns in Datasheet view to their best fit, and then save and close the table.
   a. Import the **Trip** table structure and data from the **Travel** database into a new table in the **Appalachia** database. As the source of the data, specify the Travel database, which is located in the Access1 > Case4 folder provided with your Data Files; select the option button to import tables, queries, forms, reports, macros, and modules into the current database; and in the Import Objects dialog box, select the **Trip** table, click the **Options** button, and then make sure that the correct option is selected to import the table's data and structure (definition).
   b. Do not save your import steps.

✦ **Explore** 3. Using a shortcut menu in the Navigation Pane, rename the Trip table as **Tour** to give this name to the new table in the Appalachia database.

4. Open the **Tour** table in Design view, and then delete the VIPDiscount field.

5. Change the following properties:

   a. TourID: Enter the description **Primary key**, change the field size to **3**, and enter **Tour ID** for the caption.

   b. TourName: Enter **Tour Name** for the caption, and change the field size to **35**.

   c. TourType: Enter **Tour Type** for the caption, and change the field size to **15**.

   d. PricePerPerson: Enter **Price Per Person** for the caption.

6. Save the modified table, click the Yes button when a message appears, indicating some data might be lost, and then display the table in Datasheet view. Resize all datasheet columns to their best fit, and then save and close the table.

7. In Design view, create a table using the table design shown in Figure 2-58.

| Figure 2-58 | Design for the Reservation table |
| --- | --- |

| Field Name | Data Type | Description | Field Size | Other |
| --- | --- | --- | --- | --- |
| ReservationID | Short Text | Primary key | 4 | Caption = Reservation ID |
| HikerID | Short Text | Foreign key | 3 | Caption = Hiker ID |
| TourID | Short Text | Foreign key | 3 | Caption = Tour ID |
| TourDate | Date/Time | | | Caption = Tour Date |
| People | Number | | Integer | Decimal Places = 0 |
| | | | | Default Value = [no entry] |

8. Specify **ReservationID** as the primary key, and then save the table as **Reservation**.

✦ **Explore** 9. Refer back to Figure 2-11 to review the custom date formats. Change the Format property of the TourDate field to a custom format that displays dates in a format similar to 02/15/17. Save and close the Reservation table.

10. Use the Import Text File Wizard to add data to the Reservation table. The data you need to import is contained in the Bookings text file, which is located in the Access1 > Case4 folder provided with your Data Files.

   a. Specify the Bookings text file as the source of the data.

   b. Select the option for appending the data.

   c. Select Reservation as the table.

   d. In the Import Text File Wizard dialog boxes, choose the options to import delimited data, to use a comma delimiter, and to import the data into the Reservation table. Do not save the import steps.

11. Open the **Reservation** table, and then resize columns in the table datasheet to their best fit (as necessary), verify that the date values in the StartDate field are displayed correctly according to the custom format, and then save and close the table.

12. Define the one-to-many relationships between the database tables as follows: between the primary Hiker table and the related Reservation table, and between the primary Tour table and the related Reservation table. (*Hint:* Place the Reservation table as the middle table in the Relationships window to make it easier to join the tables.) Resize the Hiker field list so that all field names are visible. Select the referential integrity option and the cascade updates option for each relationship.

13. Save the changes to the Relationships window and close it, compact and repair the Appalachia database, and then close the database.

ACCESS

# Maintaining and Querying a Database

*Updating Tables and Retrieving Care Center Information*

## Case | *Riverview Veterinary Care Center*

At a recent meeting, Kimberly Johnson and her staff discussed the importance of maintaining accurate information about the animals seen by Riverview Veterinary Care Center, as well as the owners, visits, and invoices, and regularly monitoring the business activities of the care center. For example, Kelly Flannagan, Kimberly's assistant, needs to make sure she has up-to-date contact information, such as phone numbers and email addresses, for the owners of all the animals seen by the care center. The office staff also must monitor billing activity to ensure that invoices are paid on time and in full. In addition, the staff handles marketing efforts for the care center and tracks services provided to develop new strategies for promoting these services. Kimberly is also interested in analyzing other aspects of the business related to animal visits and finances. You can satisfy all these informational needs for Riverview Veterinary Care Center by updating data in the Riverview database and by creating and using queries that retrieve information from the database.

## STARTING DATA FILES

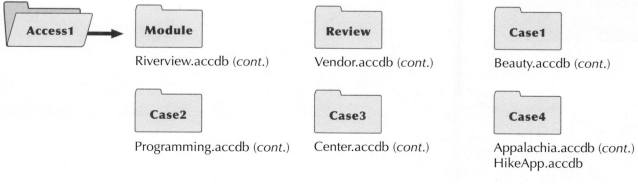

Access1 → Module
Riverview.accdb (*cont.*)

Review
Vendor.accdb (*cont.*)

Case1
Beauty.accdb (*cont.*)

Case2
Programming.accdb (*cont.*)

Case3
Center.accdb (*cont.*)

Case4
Appalachia.accdb (*cont.*)
HikeApp.accdb

# Session 3.1 Visual Overview:

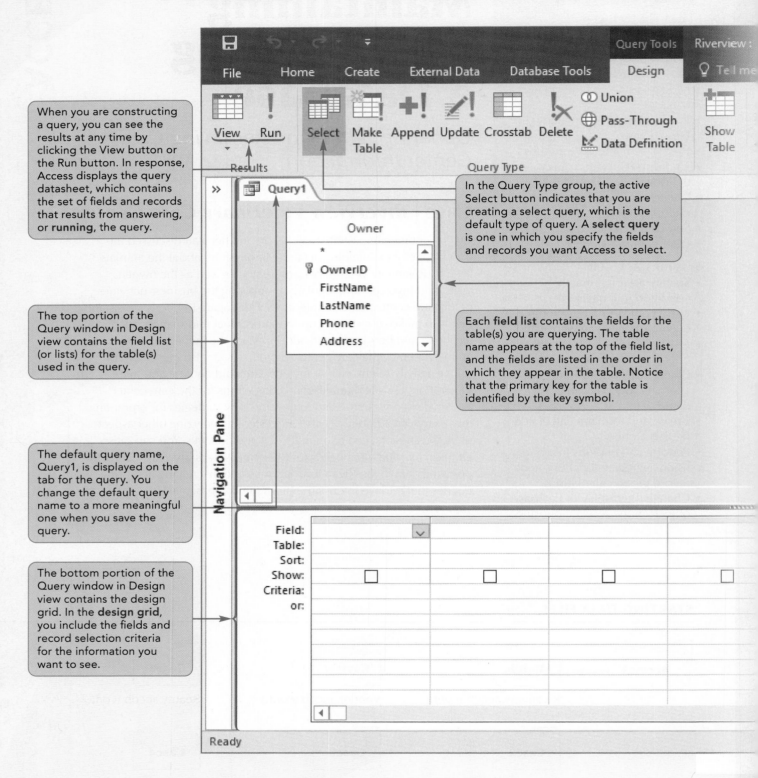

When you are constructing a query, you can see the results at any time by clicking the View button or the Run button. In response, Access displays the query datasheet, which contains the set of fields and records that results from answering, or **running**, the query.

The top portion of the Query window in Design view contains the field list (or lists) for the table(s) used in the query.

The default query name, Query1, is displayed on the tab for the query. You change the default query name to a more meaningful one when you save the query.

The bottom portion of the Query window in Design view contains the design grid. In the **design grid**, you include the fields and record selection criteria for the information you want to see.

In the Query Type group, the active Select button indicates that you are creating a select query, which is the default type of query. A **select query** is one in which you specify the fields and records you want Access to select.

Each **field list** contains the fields for the table(s) you are querying. The table name appears at the top of the field list, and the fields are listed in the order in which they appear in the table. Notice that the primary key for the table is identified by the key symbol.

# Query Window in Design View

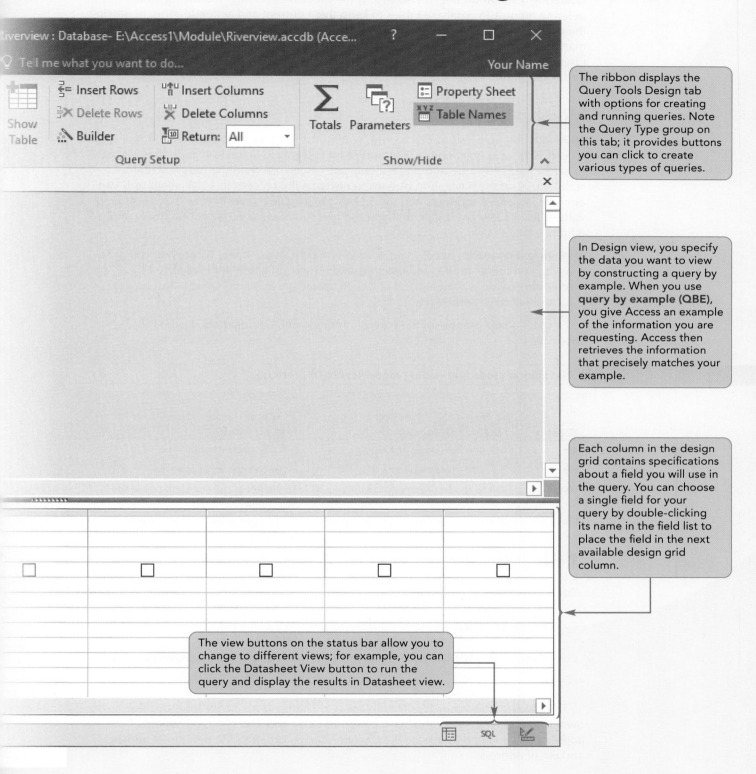

Riverview : Database- E:\Access1\Module\Riverview.accdb (Acce...    ?    —    □    ✕

Tell me what you want to do...                                    Your Name

Show Table

Insert Rows    Insert Columns    Totals    Parameters    Property Sheet
Delete Rows    Delete Columns                            Table Names
Builder        Return: All

Query Setup                                Show/Hide

The ribbon displays the Query Tools Design tab with options for creating and running queries. Note the Query Type group on this tab; it provides buttons you can click to create various types of queries.

In Design view, you specify the data you want to view by constructing a query by example. When you use **query by example (QBE)**, you give Access an example of the information you are requesting. Access then retrieves the information that precisely matches your example.

Each column in the design grid contains specifications about a field you will use in the query. You can choose a single field for your query by double-clicking its name in the field list to place the field in the next available design grid column.

The view buttons on the status bar allow you to change to different views; for example, you can click the Datasheet View button to run the query and display the results in Datasheet view.

SQL

# Updating a Database

**Updating**, or **maintaining**, a database is the process of adding, modifying, and deleting records in database tables to keep them current and accurate. After reviewing the data in the Riverview database, Kelly identified some changes that need to be made to the data. She would like you to update the field values in one record in the Owner table, correct an error in one record in the Visit table, and then delete a record in the Visit table.

## Modifying Records

To modify the field values in a record, you must first make the record the current record. Then you position the insertion point in the field value to make minor changes or select the field value to replace it entirely. Earlier you used the mouse with the scroll bars and the navigation buttons to navigate the records in a datasheet. You can also use keyboard shortcuts and the F2 key to navigate a datasheet and to select field values. The **F2 key** is a toggle that you use to switch between navigation mode and editing mode.

- In **navigation mode**, Access selects an entire field value. If you type while you are in navigation mode, your typed entry replaces the highlighted field value.
- In **editing mode**, you can insert or delete characters in a field value based on the location of the insertion point.

Figure 3-1 shows some of the navigation mode and editing mode keyboard shortcuts.

**Figure 3-1**    **Navigation mode and editing mode keyboard shortcuts**

| Press | To Move the Selection in Navigation Mode | To Move the Insertion Point in Editing Mode |
|---|---|---|
| ← | Left one field value at a time | Left one character at a time |
| → | Right one field value at a time | Right one character at a time |
| Home | Left to the first field value in the record | To the left of the first character in the field value |
| End | Right to the last field value in the record | To the right of the last character in the field value |
| ↑ or ↓ | Up or down one record at a time | Up or down one record at a time and switch to navigation mode |
| Tab or Enter | Right one field value at a time | Right one field value at a time and switch to navigation mode |
| Ctrl + Home | To the first field value in the first record | To the left of the first character in the field value |
| Ctrl + End | To the last field value in the last record | To the right of the last character in the field value |

The Owner table record Kelly wants you to change is for Taylor Johnson. This owner recently moved to another location in Cody and also changed her email address, so you need to update the Owner table record with the new street address and email address.

### To open the Owner table in the Riverview database:

**1.** Start Access and open the **Riverview** database you created and worked with earlier.

**Trouble?** If the security warning is displayed below the ribbon, click the Enable Content button.

**2.** Open the **Owner** table in Datasheet view.

The Owner table contains many fields. Sometimes, when updating data in a table, it can be helpful to remove the display of some fields on the screen.

## Hiding and Unhiding Fields

When you are viewing a table or query datasheet in Datasheet view, you might want to temporarily remove certain fields from the displayed datasheet, making it easier to focus on the data you're interested in viewing. The **Hide Fields** command allows you to remove the display of one or more fields, and the **Unhide Fields** command allows you to redisplay any hidden fields.

To make it easier to modify the owner record, you'll first hide a couple of fields in the Owner table.

### To hide fields in the Owner table and modify the owner record:

**1.** Right-click the **State** field name to display the shortcut menu, and then click **Hide Fields**. The State column is removed from the datasheet display.

**2.** Right-click the **Zip** field name, and then click **Hide Fields** on the shortcut menu. The Zip column is removed from the datasheet display.

With the fields hidden, you can now update the owner record. The record you need to modify is near the end of the table and has an OwnerID field value of 2412.

**3.** Scroll the datasheet until you see the last record in the table.

**4.** Click the OwnerID field value **2412**, for Taylor Johnson. The insertion point appears within the field value, indicating you are in editing mode.

**5.** Press the **Tab** key to move to the First Name field value, Taylor. The field value is selected, indicating you are in navigation mode.

**6.** Press the **Tab** key three times to move to the Address field and select its field value, type **458 Rose Ln**, and then press the **Tab** key twice to move to the Email field.

**7.** Type **taylor.johnson@example.net**, and then press the **Tab** key to move to the insertion point to the OwnerID field in the blank record at the bottom of the table. The changes to the record are complete. See Figure 3-2.

**Figure 3-2**     **Table after changing field values in a record**

Access saves changes to field values when you move to a new field or another record, or when you close the table. You don't have to click the Save button to save changes to field values or records.

▶ 8. Press the **Ctrl+Home** keys to move to the first field value in the first record. With the changes to the record complete, you can unhide the hidden fields.

▶ 9. Right-click any field name to display the shortcut menu, and then click **Unhide Fields**. The Unhide Columns dialog box opens. See Figure 3-3.

| Figure 3-3 | Unhide Columns dialog box |
| --- | --- |

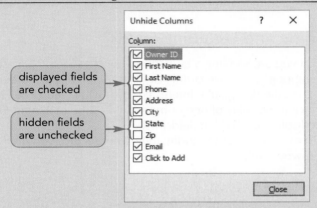

displayed fields are checked

hidden fields are unchecked

All currently displayed fields are checked in this dialog box, and all hidden fields are unchecked. To redisplay them, you simply click their check boxes to select them.

▶ 10. In the Unhide Columns dialog box, click the **State** check box to select it, click the **Zip** check box to select it, and then click the **Close** button to close the dialog box. The two hidden fields are now displayed in the datasheet.

▶ 11. Close the Owner table, and then click the **No** button in the dialog box that opens, asking if you want to save changes to the layout of the Owner table. This box appears because you hid fields and redisplayed them.

In this case, you can click either the Yes button or the No button, because no changes were actually made to the table layout or design.

Next you need to correct an error in the Visit table for a visit made by Molly, Animal ID 12312. A staff member incorrectly entered "Vaccinations" as the reason for the visit, when the animal actually came to the care center that day for a wellness exam. Ensuring the accuracy of the data in a database is an important maintenance task.

### To correct the record in the Visit table:

▶ 1. Open the **Visit** table in Datasheet view. The record containing the error is for Visit ID 1024.

▶ 2. Scroll the Visit table as necessary until you locate Visit ID **1024**, and then click at the end of the **Reason/Diagnosis** field value "Vaccinations" for this record. You are in editing mode.

**3.** Delete **Vaccinations** from the Reason/Diagnosis field, type **Wellness exam**, and then press the **Enter** key twice. The record now contains the correct value in the Reason/Diagnosis field, and this change is automatically saved in the Visit table.

The next update Kelly asks you to make is to delete a record in the Visit table. The owner of Butch, one of the animals seen by the care center, recently notified Taylor that he received an invoice for a neutering visit, but that he had canceled this scheduled appointment. Because this visit did not take place, the record for this visit needs to be deleted from the Visit table. Rather than scrolling through the table to locate the record to delete, you can use the Find command.

## Finding Data in a Table

Access provides options you can use to locate specific field values in a table. Instead of scrolling the Visit table datasheet to find the visit that you need to delete—the record for Visit ID 1128—you can use the Find command to find the record. The **Find command** allows you to search a table or query datasheet, or a form, to locate a specific field value or part of a field value. This feature is particularly useful when searching a table that contains a large number of records.

### To search for the record in the Visit table:

**TIP**

You can click any value in the column containing the field you want to search to make the field current.

**1.** Make sure the VisitID field value **1028** is still selected, and the **Home** tab is selected on the ribbon. You need to search the VisitID field to find the record containing the value 1128, so the insertion point is already correctly positioned in the field you want to search.

**2.** In the Find group, click the **Find** button. The Find and Replace dialog box opens. See Figure 3-4.

**Figure 3-4**    **Find and Replace dialog box**

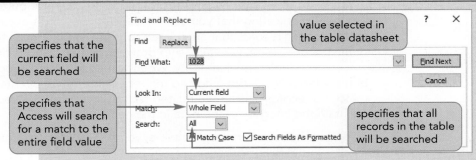

The field value 1028 appears in the Find What box because this value is selected in the table datasheet. You also can choose to search for only part of a field value, such as when you need to find all Visit IDs that start with a certain value. The Search box indicates that all the records in the table will be searched for the value you want to find. You also can choose to search up or down from the currently selected record.

**Trouble?** Some of the settings in your dialog box might be different from those shown in Figure 3-4 depending on the last search performed on the computer you're using. If so, change the settings so that they match those in the figure.

▶ **3.** Make sure the value 1028 is selected in the Find What box, type **1128** to replace the selected value, and then click the **Find Next** button. Record 50 appears with the field value you specified selected.

▶ **4.** Click the **Cancel** button to close the Find and Replace dialog box.

## Deleting Records

To delete a record, you need to select the record in Datasheet view and then delete it using the Delete button in the Records group on the Home tab or the Delete Record option on the shortcut menu.

**REFERENCE**

### Deleting a Record

- With the table open in Datasheet view, click the row selector for the record you want to delete.
- In the Records group on the Home tab, click the Delete button (or right-click the row selector for the record, and then click Delete Record on the shortcut menu).
- In the dialog box asking you to confirm the deletion, click the Yes button.

Now that you have found the record with Visit ID 1128, you can delete it. To delete a record, you must first select the entire row for the record.

### To delete the record:

▶ **1.** Click the row selector for the record containing the VisitID field value **1128**, which should still be highlighted. The entire row is selected.

▶ **2.** On the Home tab, in the Records group, click the **Delete** button. A dialog box opens indicating that you cannot delete the record because the Billing table contains records that are related to VisitID 1128. Recall that you defined a one-to-many relationship between the Visit and Billing tables and you enforced referential integrity. When you try to delete a record in the primary table (Visit), the enforced referential integrity prevents the deletion if matching records exist in the related table (Billing). This protection helps to maintain the integrity of the data in the database.

To delete the record in the Visit table, you first must delete the related records in the Billing table.

▶ **3.** Click the **OK** button in the dialog box to close it. Notice the plus sign that appears at the beginning of each record in the Visit table. The plus sign, also called the **expand indicator**, indicates that the Visit table is the primary table related to another table—in this case, the Billing table. Clicking the expand indicator displays related records from other tables in the database in a **subdatasheet**.

▶ **4.** Scroll down the datasheet until the selected record is near the top of the datasheet, so that you have room to view the related records for the visit record.

**5.** Click the **expand indicator** next to VisitID 1128. Two related records from the Billing table for this visit are displayed in the subdatasheet. See Figure 3-5.

**Figure 3-5**    **Related records from the Billing table in the subdatasheet**

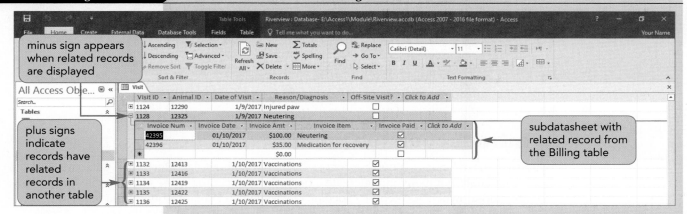

When the subdatasheet is open, you can navigate and update it, just as you can using a table datasheet. The expand indicator for an open subdatasheet is replaced by a minus sign. Clicking the minus sign, or **collapse indicator**, hides the subdatasheet.

You need to delete the records in the Billing table that are related to Visit ID 1128 before you can delete this visit record. The records are for the invoices that were mistakenly sent to the owner of Butch, who had canceled his dog's neutering visit at the care center. You could open the Billing table and find the related records. However, an easier way is to delete the records right in the subdatasheet. The records will be deleted from the Billing table automatically.

**6.** In the Billing table subdatasheet, click the row selector for invoice number **42395**, and then drag down one row. The rows are selected for both invoice number 42395 and invoice number 42396.

**7.** On the Home tab, in the Records group, click the **Delete** button. Because the deletion of records is permanent and cannot be undone, a dialog box opens asking you to confirm the deletion of two records.

**8.** Click the **Yes** button to confirm the deletion and close the dialog box. The records are removed from the Billing table, and the subdatasheet is now empty.

**9.** Click the **collapse indicator** next to VisitID 1128 to close the subdatasheet.

Now that you have deleted the related records in the Billing table, you can delete the record for Visit ID 1128. You'll use the shortcut menu to do so.

**10.** Right-click the row selector for the record for Visit ID **1128** to select the record and open the shortcut menu.

Be sure to select the correct record before deleting it.

**11.** Click **Delete Record** on the shortcut menu, and then click the **Yes** button in the dialog box to confirm the deletion. The record is deleted from the Visit table.

**12.** Close the Visit table.

*Process for Deleting Records*

When working with more complex databases that are managed by a database administrator, you typically need special permission to delete records from a table. Many companies also follow the practice of archiving records before deleting them so that the information is still available but not part of the active database.

You have finished updating the Riverview database by modifying and deleting records. Next, you'll retrieve specific data from the database to meet various requests for information about Riverview Veterinary Care Center.

# Introduction to Queries

As you have learned, a query is a question you ask about data stored in a database. For example, Kimberly might create a query to find records in the Owner table for only those owners located in a specific city. When you create a query, you tell Access which fields you need and what criteria Access should use to select the records. Access provides powerful query capabilities that allow you to do the following:

• Display selected fields and records from a table
• Sort records
• Perform calculations
• Generate data for forms, reports, and other queries
• Update data in the tables in a database
• Find and display data from two or more tables

Most questions about data are generalized queries in which you specify the fields and records you want Access to select. These common requests for information, such as "Which owners are located in Ralston?" or "How many invoices have been paid?" are select queries. The answer to a select query is returned in the form of a datasheet. The result of a query is also referred to as a **recordset** because the query produces a set of records that answers your question.

*Designing Queries vs. Using a Query Wizard*

More specialized, technical queries, such as finding duplicate records in a table, are best formulated using a Query Wizard. A Query Wizard prompts you for information by asking a series of questions and then creates the appropriate query based on your answers. For example, earlier you used the Simple Query Wizard to display only some of the fields in the Visit table; Access provides other Query Wizards for more complex queries. For common, informational queries, designing your own query is more efficient than using a Query Wizard.

The care center staff is planning an email campaign advertising a microchipping service being offered to animals seen by Riverview Veterinary Care Center. You need to create a query to display the owner ID, last name, first name, city, and email address for each record in the Owner table. You'll open the Query window in Design view to create the query.

**To open the Query window in Design view:**

▶ **1.** Close the Navigation Pane, and then, on the ribbon, click the **Create** tab.

▶ **2.** In the Queries group, click the **Query Design** button to display the Query window in Design view, with the Show Table dialog box open and the Tables tab selected. See Figure 3-6.

**Figure 3-6** ▶ Show Table dialog box

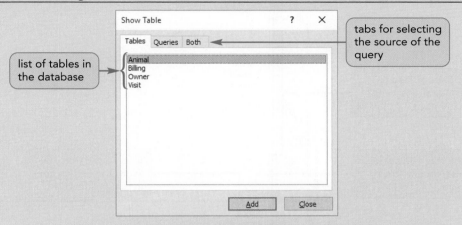

The Show Table dialog box lists all the tables in the Riverview database. You can choose to base a query on one or more tables, on other queries, or on a combination of tables and queries. The query you are creating will retrieve data from the Owner table, so you need to add this table to the Query window.

▶ **3.** In the Tables list, click **Owner**, click the **Add** button, and then click the **Close** button to close the Show Table dialog box. The Owner table's field list appears in the Query window. Refer to the Session 3.1 Visual Overview to familiarize yourself with the Query window in Design view.

**Trouble?** If you add the wrong table to the Query window, right-click the bar at the top of the field list containing the table name, and then click Remove Table on the shortcut menu. To add the correct table to the Query window, repeat Steps 2 and 3.

Now you'll create and run the query to display selected fields from the Owner table.

# Creating and Running a Query

The default table datasheet displays all the fields in the table in the same order as they appear in the table. In contrast, a query datasheet can display selected fields from a table, and the order of the fields can be different from that of the table, enabling those viewing the query results to see only the information they need and in the order they want.

You need the OwnerID, LastName, FirstName, City, and Email fields from the Owner table to appear in the query results. You'll add each of these fields to the design grid. First you'll resize the Owner table field list to display all of the fields.

### To select the fields for the query, and then run the query:

**1.** Drag the bottom border of the Owner field list to resize the field list so that all the fields in the Owner table are visible.

**2.** In the Owner field list, double-click **OwnerID** to place the field in the design grid's first column Field box. See Figure 3-7.

**Figure 3-7** **Field added to the design grid**

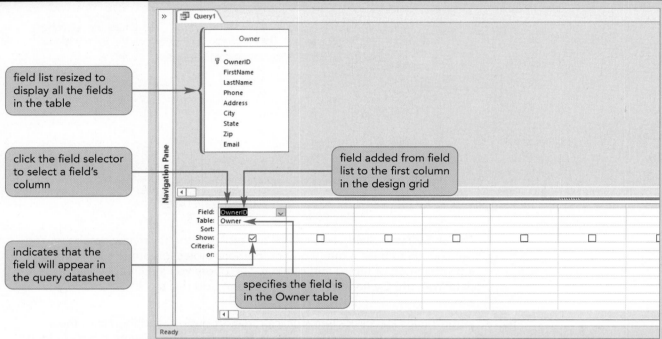

In the design grid's first column, the field name OwnerID appears in the Field box, the table name Owner appears in the Table box, and the checkmark in the Show check box indicates that the field will be displayed in the datasheet when you run the query. Sometimes you might not want to display a field and its values in the query results. For example, if you are creating a query to list all owners located in Ralston, and you assign the name "RalstonOwners" to the query, you do not need to include the City field value for each record in the query results—the query design lists only owners with the City field value of "Ralston." Even if you choose not to display a field in the query results, you can still use the field as part of the query to select specific records or to specify a particular sequence for the records in the datasheet. You can also add a field to the design grid using the arrow on the Field box; this arrow appears when you click the Field box, and if you click the arrow or the right side of an empty Field box, a menu of available fields opens.

**TIP**

You can also use the mouse to drag a field from the field list to a column in the design grid.

**3.** In the design grid, click the right side of the second column's Field box to display a menu listing all the fields in the Owner table, and then click **LastName** to add this field to the second column in the design grid.

**4.** Add the **FirstName**, **City**, and **Email** fields to the design grid in that order.

   **Trouble?** If you accidentally add the wrong field to the design grid, select the field's column by clicking the pointer ↓ on the field selector, which is the thin bar above the Field box, for the field you want to delete, and then press the Delete key (or in the Query Setup group on the Query Tools Design tab, click the Delete Columns button).

   Now that the five fields for the query have been selected, you can run the query.

**5.** On the Query Tools Design tab, in the Results group, click the **Run** button. Access runs the query and displays the results in Datasheet view. See Figure 3-8.

| Figure 3-8 | Datasheet displayed after running the query |
| --- | --- |

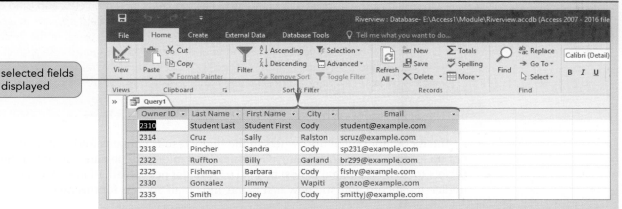

The five fields you added to the design grid appear in the datasheet in the same order as they appear in the design grid. The records are displayed in primary key sequence by OwnerID. The query selected all 25 records from the Owner table for display in the query datasheet. You will save the query as "OwnerEmail" so that you can easily retrieve the same data again.

**6.** On the Quick Access Toolbar, click the **Save** button 🖫. The Save As dialog box opens.

**7.** In the Query Name box, type **OwnerEmail** and then press the **Enter** key. The query is saved with the specified name in the Riverview database, and its name appears on the tab for the query.

**PROSKILLS**

*Decision Making: Comparing Methods for Adding All Fields to the Design Grid*

If the query you are creating includes every field from the specified table, you can use one of the following three methods to transfer all the fields from the field list to the design grid:

- Double-click (or click and drag) each field individually from the field list to the design grid. Use this method if you want the fields in your query to appear in an order that is different from the order in the field list.
- Double-click the asterisk at the top of the field list. The table name, followed by a period and an asterisk (as in "Owner.*"), appears in the Field box of the first column in the design grid, which signifies that the order of the fields is the same in the query as it is in the field list. Use this method if you don't need to sort the query or specify conditions based on the fields in the table you added in this way (for example, in a query based on more than one table). The advantage of using this method is that you do not need to change the query if you add or delete fields from the underlying table structure. Such changes are reflected automatically in the query.
- Double-click the field list title bar to select all the fields, and then click and drag one of the selected fields to the first column in the design grid. Each field appears in a separate column, and the fields are arranged in the order in which they appear in the field list. Use this method when you need to sort your query or include record selection criteria.

By choosing the most appropriate method to add all the table fields to the query design grid, you can work more efficiently and ensure that the query produces the results you want.

The record for one of the owners in the query results contains information that is not up to date. This owner, Jimmy Gonzalez, had informed the care center that he now prefers to go by the name James; he also provided a new email address. You need to update the record with the new first name and email address for this owner.

# Updating Data Using a Query

A query datasheet is temporary, and its contents are based on the criteria in the query design grid; however, you can still update the data in a table using a query datasheet. In this case, you want to make changes to a record in the Owner table. Instead of making the changes in the table datasheet, you can make them in the OwnerEmail query datasheet because the query is based on the Owner table. The underlying Owner table will be updated with the changes you make.

### To update data using the OwnerEmail query datasheet:

1. Locate the record with OwnerID 2330, Jimmy Gonzalez (record 6 in the query datasheet).

2. In the First Name column for this record, double-click **Jimmy** to select the name, and then type **James**.

3. Press the **Tab** key twice to move to the Email column, type **thewholething@example.com** and then press the **Tab** key.

4. Close the OwnerEmail query, and then open the Navigation Pane. Note that the OwnerEmail query is listed in the Queries section of the Navigation Pane.

Now you'll check the Owner table to verify that the changes you made in the query datasheet are reflected in the Owner table.

▶ **5.** Open the **Owner** table in Datasheet view, and then close the Navigation Pane.

▶ **6.** Locate the record for OwnerID 2330 (record 6). Notice that the changes you made in the query datasheet to the First Name and Email field values were made to the record in the Owner table.

▶ **7.** Close the Owner table.

Kelly also wants to view specific information in the Riverview database. She would like to review the visit data for animals while also viewing certain information about them. So, she needs to see data from both the Animal table and the Visit table at the same time.

# Creating a Multitable Query

A multitable query is a query based on more than one table. If you want to create a query that retrieves data from multiple tables, the tables must have a common field. Earlier, you established a relationship between the Animal (primary) and Visit (related) tables based on the common AnimalID field that exists in both tables, so you can now create a query to display data from both tables at the same time. Specifically, Kelly wants to view the values in the AnimalType, AnimalBreed, and AnimalName fields from the Animal table and the VisitDate and Reason fields from the Visit table.

**To create the query using the Animal and Visit tables:**

▶ **1.** On the ribbon, click the **Create** tab.

▶ **2.** In the Queries group, click the **Query Design** button. The Show Table dialog box opens in the Query window. You need to add the Animal and Visit tables to the Query window.

▶ **3.** Click **Animal** in the Tables list, click the **Add** button, click **Visit**, click the **Add** button, and then click the **Close** button to close the Show Table dialog box. The Animal and Visit field lists appear in the Query window.

▶ **4.** Resize the Animal and Visit field lists if necessary so that all the fields in each list are displayed.

The one-to-many relationship between the two tables is shown in the Query window in the same way that a relationship between two tables is shown in the Relationships window. Note that the join line is thick at both ends; this signifies that you selected the option to enforce referential integrity. If you had not selected this option, the join line would be thin at both ends, and neither the "1" nor the infinity symbol would appear, even though the tables have a one-to-many relationship.

You need to place the AnimalType, AnimalBreed, and AnimalName fields (in that order) from the Animal field list into the design grid and then place the VisitDate and Reason fields from the Visit field list into the design grid. This is the order in which Taylor wants to view the fields in the query results.

▶ **5.** In the Animal field list, double-click **AnimalType** to place this field in the design grid's first column Field box.

**6.** Repeat Step 5 to add the **AnimalBreed** and **AnimalName** fields from the Animal table to the second and third columns of the design grid.

**7.** Repeat Step 5 to add the **VisitDate** and **Reason** fields (in that order) from the Visit table to the fourth and fifth columns of the design grid. The query specifications are complete, so you can now run the query.

**8.** In the Results group on the Query Tools Design tab, click the **Run** button. After the query runs, the results are displayed in Datasheet view. See Figure 3-9.

| Figure 3-9 | Datasheet for query based on the Animal and Visit tables |

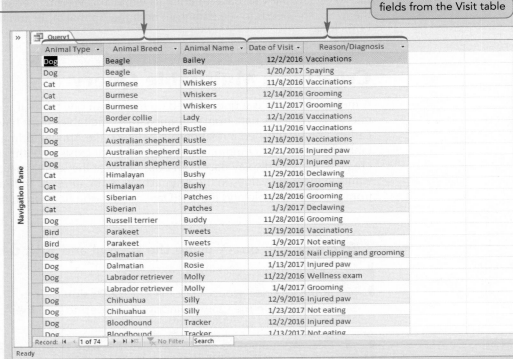

fields from the Animal table

fields from the Visit table

| Animal Type | Animal Breed | Animal Name | Date of Visit | Reason/Diagnosis |
| --- | --- | --- | --- | --- |
| Dog | Beagle | Bailey | 12/2/2016 | Vaccinations |
| Dog | Beagle | Bailey | 1/20/2017 | Spaying |
| Cat | Burmese | Whiskers | 11/8/2016 | Vaccinations |
| Cat | Burmese | Whiskers | 12/14/2016 | Grooming |
| Cat | Burmese | Whiskers | 1/11/2017 | Grooming |
| Dog | Border collie | Lady | 12/1/2016 | Vaccinations |
| Dog | Australian shepherd | Rustle | 11/11/2016 | Vaccinations |
| Dog | Australian shepherd | Rustle | 12/16/2016 | Vaccinations |
| Dog | Australian shepherd | Rustle | 12/21/2016 | Injured paw |
| Dog | Australian shepherd | Rustle | 1/9/2017 | Injured paw |
| Cat | Himalayan | Bushy | 11/29/2016 | Declawing |
| Cat | Himalayan | Bushy | 1/18/2017 | Grooming |
| Cat | Siberian | Patches | 11/28/2016 | Grooming |
| Cat | Siberian | Patches | 1/3/2017 | Declawing |
| Dog | Russell terrier | Buddy | 11/28/2016 | Grooming |
| Bird | Parakeet | Tweets | 12/19/2016 | Vaccinations |
| Bird | Parakeet | Tweets | 1/9/2017 | Not eating |
| Dog | Dalmatian | Rosie | 11/15/2016 | Nail clipping and grooming |
| Dog | Dalmatian | Rosie | 1/13/2017 | Injured paw |
| Dog | Labrador retriever | Molly | 11/22/2016 | Wellness exam |
| Dog | Labrador retriever | Molly | 1/4/2017 | Grooming |
| Dog | Chihuahua | Silly | 12/9/2016 | Injured paw |
| Dog | Chihuahua | Silly | 1/23/2017 | Not eating |
| Dog | Bloodhound | Tracker | 12/2/2016 | Injured paw |
| Dog | Bloodhound | Tracker | 1/13/2017 | Not eating |

Record: 1 of 74 No Filter Search

Ready

Only the five selected fields from the Animal and Visit tables appear in the datasheet. The records are displayed in order according to the values in the AnimalID field because it is the primary key field in the primary table, even though this field is not included in the query datasheet.

Kelly plans on frequently tracking the data retrieved by the query, so she asks you to save it as "AnimalVisits."

**9.** On the Quick Access Toolbar, click the **Save** button 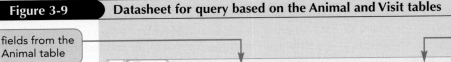. The Save As dialog box opens.

**10.** In the Query Name box, type **AnimalVisits** and then press the **Enter** key. The query is saved, and its name appears on the object tab.

Kelly decides she wants the records displayed in alphabetical order by animal type. Because the query displays data in order by the field values in the AnimalID field, which is the primary key for the Animal table, you need to sort the records by the AnimalType field to display the data in the order Kelly wants.

# Sorting Data in a Query

**Sorting** is the process of rearranging records in a specified order or sequence. Sometimes you might need to sort data before displaying or printing it to meet a specific request. For example, Kelly might want to review visit information arranged by the VisitDate field because she needs to know which months are the busiest for Riverview Veterinary Care Center in terms of animal visits. Kimberly might want to view billing information arranged by the InvoiceAmt field because she monitors the finances of the care center.

When you sort data in a query, you do not change the sequence of the records in the underlying tables. Only the records in the query datasheet are rearranged according to your specifications.

To sort records, you must select the **sort field**, which is the field used to determine the order of records in the datasheet. In this case, Kelly wants the data sorted alphabetically by animal type, so you need to specify AnimalType as the sort field. Sort fields can be Short Text, Number, Date/Time, Currency, AutoNumber, or Yes/No fields, but not Long Text, Hyperlink, or Attachment fields. You sort records in either ascending (increasing) or descending (decreasing) order. Figure 3-10 shows the results of each type of sort for these data types.

| Figure 3-10 | Sorting results for different data types |

| Data Type | Ascending Sort Results | Descending Sort Results |
| --- | --- | --- |
| Short Text | A to Z (alphabetical) | Z to A (reverse alphabetical) |
| Number | lowest to highest numeric value | highest to lowest numeric value |
| Date/Time | oldest to most recent date | most recent to oldest date |
| Currency | lowest to highest numeric value | highest to lowest numeric value |
| AutoNumber | lowest to highest numeric value | highest to lowest numeric value |
| Yes/No | yes (checkmark in check box) then no values | no then yes values |

Access provides several methods for sorting data in a table or query datasheet and in a form. One of the easiest ways is to use the AutoFilter feature for a field.

## Using an AutoFilter to Sort Data

**TIP**

You can also use the Ascending and Descending buttons in the Sort & Filter group on the Home tab to quickly sort records based on the currently selected field in a datasheet.

As you've probably noticed when working in Datasheet view for a table or query, each column heading has an arrow to the right of the field name. This arrow gives you access to the **AutoFilter** feature, which enables you to quickly sort and display field values in various ways. When you click this arrow, a menu opens with options for sorting and displaying field values. The first two options on the menu enable you to sort the values in the current field in ascending or descending order. Unless you save the datasheet or form after you've sorted the records, the rearrangement of records is temporary.

Next, you'll use an AutoFilter to sort the AnimalVisits query results by the AnimalType field.

## To sort the records using an AutoFilter:

1. Click the **arrow** on the Animal Type column heading to display the AutoFilter menu. See Figure 3-11.

**Figure 3-11**    Using AutoFilter to sort records in the datasheet

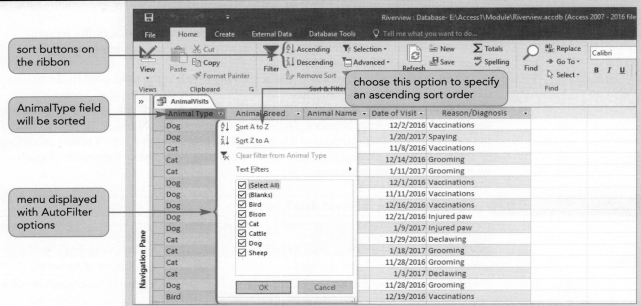

Kelly wants the data sorted in ascending (alphabetical) order by the values in the AnimalType field, so you need to select the first option in the menu.

2. Click **Sort A to Z**. The records are rearranged in ascending alphabetical order by animal type. A small, upward-pointing arrow appears on the right side of the Animal Type column heading. This arrow indicates that the values in the field have been sorted in ascending order. If you used the same method to sort the field values in descending order, a small downward-pointing arrow would appear there instead.

After viewing the query results, Kelly decides that she would also like to see the records arranged by the values in the VisitDate field, so that the data is presented in chronological order. She still wants the records to be arranged by the AnimalType field values as well. To produce the results Kelly wants, you need to sort using two fields.

## Sorting on Multiple Fields in Design View

Sort fields can be unique or nonunique. A sort field is **unique** if the value in the sort field for each record is different. The AnimalID field in the Animal table is an example of a unique sort field because each animal record has a different value in this primary key field. A sort field is **nonunique** if more than one record can have the same value for the sort field. For example, the AnimalType field in the Animal table is a nonunique sort field because more than one record can have the same AnimalType value.

**TIP**

The primary sort field is not the same as a table's primary key. A table has at most one primary key, which must be unique, whereas any field in a table can serve as a primary sort field.

When the sort field is nonunique, records with the same sort field value are grouped together, but they are not sorted in a specific order within the group. To arrange these grouped records in a specific order, you can specify a **secondary sort field**, which is a second field that determines the order of records that are already sorted by the **primary sort field** (the first sort field specified).

In Access, you can select up to 10 different sort fields. When you use the buttons on the ribbon to sort by more than one field, the sort fields must be in adjacent columns in the datasheet. (Note that you cannot use an AutoFilter to sort on more than one field. This method works for a single field only.) You can specify only one type of sort—either ascending or descending—for the selected columns in the datasheet. You select the adjacent columns, and Access sorts first by the first column and then by each remaining selected column in order from left to right.

Kelly wants the records sorted first by the AnimalType field values, as they currently are, and then by the VisitDate values. The two fields are in the correct left-to-right order in the query datasheet, but they are not adjacent, so you cannot use the Ascending and Descending buttons on the ribbon to sort them. You could move the AnimalType field to the left of the VisitDate field in the query datasheet, but both columns would have to be sorted with the same sort order. This is not what Kelly wants—she wants the AnimalType field values sorted in ascending order so that they are in the correct alphabetical order, for ease of reference; and she wants the VisitDate field values to be sorted in descending order, so that she can focus on the most recent animal visits first. To sort the AnimalType and VisitDate fields with different sort orders, you must specify the sort fields in Design view.

In the Query window in Design view, you must arrange the fields you want to sort from left to right in the design grid, with the primary sort field being the leftmost. In Design view, multiple sort fields do not have to be adjacent to each other, as they do in Datasheet view; however, they must be in the correct left-to-right order.

**REFERENCE**

### Sorting a Query Datasheet

- In the query datasheet, click the arrow on the column heading for the field you want to sort.
- In the menu that opens, click Sort A to Z for an ascending sort, or click Sort Z to A for a descending sort.

*or*

- In the query datasheet, select the column or adjacent columns on which you want to sort.
- In the Sort & Filter group on the Home tab, click the Ascending button or the Descending button.

*or*

- In Design view, position the fields serving as sort fields from left to right.
- Click the right side of the Sort box for each field you want to sort, and then click Ascending or Descending for the sort order.

To achieve the results Kelly wants, you need to modify the query in Design view to specify the sort order for the two fields.

**TIP**

In Design view, the sort fields do not have to be adjacent, and fields that are not sorted can appear between the sort fields.

### To select the two sort fields in Design view:

1. On the Home tab, in the Views group, click the **View** button to open the query in Design view. The fields are currently in the correct left-to-right order in the design grid, so you only need to specify the sort order for the two fields.

   First, you need to specify an ascending sort order for the AnimalType field. Even though the records are already sorted by the values in this field, you need to modify the query so that this sort order, and the sort order you will specify for the VisitDate field, are part of the query's design. Any time the query is run, the records will be sorted according to these specifications.

2. Click the right side of the **AnimalType Sort** box to display the arrow and the sort options, and then click **Ascending**. You've selected an ascending sort order for the AnimalType field, which will be the primary sort field. The AnimalType field is a Short Text field, and an ascending sort order will display the field values in alphabetical order.

3. Click the right side of the **VisitDate Sort** box, click **Descending**, and then click in one of the empty text boxes below the VisitDate field to deselect the setting. You've selected a descending sort order for the VisitDate field, which will be the secondary sort field because it appears to the right of the primary sort field (AnimalType) in the design grid. The VisitDate field is a Date/Time field, and a descending sort order will display the field values with the most recent dates first. See Figure 3-12.

**Figure 3-12** | **Selecting two sort fields in Design view**

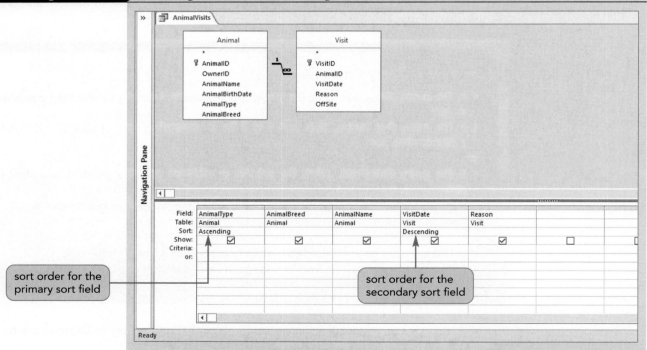

sort order for the primary sort field

sort order for the secondary sort field

You have finished your query changes, so now you can run the query and then save the modified query with the same name.

**4.** On the Query Tools Design tab, in the Results group, click the **Run** button. After the query runs, the records appear in the query datasheet in ascending order based on the values in the AnimalType field. Within groups of records with the same AnimalType field value, the records appear in descending order by the values of the VisitDate field. See Figure 3-13.

| Figure 3-13 | Datasheet sorted on two fields |
|---|---|

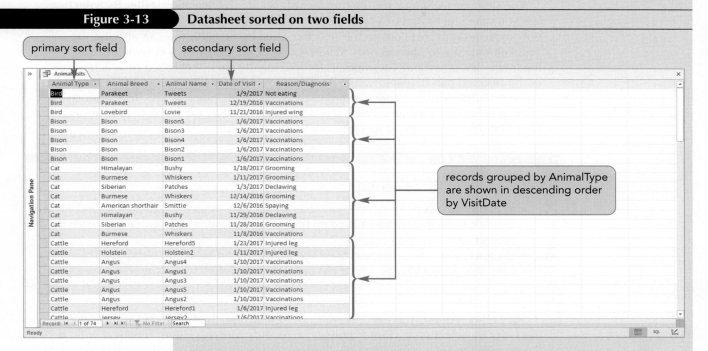

primary sort field

secondary sort field

records grouped by AnimalType are shown in descending order by VisitDate

When you save the query, all of your design changes—including the selection of the sort fields—are saved with the query. The next time Kelly runs the query, the records will appear sorted by the primary and secondary sort fields.

**5.** On the Quick Access Toolbar, click the **Save** button 🖫 to save the revised AnimalVisits query.

Kelly knows that Riverview Veterinary Care Center has seen an increase in the number of dogs receiving care. She would like to focus briefly on the information for that animal type only. Also, she is interested in knowing how many dogs have had recent vaccinations. She is concerned that, although more dogs are being brought to the care center, not enough of them are receiving regular vaccinations. Selecting only the records with an AnimalType field value of "Dog" and a Reason field value beginning with "Vaccination" is a temporary change that Kelly wants in the query datasheet, so you do not need to switch to Design view and change the query. Instead, you can apply a filter.

# Filtering Data

A **filter** is a set of restrictions you place on the records in an open datasheet or form to *temporarily* isolate a subset of the records. A filter lets you view different subsets of displayed records so that you can focus on only the data you need. Unless you save a query or form with a filter applied, an applied filter is not available the next time you run the query or open the form.

The simplest technique for filtering records is Filter By Selection. **Filter By Selection** lets you select all or part of a field value in a datasheet or form and then display only those records that contain the selected value in the field. You can also use the AutoFilter feature to filter records. When you click the arrow on a column heading, the menu that opens provides options for filtering the datasheet based on a field value or the selected part of a field value. Another technique for filtering records is to use **Filter By Form**, which changes your datasheet to display blank fields. Then you can select a value using the arrow that appears when you click any blank field to apply a filter that selects only those records containing that value.

**REFERENCE**

### Using Filter By Selection

- In the datasheet or form, select the part of the field value that will be the basis for the filter; or, if the filter will be based on the entire field value, click anywhere within the field value.
- On the Home tab, in the Sort & Filter group, click the Selection button.
- Click the type of filter you want to apply.

For Kelly's request, you need to select an AnimalType field value of Dog and then use Filter By Selection to display only those records with this value. Then you will filter the records further by selecting only those records with a Reason value that begins with "Vaccination" (for visits that include a single vaccination or multiple vaccinations).

### To display the records using Filter By Selection:

1. In the query datasheet, locate the first occurrence of an AnimalType field containing the value **Dog**, and then click anywhere within that field value.

2. On the Home tab, in the Sort & Filter group, click the **Selection** button. A menu opens with options for the type of filter to apply. See Figure 3-14.

**Figure 3-14**  **Using Filter By Selection**

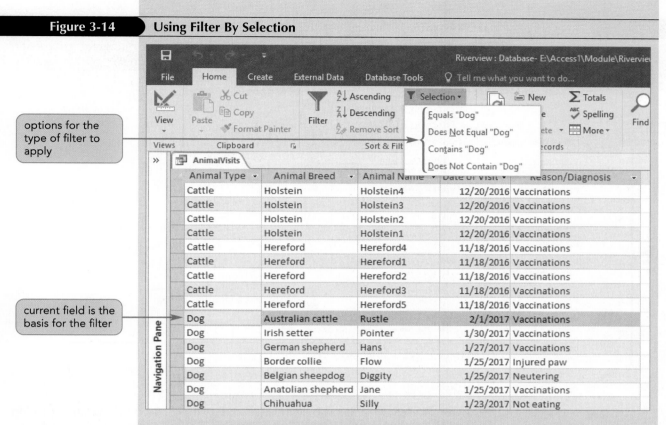

options for the type of filter to apply

current field is the basis for the filter

The menu provides options for displaying only those records with an AnimalType field value that equals the selected value (in this case, Dog); does not equal the value; contains the value somewhere within the field; or does not contain the value somewhere within the field. You want to display all the records whose AnimalType field value equals Dog.

3. In the Selection menu, click **Equals "Dog"**. Only the 25 records that have an AnimalType field value of Dog appear in the datasheet. See Figure 3-15.

Your Name

**Figure 3-15** Datasheet after applying the filter

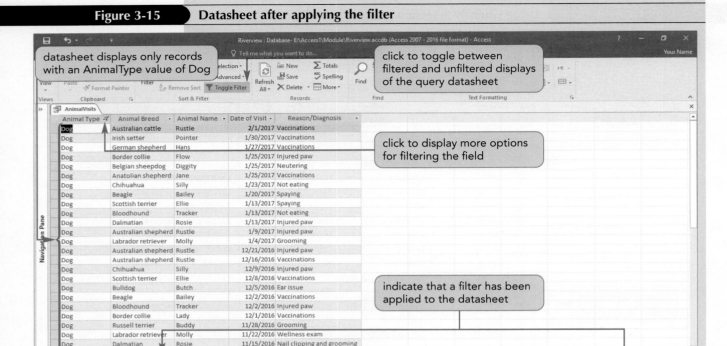

Next, Kelly wants to view only those records with a Reason field value beginning with the word "Vaccination" so she can view the records for visits that involved one or more vaccinations. You need to apply an additional filter to the datasheet.

4. In any Reason field value beginning with the word "Vaccination," select only the text **Vaccination**.

5. In the Sort & Filter group, click the **Selection** button. The same four filter types are available for this selection as when you filtered the AnimalType field.

6. On the Selection menu, click **Begins With "Vaccination"**. The first filter is applied to the query datasheet, which now shows only the nine records for dogs who have had one or more vaccinations at the care center.

**Trouble?** If you do not see the Begins With "Vaccination" option, click anywhere in the datasheet to close the Selection menu, and then repeat Steps 4–6, being sure not to select the letter "s" at the end of the word "Vaccination."

Now you can redisplay all the query records by clicking the Toggle Filter button, which you use to switch between the filtered and unfiltered displays.

**TIP**

The ScreenTip for this button is Remove Filter.

7. In the Sort & Filter group, click the **Toggle Filter** button. The filter is removed, and all 74 records appear in the query datasheet.

8. Close the AnimalVisits query. A dialog box opens, asking if you want to save your changes to the design of the query—in this case, the filtered display, which is still available through the Toggle Filter button. Kelly does not want the query saved with the filter because she doesn't need to view the filtered information on a regular basis.

9. Click the **No** button to close the query without saving the changes.

10. If you are not continuing to Session 3.2, click the **File** tab, and then click **Close** in the navigation bar to close the Riverview database.

REVIEW

## Session 3.1 Quick Check

1. In Datasheet view, what is the difference between navigation mode and editing mode?
2. What command can you use in Datasheet view to remove the display of one or more fields from the datasheet?
3. What is a select query?
4. Describe the field list and the design grid in the Query window in Design view.
5. How are a table datasheet and a query datasheet similar? How are they different?
6. For a Date/Time field, how do the records appear when sorted in ascending order?
7. When you define multiple sort fields in Design view, describe how the sort fields must be positioned in the design grid.
8. A(n) _____ is a set of restrictions you place on the records in an open datasheet or form to isolate a subset of records temporarily.

# Session 3.2 Visual Overview:

When creating queries in Design view, you can enter criteria so that only selected records are displayed in the query results.

| Field: | AnimalName | AnimalBirthDate | AnimalType | VisitDate | Reason |
|---|---|---|---|---|---|
| Table: | Animal | Animal | Animal | Visit | Visit |
| Sort: | | | | | |
| Show: | ☑ | ☑ | ☑ | ☑ | ☑ |
| Criteria: | | | "Bird" | | |
| or: | | | | | |

To define a condition for a field, you place the condition in the field's Criteria box in the design grid.

To indicate which records you want to select, you must specify a condition as part of the query. A **condition** is a criterion, or rule, that determines which records are selected.

| Field: | InvoiceNum | InvoiceDate | InvoiceAmt | |
|---|---|---|---|---|
| Table: | Billing | Billing | Billing | |
| Sort: | | | | |
| Show: | ☑ | ☑ | ☑ | ☐ |
| Criteria: | | | >100 | |
| or: | | | | |

A condition usually consists of an operator, often a comparison operator, and a value. A **comparison operator** compares the value in a field to the condition value and selects all the records for which the condition is true.

| Field: | VisitID | AnimalID | VisitDate | Reason |
|---|---|---|---|---|
| Table: | Visit | Visit | Visit | Visit |
| Sort: | | | | |
| Show: | ☑ | ☑ | ☑ | ☑ |
| Criteria: | | | Between #1/1/2017# And #1/15/2017# | |
| or: | | | | |

Most comparison operators (such as Between...And...) select records that match a range of values for the condition—in this case, all records with dates that fall within the range shown.

# Selection Criteria in Queries

The results of a query containing selection criteria include only the records that meet the specified criteria.

**BirdAnimalType**

| Animal Name | Animal Birth Date | Animal Type | Date of Visit |
|---|---|---|---|
| Tweets | 11/12/2010 | Bird | 12/19/2016 |
| Tweets | 11/12/2010 | Bird | 1/9/2017 |
| Lovie | 02/03/2002 | Bird | 11/21/2016 |
| * | | | |

The results of this query show only birds because the condition "Bird" in the AnimalType field's Criteria box specifies that the query should select records only with AnimalType field values of bird. This type of condition is called an **exact match** because the value in the specified field must match the condition exactly in order for the record to be included in the query results.

**LargeInvoiceAmts**

| Invoice Num | Invoice Date | Invoice Amt |
|---|---|---|
| 42145 | 11/22/2016 | $275.00 |
| 42182 | 11/30/2016 | $225.00 |
| 42320 | 01/04/2017 | $225.00 |
| 42435 | 01/16/2017 | $125.00 |
| 42525 | 01/26/2017 | $125.00 |
| * | | $0.00 |

The results of this query show only those invoices with amounts greater than $100 because the condition >100, which uses the greater than comparison operator, specifies that query should select records only with InvoiceAmt field values over $100.

**EarlyJanuaryVisits**

| Visit ID | Animal ID | Date of Visit | Reason/Diagnosis |
|---|---|---|---|
| 1098 | 12296 | 1/3/2017 | Declawing |
| 1101 | 12312 | 1/4/2017 | Grooming |
| 1120 | 12304 | 1/9/2017 | Not eating |
| 1124 | 12290 | 1/9/2017 | Injured paw |
| 1140 | 12282 | 1/11/2017 | Grooming |
| 1148 | 12308 | 1/13/2017 | Injured paw |
| 1152 | 12318 | 1/13/2017 | Not eating |
| 1156 | 12322 | 1/13/2017 | Spaying |
| * | | | |

The results of this query show only those visits that took place in the first half of January 2017 because the condition in the VisitDate Criteria box specifies that the query should select records only with a visit date between 1/1/2017 and 1/15/2017.

# Defining Record Selection Criteria for Queries

Kimberly is considering offering a workshop on dog care at the care center, with a special emphasis on the needs of older dogs. To prepare for this, she is interested in knowing more about the level of care provided to the dogs that have visited the care center, as well as where these dogs live. For this request, you could create a query to select the correct fields and all records in the Owner, Animal, and Visit tables, select an AnimalType field value of Dog in the query datasheet, and then click the Selection button and choose the appropriate filter option to display the information for only those animals that are dogs. However, a faster way of accessing the data Kimberly needs is to create a query that displays the selected fields and only those records in the Owner, Animal, and Visit tables that satisfy a condition.

Just as you can display selected fields from a database in a query datasheet, you can display selected records. To identify which records you want to select, you must specify a condition as part of the query, as illustrated in the Session 3.2 Visual Overview. A condition usually includes one of the comparison operators shown in Figure 3-16.

**Figure 3-16**     **Access comparison operators**

| Operator | Meaning | Example |
|---|---|---|
| = | equal to (optional; default operator) | ="Hall" |
| <> | not equal to | <>"Hall" |
| < | less than | <#1/1/99# |
| <= | less than or equal to | <=100 |
| > | greater than | >"C400" |
| >= | greater than or equal to | >=18.75 |
| Between … And … | between two values (inclusive) | Between 50 And 325 |
| In () | in a list of values | In ("Hall", "Seeger") |
| Like | matches a pattern that includes wildcards | Like "706*" |

## Specifying an Exact Match

For Kimberly's request, you need to first create a query that will display only those records in the Animal table with the value Dog in the AnimalType field. This type of condition is an exact match because the value in the specified field must match the condition exactly in order for the record to be included in the query results. You'll create the query in Design view.

### To create the query in Design view:

1. If you took a break after the previous session, make sure that the Riverview database is open and the Navigation Pane is closed, and then on the ribbon, click the **Create** tab.

2. In the Queries group, click the **Query Design** button. The Show Table dialog box opens. You need to add the Owner, Animal, and Visit tables to the Query window.

3. Click **Owner** in the Tables list, click the **Add** button, click **Animal**, click the **Add** button, click **Visit**, click the **Add** button, and then click the **Close** button. The field lists for the Owner, Animal, and Visit tables appear in the top portion of the window, and join lines indicating one-to-many relationships connect the tables.

4. Resize all three field lists so that all the fields are displayed.

5. Add the following fields from the Animal table to the design grid in this order: **AnimalName**, **AnimalBirthDate**, and **AnimalType**.

Kimberly also wants information from the Visit table and the Owner table included in the query results.

6. Add the following fields from the Visit table to the design grid in this order: **VisitDate** and **Reason**.

7. Add the following fields from the Owner table to the design grid in this order: **FirstName**, **LastName**, **Phone**, and **Email**. All the fields needed for the query appear in the design grid. See Figure 3-17.

**Figure 3-17** 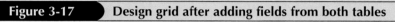 **Design grid after adding fields from both tables**

enter condition here

To display the information Kimberly wants, you need to enter the condition for the AnimalType field in its Criteria box, as shown in Figure 3-17. Kimberly wants to display only those records with an AnimalType field value of Dog.

**To enter the exact match condition, and then save and run the query:**

1. Click the **AnimalType Criteria** box, type **Dog**, and then press the **Enter** key. The condition changes to "Dog".

Access automatically enclosed the condition you typed in quotation marks. You must enclose text values in quotation marks when using them as selection criteria. If you omit the quotation marks, however, Access will include them automatically in most cases. Some words—including "in" and "select"—are special keywords in Access that are reserved for functions and commands. If you want to enter one of these keywords as the condition, you must type the quotation marks around the text or an error message will appear indicating the condition cannot be entered.

2. Save the query with the name **DogAnimalType**. The query is saved, and its name is displayed on the object tab.

3. Run the query. After the query runs, the selected field values for only those records with an AnimalType field value of Dog are shown. A total of 25 records is selected and displayed in the datasheet. See Figure 3-18.

**Figure 3-18**    **Datasheet displaying selected fields and records**

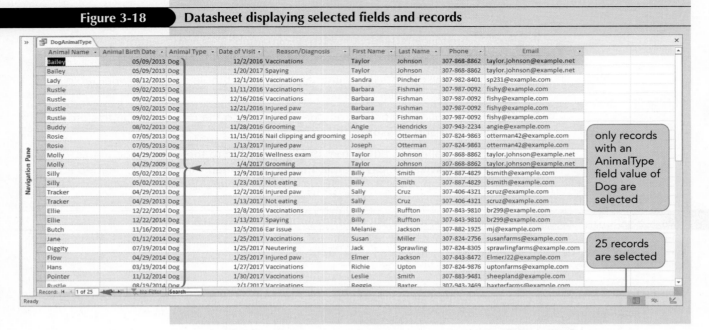

Kimberly realizes that it's not necessary to include the AnimalType field values in the query results. The name of the query, DogAnimalType, indicates that the query design includes all animals with an AnimalType of Dog, so the AnimalType field values are unnecessary and repetitive in the query results. Also, she decides that she would prefer the query datasheet to show the fields from the Owner table first, followed by the Animal table fields and then the Visit table fields. You need to modify the query to produce the results Kimberly wants.

## Modifying a Query

After you create a query and view the results, you might need to make changes to the query if the results are not what you expected or require. First, Kimberly asks you to modify the DogAnimalType query so that it does not display the AnimalType field values in the query results.

### To remove the display of the AnimalType field values:

▶ 1. On the Home tab, in the Views group, click the **View** button. The DogAnimalType query opens in Design view.

You need to keep the AnimalType field as part of the query design because it contains the defined condition for the query. You only need to remove the display of the field's values from the query results.

▶ 2. Click the **AnimalType Show** check box to remove the checkmark. The query will still find only those records with the value Dog in the AnimalType field, but the query results will not display these field values.

Next, you need to change the order of the fields in the query so that the owner information is listed first.

**To move the Owner table fields to precede the Animal and Visit table fields:**

1. Position the pointer on the FirstName field selector until the pointer changes to ⬇, and then click to select the field. See Figure 3-19.

**Figure 3-19**    **Selected FirstName field**

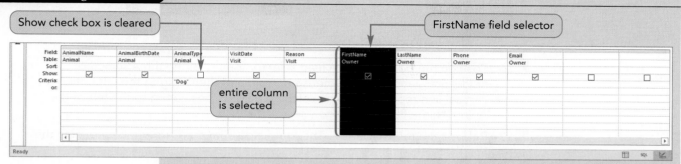

Show check box is cleared

FirstName field selector

entire column is selected

2. Position the pointer on the FirstName field selector, and then press and hold the mouse button; notice that the pointer changes to ⬚, and a black vertical line appears to the left of the selected field. This line represents the selected field when you drag the mouse to move it.

3. Drag the pointer to the left until the vertical line representing the selected field is positioned to the left of the AnimalName field. See Figure 3-20.

**Figure 3-20**    **Dragging the field in the design grid**

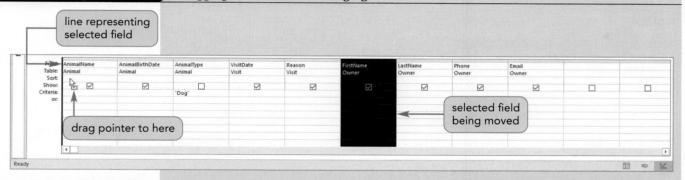

line representing selected field

drag pointer to here

selected field being moved

**TIP**

Instead of moving a field by dragging, you can also delete the field and then add it back to the design grid in the location you want.

4. Release the mouse button. The FirstName field moves to the left of the AnimalName field.

You can also select and move multiple fields at once. You need to select and move the LastName, Phone, and Email fields so that they appear directly after the FirstName field in the query design. To select multiple fields, you click and drag the mouse over the field selectors for the fields you want.

5. Point to the LastName field selector. When the pointer changes to ⬇, press and hold the mouse button, drag to the right to select the Phone and Email fields, and then release the mouse button. All three fields are now selected. See Figure 3-21.

| Figure 3-21 | Multiple fields selected to be moved |

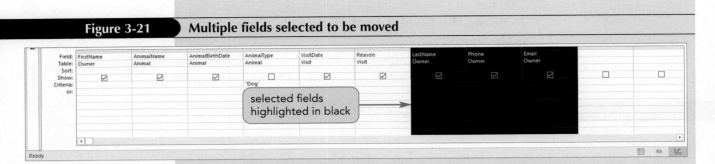

6. Position the pointer on the field selector for any of the three selected fields, press and hold the mouse button, and then drag to the left until the vertical line representing the selected fields is positioned to the left of the AnimalName field.

7. Release the mouse button. The four fields from the Owner table are now the first four fields in the query design.

You have finished making the modifications to the query Kimberly requested, so you can now run the query.

8. Run the query. The results of the modified query are displayed. See Figure 3-22.

| Figure 3-22 | Results of the modified query |

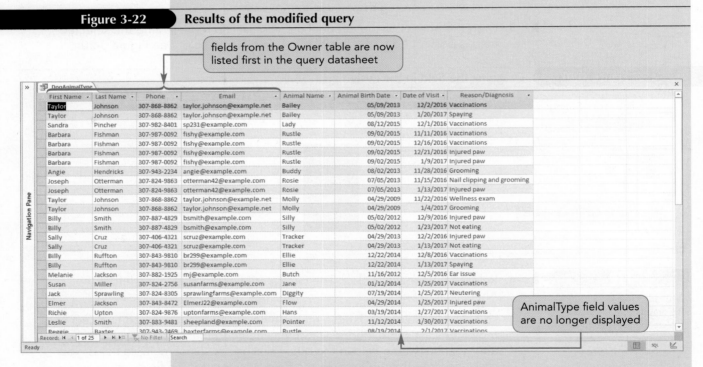

Note that the AnimalType field values are no longer displayed in the query results.

9. Save and close the DogAnimalType query.

Kimberly asks you to create a new query. She is interested to know which animals of all animal types that have not been to the care center recently, so that her staff can follow up with their owners by sending them reminder notes or emails. To create the query that will produce the results Kimberly wants, you need to use a comparison operator to match a range of values—in this case, any VisitDate value less than 1/1/2017. Because this new query will include information from several of the same fields as the DogAnimalType query, you can use that query as a starting point in designing this new query.

## Using a Comparison Operator to Match a Range of Values

As you know, after you create and save a query, you can double-click the query name in the Navigation Pane to run the query again. You can then click the View button to change its design. You can also use an existing query as the basis for creating another query. Because the design of the query you need to create next is similar to the DogAnimalType query, you will copy, paste, and rename this query to create the new query. Using this approach keeps the DogAnimalType query intact.

### To create the new query by copying the DogAnimalType query:

1. Open the Navigation Pane. Note that the DogAnimalType query is listed in the Queries section.

    You need to use the shortcut menu to copy the DogAnimalType query and paste it in the Navigation Pane; then you'll give the copied query a different name.

2. In the Queries section of the Navigation Pane, right-click **DogAnimalType** to select it and display the shortcut menu.

3. Click **Copy** on the shortcut menu.

4. Right-click the empty area near the bottom of the Navigation Pane, and then click **Paste** on the shortcut menu. The Paste As dialog box opens with the text "Copy Of DogAnimalType" in the Query Name box. Because Kimberly wants the new query to show data for animals that have not visited the care center recently, you'll name the new query "EarlierVisits."

5. In the Query Name box, type **EarlierVisits** and then press the **Enter** key. The new query appears in the Queries section of the Navigation Pane.

6. Double-click the **EarlierVisits** query to open, or run, the query. The design of this query is currently the same as the original DogAnimalType query.

7. Close the Navigation Pane.

Next, you need to open the query in Design view and modify its design to produce the results Kimberly wants—to display records for all animals and only those records with VisitDate field values that are earlier than, or less than, 1/1/2017.

## To modify the design of the new query:

▶ **1.** Display the query in Design view.

▶ **2.** Click the **VisitDate Criteria** box, type **<1/1/2017** and then press the **Tab** key. Note that Access automatically encloses the date criteria with number signs. The condition specifies that a record will be selected only if its VisitDate field value is less than (earlier than) 1/1/2017. See Figure 3-23.

**Figure 3-23**      **Criteria entered for the VisitDate field**

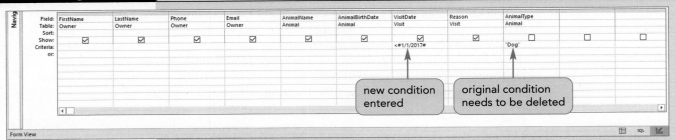

Before you run the query, you need to delete the condition for the AnimalType field. Recall that the AnimalType field is part of the query, but its values are not displayed in the query results. When you modified the query to remove the AnimalType field values from the query results, Access moved the field to the end of the design grid. You need to delete the AnimalType field's condition, specify that the AnimalType field values should be included in the query results, and then move the field back to its original position following the AnimalBirthDate field.

▶ **3.** Press the **Tab** key to select the condition for the AnimalType field, and then press the **Delete** key. The condition for the AnimalType field is removed.

▶ **4.** Click the **Show** check box for the AnimalType field to insert a checkmark so that the field values will be displayed in the query results.

▶ **5.** Use the pointer to select the AnimalType field, drag the selected field to position it to the left of the VisitDate field, and then click in an empty box to deselect the AnimalType field. See Figure 3-24.

**Figure 3-24**      **Design grid after moving the AnimalType field**

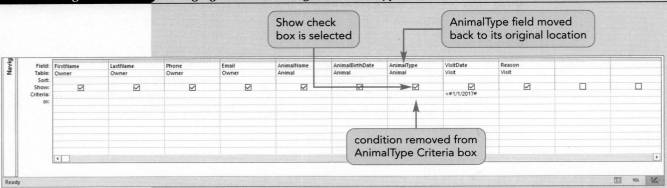

▶ **6.** Run the query. The query datasheet displays the selected fields for only those records with a VisitDate field value less than 1/1/2017, a total of 34 records. See Figure 3-25.

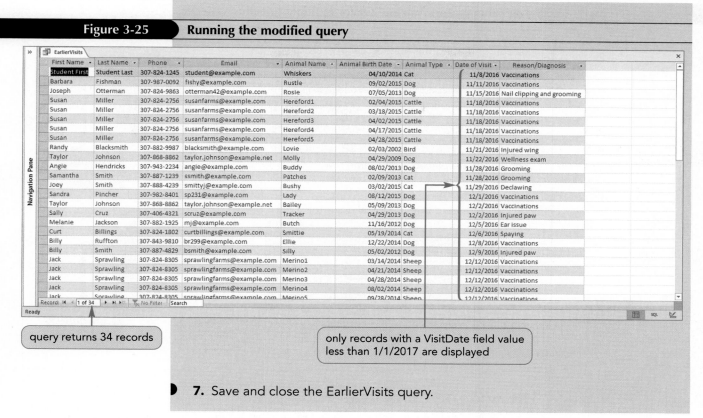

Figure 3-25     Running the modified query

query returns 34 records

only records with a VisitDate field value less than 1/1/2017 are displayed

**7.** Save and close the EarlierVisits query.

Kimberly continues to analyze animal visits to Riverview Veterinary Care Center. Although the care center offers payment plans and pet insurance options, she realizes that owners of younger animals seen off-site might not see the literature about these options that is available in the care center's waiting room. With this in mind, she would like to see a list of all animals that are less than a year old and that the care center has visited off-site. She wants to track these animals in particular so that her staff can contact their owners to review payment plans and pet insurance options. To produce this list, you need to create a query containing two conditions—one for the animal's date of birth and another for whether each visit was off-site.

# Defining Multiple Selection Criteria for Queries

Multiple conditions require you to use **logical operators** to combine two or more conditions. When you want a record selected only if two or more conditions are met, you need to use the **And logical operator**. In this case, Kimberly wants to see only those records with an AnimalBirthDate field value greater than or equal to 7/1/2015 *and* an OffSite field value of "Yes" (indicating a checked box). If you place conditions in separate fields in the *same* Criteria row of the design grid, all conditions in that row must be met in order for a record to be included in the query results. However, if you place conditions in *different* Criteria rows, a record will be selected if at least one of the conditions is met. If none of the conditions are met, Access does not select the record. When you place conditions in different Criteria rows, you are using the **Or logical operator**. Figure 3-26 illustrates the difference between the And and Or logical operators.

| Figure 3-26 | Logical operators And and Or for multiple selection criteria |

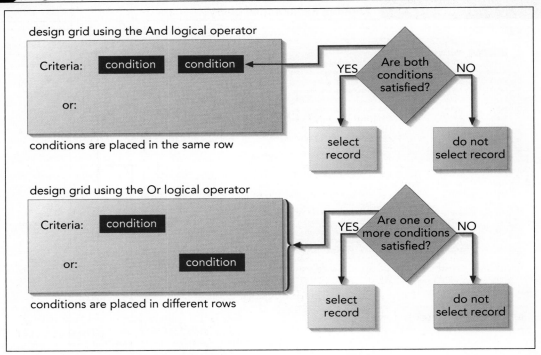

## The And Logical Operator

To create the query for Kimberly, you need to use the And logical operator to show only the records for animals that were born on or after 7/1/2015 *and* who have had an off-site visit. You'll create a new query based on the Owner, Animal, and Visit tables to produce the necessary results. In the query design, both conditions you specify will appear in the same Criteria row; therefore, the query will select records only if both conditions are met.

### To create a new query using the And logical operator:

1. On the ribbon, click the **Create** tab.

2. In the Queries group, click the **Query Design** button.

3. Add the **Owner**, **Animal**, and **Visit** tables to the Query window in that order, and then close the Show Table dialog box. Resize all three field lists to display all the field names.

4. Add the **AnimalName** and **AnimalBirthDate** fields from the Animal table to the design grid.

5. Add the **FirstName**, **LastName**, and **Phone** fields from the Owner field list to the design grid.

6. Add the **VisitDate** and **OffSite** fields from the Visit table to the design grid.

   Now you need to enter the two conditions for the query.

7. Click the **AnimalBirthDate Criteria** box, and then type **>=7/1/2015**.

8. Press the **Tab** key five times to move to the **OffSite** box, type **Yes**, and then press the **Tab** key. Notice that for a Yes/No field such as OffSite, the criteria value is not automatically enclosed in quotes. See Figure 3-27.

**Figure 3-27**  Query to find younger animals who have had off-site visits

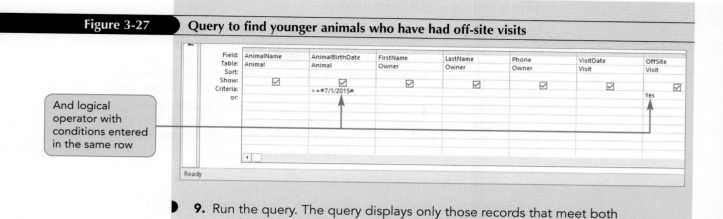

**And logical operator with conditions entered in the same row**

9. Run the query. The query displays only those records that meet both conditions: an AnimalBirthDate field value greater than or equal to 7/1/2015 *and* an OffSite field value of Yes. 14 records are displayed for 14 different animals. See Figure 3-28.

**Figure 3-28**  Results of query using the And logical operator

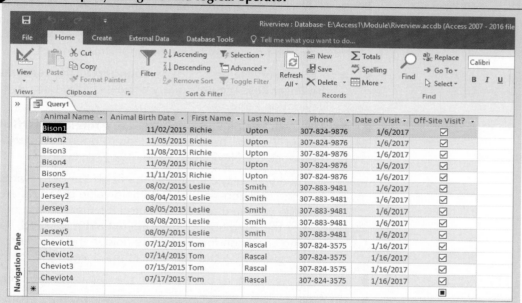

10. On the Quick Access Toolbar, click the **Save** button, and then save the query as **YoungerAndOffsiteAnimals**.

11. Close the query.

Kimberly meets with staff members to discuss the issue of owners with younger animals being informed of the care center's payment plans and insurance options. After viewing the results of the YoungerAndOffsiteAnimals query, the group agrees that the care center should reach out to the owners of all younger animals regarding these services, because first-time owners are more likely to be unaware of the care center's options. In addition, the care center should contact the owner of any animal that has received an off-site visit, because these owners are less likely to have seen the care center's waiting room literature on these payment options. To help with their planning, Kimberly asks you to produce a list of all animals that were born on or after 7/1/2015 or that received an off-site visit. To create this query, you need to use the Or logical operator.

## The Or Logical Operator

To create the query that Kimberly requested, your query must select a record when either one of two conditions is satisfied or when both conditions are satisfied. That is, a record is selected if the AnimalBirthDate field value is greater than or equal to 7/1/2015 *or* if the OffSite field value is Yes *or* if both conditions are met. You will enter the condition for the AnimalBirthDate field in the Criteria row and the condition for the OffSite field in the "or" criteria row, thereby using the Or logical operator.

To display the information, you'll create a new query based on the existing YoungerAndOffsiteAnimals query, since it already contains the necessary fields. Then you'll specify the conditions using the Or logical operator.

**To create a new query using the Or logical operator:**

▶ **1.** Open the Navigation Pane. You'll use the shortcut menu to copy and paste the YoungerAndOffsiteAnimals query to create the new query.

▶ **2.** In the Queries section of the Navigation Pane, right-click **YoungerAndOffsiteAnimals**, and then click **Copy** on the shortcut menu.

▶ **3.** Right-click the empty area near the bottom of the Navigation Pane, and then click **Paste** on the shortcut menu. The Paste As dialog box opens with the text "Copy Of YoungerAndOffsiteAnimals" in the Query Name box. You'll name the new query "YoungerOrOffsiteAnimals."

▶ **4.** In the Query Name box, type **YoungerOrOffsiteAnimals** and then press the **Enter** key. The new query appears in the Queries section of the Navigation Pane.

▶ **5.** In the Navigation Pane, right-click the **YoungerOrOffsiteAnimals** query, click **Design View** on the shortcut menu to open the query in Design view, and then close the Navigation Pane.

The query already contains all the fields Kimberly wants to view, as well as the first condition—a BirthDate field value greater than or equal to 7/1/2015. Because you want records selected if either the condition for the BirthDate field or the condition for the OffSite field is satisfied, you must delete the existing condition for the OffSite field in the Criteria row and then enter this same condition in the "or" row of the design grid for the OffSite field.

▶ **6.** In the design grid, delete **Yes** in the OffSite Criteria box.

▶ **7.** Press the ↓ key to move to the "or" row for the OffSite field, type **Yes**, and then press the **Tab** key. See Figure 3-29.

**Figure 3-29** **Query window with the Or logical operator**

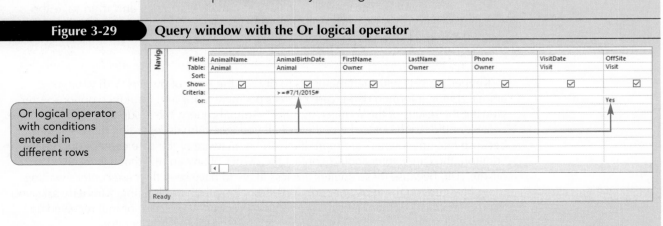

Or logical operator with conditions entered in different rows

To better analyze the data, Kimberly wants the list displayed in descending order by AnimalBirthDate.

▶ **8.** Click the right side of the **AnimalBirthDate Sort** box, and then click **Descending**.

▶ **9.** Run the query. The query datasheet displays only those records that meet either condition: a BirthDate field value greater than or equal to 7/1/2015 *or* an OffSite field value of Yes. The query also returns records that meet both conditions. The query displays a total of 43 records. The records in the query datasheet appear in descending order based on the values in the AnimalBirthDate field. See Figure 3-30.

| Figure 3-30 | Results of query using the Or logical operator |

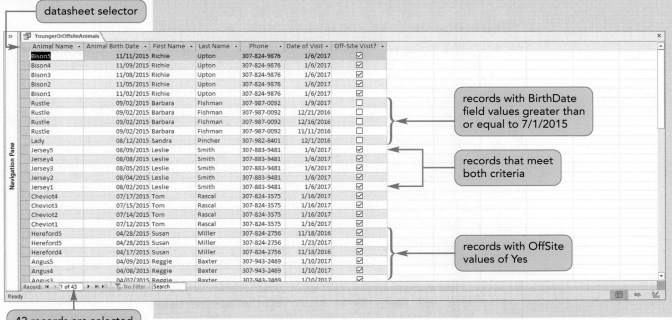

datasheet selector

records with BirthDate field values greater than or equal to 7/1/2015

records that meet both criteria

records with OffSite values of Yes

43 records are selected

**INSIGHT**

## Understanding the Results of Using And vs. Or

When you use the And logical operator to define multiple selection criteria in a query, you *narrow* the results produced by the query because a record must meet more than one condition to be included in the results. For example, the YoungerAndOffsiteAnimals query you created resulted in only 14 records. When you use the Or logical operator, you *broaden* the results produced by the query because a record must meet only one of the conditions to be included in the results. For example, the YoungerOrOffsiteAnimals query you created resulted in 43 records. This is an important distinction to keep in mind when you include multiple selection criteria in queries, so that the queries you create will produce the results you want.

Kimberly would like to spend some time reviewing the results of the YoungerOrOffsiteAnimals query. To make this task easier, she asks you to change how the datasheet is displayed.

# Changing a Datasheet's Appearance

You can make many formatting changes to a datasheet to improve its appearance or readability. Many of these modifications are familiar types of changes you can also make in Word documents or Excel spreadsheets, such as modifying the font type, size, color, and the alignment of text. You can also apply different colors to the rows and columns in a datasheet to enhance its appearance.

## Modifying the Font Size

Depending on the size of the monitor you are using or the screen resolution, you might need to increase or decrease the size of the font in a datasheet to view more or fewer columns of data. Kimberly asks you to change the font size in the query datasheet from the default 11 points to 14 points so that she can read the text more easily.

**To change the font size in the datasheet:**

1. On the Home tab, in the Text Formatting group, click the **Font Size** arrow, and then click **14**. The font size for the entire datasheet increases to 14 points.

   Next, you need to resize the columns to their best fit, so that all field values are displayed. Instead of resizing each column individually, you'll use the datasheet selector to select all the columns and resize them at the same time.

2. Click the **datasheet selector**. All the columns in the datasheet are selected.

3. Move the pointer to one of the vertical lines separating two columns in the datasheet until the pointer changes to ↔, and then double-click the vertical line. All the columns visible on the screen are resized to their best fit. Scroll down and repeat the resizing, as necessary, to make sure that all field values are fully displayed.

   **Trouble?** If all the columns are not visible on your screen, you need to scroll the datasheet to the right to make sure all field values for all columns are fully displayed. If you need to resize any columns, click a field value first to deselect the columns before resizing an individual column.

4. Click any value in the Animal Name column to make it the current field and to deselect the columns in the datasheet.

## Changing the Alternate Row Color in a Datasheet

Access uses themes to format the objects in a database. A **theme** is a predefined set of formats including colors, fonts, and other effects that enhance an object's appearance and usability. When you create a database, Access applies the Office theme to objects as you create them. By default, the Office theme formats every other row in a datasheet with a gray background color to distinguish one row from another, making it easier to view and read the contents of a datasheet. The gray alternate row color provides a subtle difference compared to the rows that have the default white color. You can change the alternate row color in a datasheet to something more noticeable using the Alternate Row Color button in the Text Formatting group on the Home tab. Kimberly suggests that you change the alternate row color in the datasheet to see the effect of using this feature.

## To change the alternate row color in the datasheet:

**1.** On the Home tab, in the Text Formatting group, click the **Alternate Row Color button arrow** ⊞ ▾ to display the gallery of color choices. See Figure 3-31.

**Figure 3-31**   Gallery of color choices for alternate row color

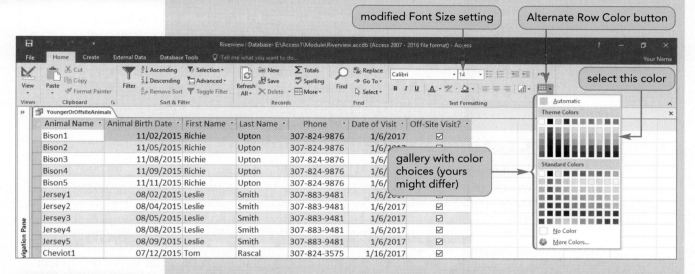

modified Font Size setting

Alternate Row Color button

select this color

gallery with color choices (yours might differ)

---

**TIP**

The name of the color appears in a ScreenTip when you point to a color in the gallery.

The Theme Colors section provides colors from the default Office theme, so that your datasheet's color scheme matches the one in use for the database. The Standard Colors section provides many standard color choices. You might also see a Recent Colors section, with colors that you have recently used in a datasheet. The No Color option, which appears at the bottom of the gallery, sets each row's background color to white. If you want to create a custom color, you can do so using the More Colors option. You'll use one of the theme colors.

**2.** In the Theme Colors section, click the **Green, Accent 6, Lighter 60%** color (third row, tenth color). The alternate row color is applied to the query datasheet. See Figure 3-32.

**Figure 3-32**   Datasheet formatted with alternate row color

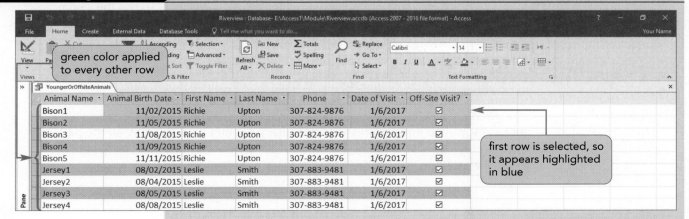

green color applied to every other row

first row is selected, so it appears highlighted in blue

Every other row in the datasheet uses the selected theme color. Kimberly likes how the datasheet looks with this color scheme, so she asks you to save the query.

▶ **3.** Save and close the YoungerOrOffsiteAnimals query. The query is saved with both the increased font size and the green alternate row color.

Next, Kimberly turns her attention to some financial aspects of operating the care center. She wants to use the Riverview database to perform calculations. She is considering imposing a 2% late fee on unpaid invoices and wants to know exactly what the late fee charges would be, should she decide to institute such a policy in the future. To produce the information for Kimberly, you need to create a calculated field.

# Creating a Calculated Field

In addition to using queries to retrieve, sort, and filter data in a database, you can use a query to perform calculations. To perform a calculation, you define an **expression** containing a combination of database fields, constants, and operators. For numeric expressions, the data types of the database fields must be Number, Currency, or Date/Time; the constants are numbers such as .02 (for the 2% late fee); and the operators can be arithmetic operators (+ – * /) or other specialized operators. In complex expressions, you can enclose calculations in parentheses to indicate which one should be performed first; any calculation within parentheses is completed before calculations outside the parentheses. In expressions without parentheses, Access performs basic calculations using the following order of precedence: multiplication and division before addition and subtraction. When operators have equal precedence, Access calculates them in order from left to right.

To perform a calculation in a query, you add a calculated field to the query. A **calculated field** is a field that displays the results of an expression. A calculated field that you create with an expression appears in a query datasheet or in a form or report; however, it does not exist in a database. When you run a query that contains a calculated field, Access evaluates the expression defined by the calculated field and displays the resulting value in the query datasheet, form, or report.

To enter an expression for a calculated field, you can type it directly in a Field box in the design grid. Alternately, you can open the Zoom box or Expression Builder and use either one to enter the expression. The **Zoom box** is a dialog box that you can use to enter text, expressions, or other values. To use the Zoom box, however, you must know all the parts of the expression you want to create. **Expression Builder** is an Access tool that makes it easy for you to create an expression; it contains a box for entering the expression, an option for displaying and choosing common operators, and one or more lists of expression elements, such as table and field names. Unlike a Field box, which is too narrow to show an entire expression at one time, the Zoom box and Expression Builder are large enough to display longer expressions. In most cases, Expression Builder provides the easiest way to enter expressions because you don't have to know all the parts of the expression; you can choose the necessary elements from the Expression Builder dialog box, which also helps to prevent typing errors.

**REFERENCE**

**Creating a Calculated Field Using Expression Builder**

- Create and save the query in which you want to include a calculated field.
- Open the query in Design view.
- In the design grid, click the Field box in which you want to create an expression.
- In the Query Setup group on the Query Tools Design tab, click the Builder button.
- Use the expression elements and common operators to build the expression, or type the expression directly in the expression box.
- Click the OK button.

To produce the information Kimberly wants, you need to create a new query based on the Billing and Visit tables and, in the query, create a calculated field that will multiply each InvoiceAmt field value by .02 to calculate the proposed 2% late fee.

### To create the new query:

1. On the ribbon, click the **Create** tab.

2. In the Queries group, click the **Query Design** button. The Show Table dialog box opens.

   Kimberly wants to see data from both the Visit and Billing tables, so you need to add these two tables to the Query window.

3. Add the **Visit** and **Billing** tables to the Query window, and resize the field lists as necessary so that all the field names are visible. The field lists appear in the Query window, and the one-to-many relationship between the Visit (primary) and Billing (related) tables is displayed.

4. Add the following fields to the design grid in the order given: **VisitID**, **AnimalID**, and **VisitDate** from the Visit table; and **InvoiceItem**, **InvoicePaid**, and **InvoiceAmt** from the Billing table.

   Kimberly is interested in viewing data only for unpaid invoices because a late fee would apply only to them, so you need to enter the necessary condition for the InvoicePaid field. Recall that InvoicePaid is a Yes/No field. The condition you need to enter is the word "No" in the Criteria box for this field, so that Access will retrieve the records for unpaid invoices only.

5. In the **InvoicePaid Criteria box**, type **No**. As soon as you type the letter "N," a menu appears with options for entering various functions for the criteria. You don't need to enter a function, so you can close this menu.

> You must close the menu or you'll enter a function, which will cause an error.

6. Press the **Esc** key to close the menu.

7. Press the **Tab** key. The query name you'll use will indicate that the data is for unpaid invoices, so you don't need to include the InvoicePaid values in the query results.

8. Click the **InvoicePaid Show** check box to remove the checkmark.

9. Save the query with the name **UnpaidInvoiceLateFee**.

Now you can use Expression Builder to create the calculated field for the InvoiceAmt field.

## To create the calculated field:

▸ **1.** Click the blank Field box to the right of the InvoiceAmt field. This field will contain the expression.

▸ **2.** On the Query Tools Design tab, in the Query Setup group, click the **Builder** button. The Expression Builder dialog box opens.

The insertion point is positioned in the large box at the top of the dialog box, ready for you to enter the expression. The Expression Categories section of the dialog box lists the fields from the query so you can include them in the expression. The Expression Elements section contains options for including other elements in the expression, including functions, constants, and operators. If the expression you're entering is a simple one, you can type it in the box; if it's more complex, you can use the options in the Expression Elements section to help you build the expression.

The expression for the calculated field will multiply the InvoiceAmt field values by the numeric constant .02 (which represents a 2% late fee).

▸ **3.** In the Expression Categories section of the dialog box, double-click **InvoiceAmt**. The field name is added to the expression box, within brackets and with a space following it. In an expression, all field names must be enclosed in brackets.

Next you need to enter the multiplication operator, which is the asterisk (*), followed by the constant.

▸ **4.** Type * (an asterisk) and then type **.02**. You have finished entering the expression. See Figure 3-33.

**Figure 3-33** Completed expression for the calculated field

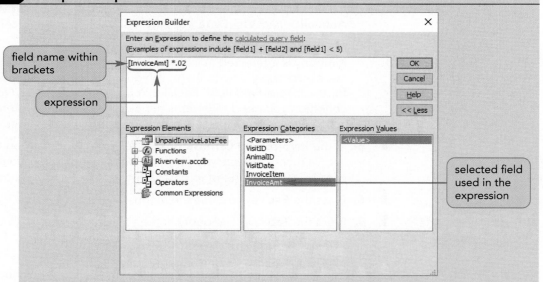

If you're not sure which operator to use, you can click Operators in the Expression Elements section to display a list of available operators in the center section of the dialog box.

▸ **5.** Click the **OK** button. The Expression Builder dialog box closes, and the expression is added to the design grid in the Field box for the calculated field.

When you create a calculated field, Access uses the default name "Expr1" for the field. You need to specify a more meaningful field name so it will appear in the query results. You'll enter the name "LateFee," which better describes the field's contents.

**6.** Click to the left of the text "Expr1:" at the beginning of the expression, and then press the **Delete** key five times to delete the text **Expr1**. *Do not delete the colon*; it is needed to separate the calculated field name from the expression.

**7.** Type **LateFee**. Next, you'll set this field's Caption property so that the field name will appear as "Late Fee" in the query datasheet.

**8.** On the Query Tools Design tab, in the Show/Hide group, click the **Property Sheet** button. The Property Sheet for the current field, LateFee, opens on the right side of the window. See Figure 3-34.

| Figure 3-34 | Property Sheet for the calculated field |
| --- | --- |

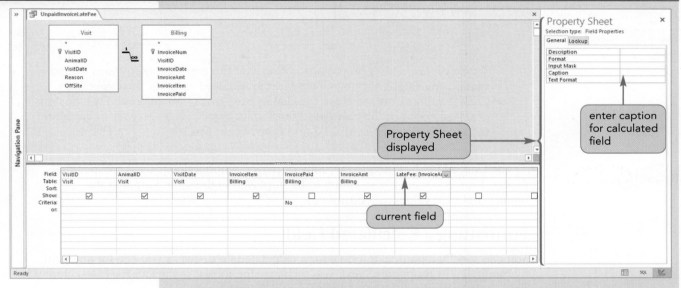

**9.** In the Property sheet, click in the Caption box, type **Late Fee** and then close the Property Sheet.

**10.** Run the query. The query datasheet is displayed and contains the specified fields and the calculated field with the caption "Late Fee." See Figure 3-35.

**Figure 3-35** Datasheet displaying the calculated field

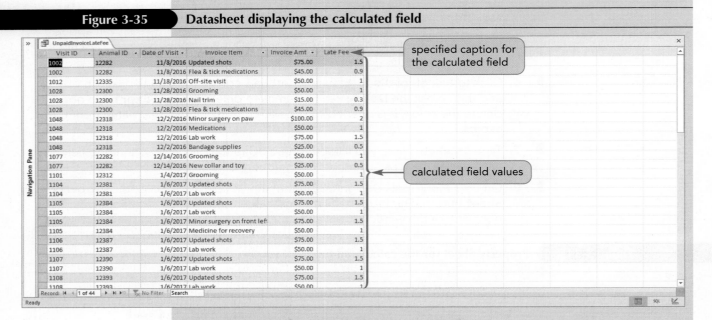

**Trouble?** If a dialog box opens noting that the expression contains invalid syntax, you might not have included the required colon in the expression. Click the OK button to close the dialog box, resize the column in the design grid that contains the calculated field to its best fit, change your expression to LateFee: [InvoiceAmt]*0.02 and then repeat Step 10.

The LateFee field values are currently displayed without dollar signs and decimal places. Kimberly wants these values to be displayed in the same format as the InvoiceAmt field values for consistency.

## Formatting a Calculated Field

You can specify a particular format for a calculated field, just as you can for any field, by modifying its properties. Next, you'll change the format of the LateFee calculated field so that all values appear in the Currency format.

**To format the calculated field:**

1. Switch to Design view.

2. In the design grid, click in the **LateFee** calculated field to make it the current field, if necessary.

3. On the Query Tools Design tab, in the Show/Hide group, click the **Property Sheet** button to open the Property Sheet for the calculated field.

   You need to change the Format property to Currency, which displays values with a dollar sign and two decimal places.

4. In the Property Sheet, click the right side of the **Format** box to display the list of formats, and then click **Currency**.

5. Close the Property Sheet, and then run the query. The amounts in the LateFee calculated field are now displayed with dollar signs and two decimal places.

6. Save and close the UnpaidInvoiceLateFee query.

**PROSKILLS**

*Problem Solving: Creating a Calculated Field vs. Using the Calculated Field Data Type*

You can also create a calculated field using the Calculated Field data type, which lets you store the result of an expression as a field in a table. However, database experts caution users against storing calculations in a table for several reasons. First, storing calculated data in a table consumes valuable space and increases the size of the database. The preferred approach is to use a calculated field in a query; with this approach, the result of the calculation is not stored in the database—it is produced only when you run the query—and it is always current. Second, the Calculated Field data type provides limited options for creating a calculation, whereas a calculated field in a query provides more functions and options for creating expressions. Third, including a field in a table using the Calculated Field data type limits your options if you need to upgrade the database at some point to a more robust DBMS, such as Oracle or SQL Server, that doesn't support this data type; you would need to redesign your database to eliminate this data type. Finally, most database experts agree that including a field in a table whose value is dependent on other fields in the table violates database design principles. To avoid such problems, it's best to create a query that includes a calculated field to perform the calculation you want, instead of creating a field in a table that uses the Calculated Field data type.

To better analyze costs at Riverview Veterinary Care Center, Kimberly wants to view more detailed information about invoices for animal care. Specifically, she would like to know the minimum, average, and maximum invoice amounts. She asks you to determine these statistics from data in the Billing table.

# Using Aggregate Functions

You can calculate statistical information, such as totals and averages, on the records displayed in a table datasheet or selected by a query. To do this, you use the Access aggregate functions. **Aggregate functions** perform arithmetic operations on selected records in a database. Figure 3-36 lists the most frequently used aggregate functions.

**Figure 3-36** Frequently used aggregate functions

| Aggregate Function | Determines | Data Types Supported |
|---|---|---|
| Average | Average of the field values for the selected records | AutoNumber, Currency, Date/Time, Number |
| Count | Number of records selected | AutoNumber, Currency, Date/Time, Long Text, Number, OLE Object, Short Text, Yes/No |
| Maximum | Highest field value for the selected records | AutoNumber, Currency, Date/Time, Number, Short Text |
| Minimum | Lowest field value for the selected records | AutoNumber, Currency, Date/Time, Number, Short Text |
| Sum | Total of the field values for the selected records | AutoNumber, Currency, Date/Time, Number |

# Working with Aggregate Functions Using the Total Row

If you want to quickly perform a calculation using an aggregate function in a table or query datasheet, you can use the Totals button in the Records group on the Home tab. When you click this button, a row labeled "Total" appears at the bottom of the datasheet. You can then choose one of the aggregate functions for a field in the datasheet, and the results of the calculation will be displayed in the Total row for that field.

Kimberly wants to know the total amount of all invoices for the care center. You can quickly display this amount using the Sum function in the Total row in the Billing table datasheet.

### To display the total amount of all invoices in the Billing table:

1. Open the Navigation Pane, open the **Billing** table in Datasheet view, and then close the Navigation Pane.

2. Make sure the Home tab is displayed.

3. In the Records group, click the **Totals** button. A row with the label "Total" is added to the bottom of the datasheet.

4. Scroll to the bottom of the datasheet to view the Total row. You want to display the sum of all the values in the Invoice Amt column.

5. In the Total row, click the **Invoice Amt** field. An arrow appears on the left side of the field.

6. Click the **arrow** to display the menu of aggregate functions. The functions displayed depend on the data type of the current field; in this case, the menu provides functions for a Currency field. See Figure 3-37.

| Figure 3-37 | Using aggregate functions in the Total row |
| --- | --- |

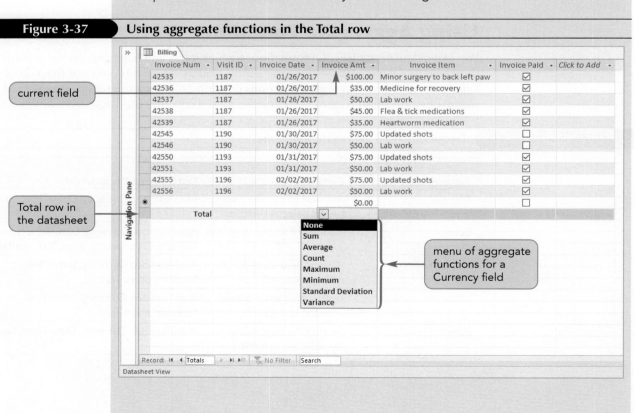

> **7.** Click **Sum** in the menu. All the values in the Invoice Amt column are added, and the total $12,015.00 appears in the Total row for the column.
>
> Kimberly doesn't want to change the Billing table to always display this total. You can remove the Total row by clicking the Totals button again; this button works as a toggle to switch between the display of the Total row with the results of any calculations in the row, and the display of the datasheet without this row.
>
> **8.** In the Records group, click the **Totals** button. The Total row is removed from the datasheet.
>
> **9.** Close the Billing table without saving the changes.

Kimberly wants to know the minimum, average, and maximum invoice amounts for Riverview Veterinary Care Center. To produce this information for Kimberly, you need to use aggregate functions in a query.

## Creating Queries with Aggregate Functions

Aggregate functions operate on the records that meet a query's selection criteria. You specify an aggregate function for a specific field, and the appropriate operation applies to that field's values for the selected records.

To display the minimum, average, and maximum of all the invoice amounts in the Billing table, you will use the Minimum, Average, and Maximum aggregate functions for the InvoiceAmt field.

### To calculate the minimum of all invoice amounts:

> **1.** Create a new query in Design view, add the **Billing** table to the Query window, and then resize the Billing field list to display all fields.
>
> To perform the three calculations on the InvoiceAmt field, you need to add the field to the design grid three times.
>
> **2.** In the Billing field list, double-click **InvoiceAmt** three times to add three copies of the field to the design grid.
>
> You need to select an aggregate function for each InvoiceAmt field. When you click the Totals button in the Show/Hide group on the Design tab, a row labeled "Total" is added to the design grid. The Total row provides a list of the aggregate functions that you can select.
>
> **3.** On the Query Tools Design tab, in the Show/Hide group, click the **Totals** button. A new row labeled "Total" appears between the Table and Sort rows in the design grid. The default entry for each field in the Total row is the Group By operator, which you will learn about later in this module. See Figure 3-38.

**Figure 3-38** **Total row inserted in the design grid**

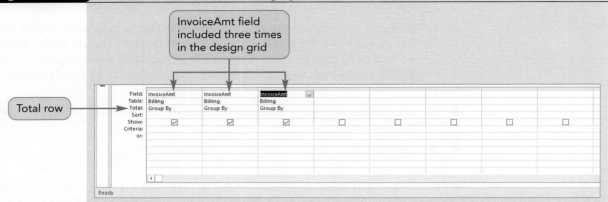

InvoiceAmt field included three times in the design grid

Total row

In the Total row, you specify the aggregate function you want to use for a field.

▶ **4.** Click the right side of the first column's **Total** box, and then click **Min**. This field will calculate the minimum amount of all the InvoiceAmt field values.

When you run the query, Access automatically will assign a datasheet column name of "MinOfInvoiceAmt" for this field. You can change the datasheet column name to a more descriptive or readable name by entering the name you want in the Field box. However, you must also keep the InvoiceAmt field name in the Field box because it identifies the field to use in the calculation. The Field box will contain the datasheet column name you specify followed by the field name (InvoiceAmt) with a colon separating the two names.

▶ **5.** In the first column's Field box, click to the left of InvoiceAmt, and then type **MinimumInvoiceAmt:** (including the colon).

Be sure to type the colon following the name or the query will not work correctly.

▶ **6.** Resize the column so that you can see the complete field name, MinimumInvoiceAmt:InvoiceAmt.

Next, you need to set the Caption property for this field so that the field name appears with spaces between words in the query datatsheet.

▶ **7.** On the Query Tools Design tab, in the Show/Hide group, click the **Property Sheet** button to open the Property Sheet for the current field.

▶ **8.** In the Caption box, type **Minimum Invoice Amt**, and then close the Property Sheet.

You'll follow the same process to complete the query by calculating the average and maximum invoice amounts.

**To calculate the average and maximum of all invoice amounts:**

▶ **1.** Click the right side of the second column's **Total** box, and then click **Avg**. This field will calculate the average of all the InvoiceAmt field values.

▶ **2.** In the second column's Field box, click to the left of InvoiceAmt, and then type **AverageInvoiceAmt:**.

▶ **3.** Resize the second column to fully display the field name, AverageInvoiceAmt:InvoiceAmt.

**4.** Open the Property Sheet for the current field, and then set its Caption property to **Average Invoice Amt**.

**5.** Click the right side of the third column's **Total** box, and then click **Max**. This field will calculate the maximum amount of all the InvoiceAmt field values.

**6.** In the third column's Field box, click to the left of InvoiceAmt, and then type **MaximumInvoiceAmt:**.

**7.** Resize the third column to fully display the field name, MaximumInvoiceAmt:InvoiceAmt.

**8.** In the Property Sheet, set the Caption property to **Maximum Invoice Amt**, and then close the Property Sheet. See Figure 3-39.

**Figure 3-39**    **Query with aggregate functions entered**

functions entered and columns resized

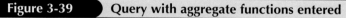
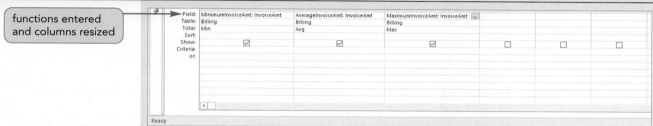

**Trouble?** Carefully compare your field names to those shown in the figure to make sure they match exactly; otherwise the query will not work correctly.

**9.** Run the query. One record displays containing the three aggregate function results. The single row of summary statistics represents calculations based on all the records selected for the query—in this case, all 202 records in the Billing table.

**10.** Resize all columns to their best fit so that the column names are fully displayed, and then click the field value in the first column to deselect the value and view the results. See Figure 3-40.

**Figure 3-40**    **Result of the query using aggregate functions**

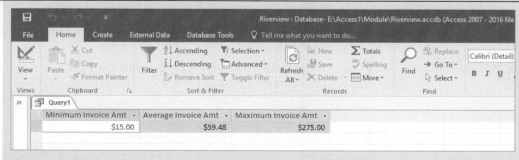

**11.** Save the query as **InvoiceAmtStatistics**.

Kimberly would like to view the same invoice amount statistics (minimum, average, and maximum) as they relate to both appointments at the care center and off-site visits.

## Using Record Group Calculations

In addition to calculating statistical information on all or selected records in selected tables, you can calculate statistics for groups of records. The **Group By operator** divides the selected records into groups based on the values in the specified field. Those records with the same value for the field are grouped together, and the datasheet displays one record for each group. Aggregate functions, which appear in the other columns of the design grid, provide statistical information for each group.

To create a query for Kimberly's latest request, you will modify the current query by adding the OffSite field and assigning the Group By operator to it. The Group By operator will display the statistical information grouped by the values of the OffSite field for all the records in the query datasheet. To create the new query, you will save the InvoiceAmtStatistics query with a new name, keeping the original query intact, and then modify the new query.

### To create a new query with the Group By operator:

▶ 1. Display the InvoiceAmtStatistics query in Design view. Because the query is open, you can use Backstage view to save it with a new name, keeping the original query intact.

▶ 2. Click the **File** tab to display Backstage view, and then click **Save As** in the navigation bar. The Save As screen opens.

▶ 3. In the File Types section on the left, click **Save Object As**. The right side of the screen changes to display options for saving the current database object as a new object.

▶ 4. Click the **Save As** button. The Save As dialog box opens, indicating that you are saving a copy of the InvoiceAmtStatistics query.

▶ 5. Type **InvoiceAmtStatisticsByOffsite** to replace the selected name, and then press the **Enter** key. The new query is saved with the name you specified and appears in Design view.

You need to add the OffSite field to the query. This field is in the Visit table. To include another table in an existing query, you open the Show Table dialog box.

**TIP**

You could also open the Navigation Pane and drag the Visit table from the pane to the Query window.

▶ 6. On the Query Tools Design tab, in the Query Setup group, click the **Show Table** button to open the Show Table dialog box.

▶ 7. Add the **Visit** table to the Query window, and then resize the Visit field list if necessary.

▶ 8. Drag the **OffSite** field from the Visit field list to the first column in the design grid. When you release the mouse button, the OffSite field appears in the design grid's first column, and the existing fields shift to the right. Group By, the default option in the Total row, appears for the OffSite field.

▶ 9. Run the query. The query displays two records—one for each OffSite group, Yes and No. Each record contains the OffSite field value for the group and the three aggregate function values. The summary statistics represent calculations based on the 202 records in the Billing table. See Figure 3-41.

| Figure 3-41 | Aggregate functions grouped by OffSite |

record groups

aggregate function results

Kimberly notes that the minimum and average invoice amounts for off-site visits are slightly higher than those for visits to the care center, while the maximum amount is higher for visits to the care center.

**10.** Save and close the query.

**11.** Open the Navigation Pane.

You have created and saved many queries in the Riverview database. The Navigation Pane provides options for opening and managing the queries you've created, as well as the other objects in the database, such as tables, forms, and reports.

# Working with the Navigation Pane

As noted earlier, the Navigation Pane is the main area for working with the objects in a database. As you continue to create objects in your database, you might want to display and work with them in different ways. The Navigation Pane provides options for grouping database objects in various ways to suit your needs. For example, you might want to view only the queries created for a certain table or all the query objects in the database.

As you know, the Navigation Pane divides database objects into categories. Each category contains groups, and each group contains one or more objects. The default category is **Object Type**, which arranges objects by type—tables, queries, forms, and reports. The default group is **All Access Objects**, which displays all objects in the database. You can also choose to display only one type of object, such as tables.

The default group name, All Access Objects, appears at the top of the Navigation Pane. Currently, each object type—Tables, Queries, Forms, and Reports—is displayed as a heading, and the objects related to each type are listed below the heading. To group objects differently, you can select another category by using the Navigation Pane menu. You'll try this next.

**TIP**

You can hide the display of a group's objects by clicking the button to the right of the group name; click the button again to expand the group and display its objects.

### To group objects differently in the Navigation Pane:

**1.** At the top of the Navigation Pane, click the **All Access Objects** button ⊙. A menu opens with options for choosing different categories and groups. See Figure 3-42.

**Figure 3-42** **Navigation Pane menu**

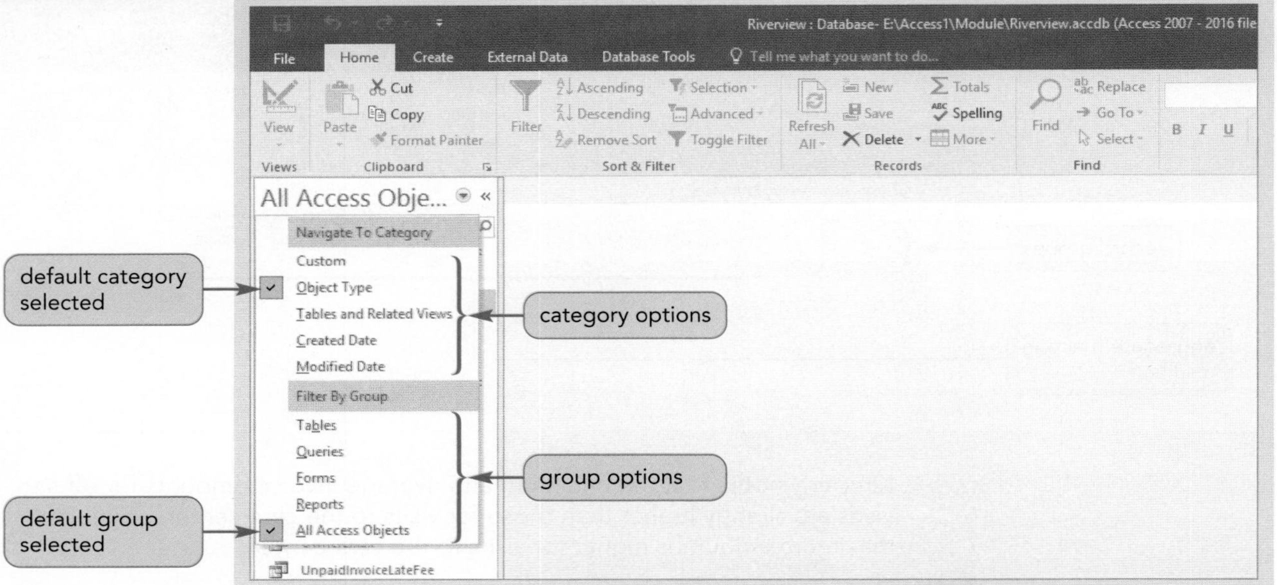

default category selected

category options

default group selected

group options

The top section of the menu provides the options for choosing a different category. The Object Type category has a checkmark next to it, signifying that it is the currently selected category. The lower section of the menu provides options for choosing a different group; these options might change depending on the selected category.

2. In the Navigate To Category section, click **Tables and Related Views**. The Navigation Pane is now grouped into categories of tables, and each table in the database—Visit, Billing, Owner, and Animal—is its own group. All database objects related to a table are listed below the table's name. Notice the UnpaidInvoiceLateFee query is based on both the Visit and Billing tables, so it is listed in the group for both tables. See Figure 3-43.

**Figure 3-43**     Database objects grouped by table in the Navigation Pane

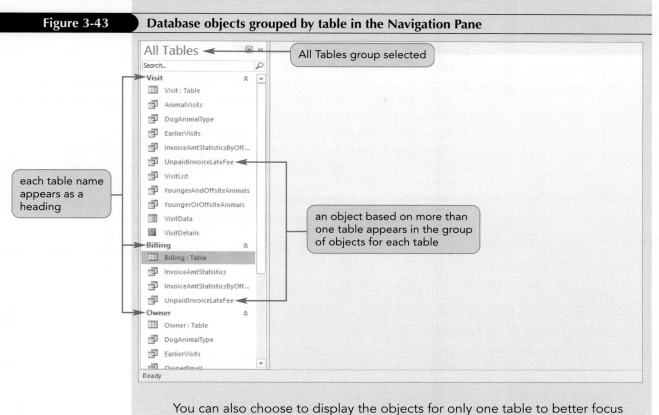

each table name appears as a heading

All Tables group selected

an object based on more than one table appears in the group of objects for each table

You can also choose to display the objects for only one table to better focus on that table.

▶ **3.** At the top of the Navigation Pane, click the **All Tables** button ⊙ to display the Navigation Pane menu, and then click **Owner**. The Navigation Pane now shows only the objects related to the Owner table—the table itself plus the five queries you created that include fields from the Owner table.

▶ **4.** At the top of the Navigation Pane, click the **Owner** button ⊙, and then click **Object Type** to return to the default display of the Navigation Pane.

▶ **5.** Compact and repair the Riverview database, and then close the database.

**Trouble?** If a dialog box opens and warns that this action will cause Microsoft Access to empty the Clipboard, click the Yes button to continue.

The default All Access Objects category is a predefined category. You can also create custom categories to group objects in the way that best suits how you want to manage your database objects. As you continue to build a database and the list of objects grows, creating a custom category can help you to work more efficiently with the objects in the database.

The queries you've created and saved will help Kimberly and her staff to monitor and analyze the business activity of Riverview Veterinary Care Center and its patients. Now any staff member can run the queries at any time, modify them as needed, or use them as the basis for designing new queries to meet additional information requirements.

REVIEW

## Session 3.2 Quick Check

1. A(n) _____ is a criterion, or rule, that determines which records are selected for a query datasheet.

2. In the design grid, where do you place the conditions for two different fields when you use the And logical operator, and where do you place them when you use the Or logical operator?

3. To perform a calculation in a query, you define a(n) _____ containing a combination of database fields, constants, and operators.

4. Which Access tool do you use to create an expression for a calculated field in a query?

5. What is an aggregate function?

6. The _____ operator divides selected records into groups based on the values in a field.

7. What is the default category for the display of objects in the Navigation Pane?

## Review Assignments

**Data File needed for the Review Assignments: Vendor.accdb** *(cont. from Module 2)*

Kimberly asks you to update some information in the Vendor database and also to retrieve specific information from the database. Complete the following:

1. Open the **Vendor** database you created and worked with in previous modules, and then click the Enable Content button next to the security warning, if necessary.

2. Open the **Supplier** table in Datasheet view, and then change the following field values for the record with the Supplier ID GGF099: Address to **738 26th St**, Contact Phone to **321-296-1958**, Contact First Name to **Carmela**, and Contact Last Name to **Montoya**. Close the table.

3. Create a query based on the Supplier table. Include the following fields in the query, in the order shown: Company, Category, ContactFirst, ContactLast, Phone, and City. Sort the query in ascending order based on the Category field values. Save the query as **ContactList**, and then run the query.

4. Use the ContactList query datasheet to update the Supplier table by changing the Phone field value for A+ Labs to **402-495-3957**.

5. Change the size of the font in the ContactList query datasheet to 12 points. Resize columns, as necessary, so that all field values and column headings are visible.

6. Change the alternate row color in the ContactList query datasheet to the Theme Color named Gold, Accent 4, Lighter 60%, and then save and close the query.

7. Create a query based on the Supplier and Product tables. Select the Company, Category, and State fields from the Supplier table, and the ProductName, Price, Units, and Weight fields from the Product table. Sort the query results in descending order based on price. Select only those records with a Category field value of Supplies, but do not display the Category field values in the query results. Save the query as **SupplyProducts**, run the query, and then close it.

8. Create a query that lists all products that cost more than $50 and are temperature controlled. Display the following fields from the Product table in the query results: ProductID, ProductName, Price, Units, and Sterile. (*Hint*: The TempControl field is a Yes/No field that should not appear in the query results.) Save the query as **HighPriceAndTempControl**, run the query, and then close it.

9. Create a query that lists information about suppliers who sell equipment or sterile products. Include the Company, Category, ContactFirst, and ContactLast fields from the Supplier table; and the ProductName, Price, TempControl, and Sterile fields from the Product table. Save the query as **EquipmentOrSterile**, run the query, and then close it.

10. Create a query that lists all resale products, along with a 10% markup amount based on the price of the product. Include the Company field from the Supplier table and the following fields from the Product table in the query: ProductID, ProductName, and Price. Save the query as **ResaleProductsWithMarkup**. Display the discount in a calculated field named **Markup** that determines a 10% markup based on the Price field values. Set the Caption property **Markup** for the calculated field. Display the query results in descending order by Price. Save and run the query.

11. Modify the format of the Markup field in the ResaleProductsWithMarkup query so that it uses the Standard format and two decimal places. Run the query, resize all columns in the datasheet to their best fit, and then save and close the query.

12. Create a query that calculates the lowest, highest, and average prices for all products using the field names **MinimumPrice**, **MaximumPrice**, and **AveragePrice**, respectively. Set the Caption property for each field to include a space between the two words in the field name. Run the query, resize all columns in the datasheet to their best fit, save the query as **PriceStatistics**, and then close it.

13. In the Navigation Pane, copy the PriceStatistics query, and then rename the copied query as **PriceStatisticsBySupplier**.

14. Modify the PriceStatisticsBySupplier query so that the records are grouped by the Company field in the Supplier table. The Company field should appear first in the query datasheet. Save and run the query, and then close it.

15. Compact and repair the Vendor database, and then close it.

## Case Problem 1

**Data File needed for this Case Problem: Beauty.accdb** *(cont. from Module 2)*

*Beauty To Go*  Sue Miller needs to modify a few records in the Beauty database and analyze the data for customers that subscribe to her business. To help Sue, you'll update the Beauty database and create queries to answer her questions. Complete the following:

1. Open the **Beauty** database you created and worked with in previous modules, and then click the Enable Content button next to the security warning, if necessary.

2. In the **Member** table, find the record for MemberID 2163, and then change the Street value to **844 Sanford Ln** and the Zip to **32804**.

3. In the **Member** table, find the record for MemberID 2169, and then delete the record. Close the Member table.

4. Create a query that lists customers who did not have to pay a fee when they signed up for their current option. In the query results, display the FirstName, LastName, and OptionBegin fields from the Member table, and the OptionCost field from the Option table. Sort the records in ascending order by the option start date. Select records only for customers whose fees were waived. (*Hint*: The FeeWaived field is a Yes/No field that should not appear in the query results.) Save the query as **NoFees**, and then run the query.

5. Use the NoFees query datasheet to update the Member table by changing the Last Name value for Gilda Packson to **Washington**.

6. Use the NoFees query datasheet to display the total Option Cost for the selected members. Save and close the query.

7. Create a query that lists the MemberID, FirstName, LastName, OptionBegin, OptionDescription, and OptionCost fields for customers who signed up with Beauty To Go between January 1, 2017 and January 31, 2017. Save the query as **JanuaryOptions**, run the query, and then close it.

8. Create a query that lists all customers who live in Celebration and whose options end on or after 4/1/2017. Display the following fields from the Member table in the query results: MemberID, FirstName, LastName, Phone, and OptionEnd. (*Hint*: The City field values should not appear in the query results.) Sort the query results in ascending order by last name. Save the query as **CelebrationAndEndDate**, run the query, and then close it.

9. Copy and paste the CelebrationAndEndDate query to create a new query named **CelebrationOrEndDate**. Modify the new query so that it lists all members who live in Celebration or whose memberships expire on or after 4/1/2017. Display the City field values in the query results following the Phone field values, and sort the query results in ascending order by city (this should be the only sort in the query). Save and run the query.

10. Change the size of the font in the CelebrationOrEndDate query datasheet to 14 points. Resize columns, as necessary, so that all field values and column headings are visible.

11. Change the alternate row color in the CelebrationOrEndDate query datasheet to the Theme Color named Green, Accent 6, Lighter 80%, and then save and close the query.

12. Create a query that calculates the lowest, highest, and average cost for all options using the field names **LowestCost**, **HighestCost**, and **AverageCost**, respectively. Set the Caption property for each field to include a space between the two words in the field name. Run the query, resize all columns in the datasheet to their best fit, save the query as **CostStatistics**, and then close it.

13. Copy and paste the CostStatistics query to create a new query named **CostStatisticsByZip**.

14. Modify the CostStatisticsByZip query to display the same statistics grouped by Zip, with Zip appearing as the first field. (*Hint*: Add the Member table to the query.) Run the query, and then save and close it.

15. Compact and repair the Beauty database, and then close it.

## Case Problem 2

**Data File needed for this Case Problem: Programming.accdb (*cont. from Module 2*)**

***Programming Pros***    After reviewing the Programming database, Brent Hovis wants to modify some records and then view specific information about the students, tutors, and contracts for his tutoring services company. He asks you to update and query the Programming database to perform these tasks. Complete the following:

1. Open the **Programming** database you created and worked with in previous modules, and then click the Enable Content button next to the security warning, if necessary.

2. In the **Tutor** table, change the following information for the record with TutorID 1048: Major is **Computer Science** and Year In School is **Graduate**. Close the table.

3. In the **Student** table, find the record with the StudentID RAM4025, and then delete the related record in the subdatasheet for this student. Delete the record for StudentID RAM4025, and then close the Student table.

4. Create a query based on the Student table that includes the LastName, FirstName, and CellPhone fields, in that order. Save the query as **StudentCellList**, and then run the query.

5. In the results of the StudentCellList query, change the cell phone number for Hidalgo Hickman to **919-301-2209**. Close the query.

6. Create a query based on the Tutor and Contract tables. Display the LastName field from the Tutor table, and the StudentID, ContractDate, SessionType, Length, and Cost fields, in that order, from the Contract table. Sort first in ascending order by the tutor's last name, and then in ascending order by the StudentID. Save the query as **SessionsByTutor**, run the query, and then close it.

7. Copy and paste the SessionsByTutor query to create a new query named **GroupSessions**. Modify the new query so that it displays the same information for records with a Group session type only. Do not display the SessionType field values in the query results. Save and run the query, and then close it.

8. Create and save a query that produces the results shown in Figure 3-44. Close the query when you are finished.

**Figure 3-44** **RaleighPrivate query results**

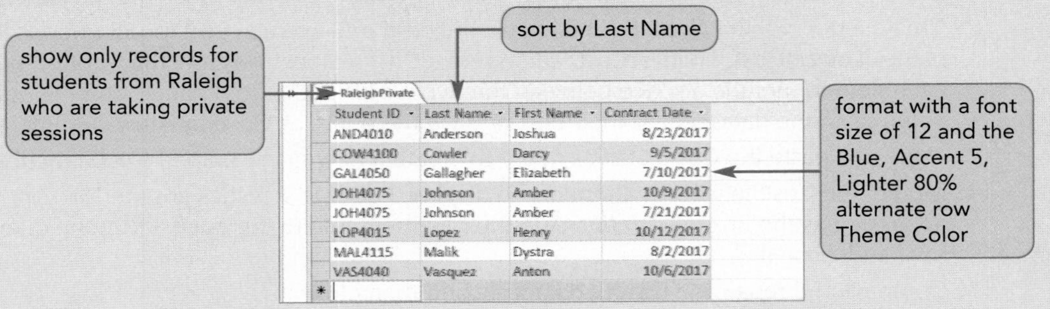

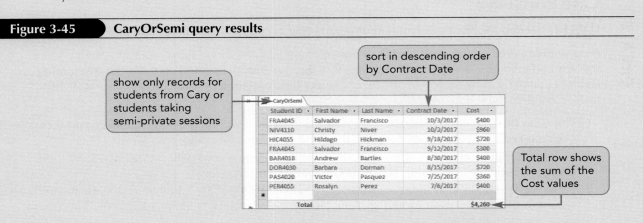

show only records for students from Raleigh who are taking private sessions
sort by Last Name
format with a font size of 12 and the Blue, Accent 5, Lighter 80% alternate row Theme Color
RaleighPrivate

| Student ID | Last Name | First Name | Contract Date |
|---|---|---|---|
| AND4010 | Anderson | Joshua | 8/23/2017 |
| COW4100 | Cowler | Darcy | 9/5/2017 |
| GAL4050 | Gallagher | Elizabeth | 7/10/2017 |
| JOH4075 | Johnson | Amber | 10/9/2017 |
| JOH4075 | Johnson | Amber | 7/21/2017 |
| LOP4015 | Lopez | Henry | 10/12/2017 |
| MAL4115 | Malik | Dystra | 8/2/2017 |
| VAS4040 | Vasquez | Anton | 10/6/2017 |

9. Create and save a query that produces the results shown in Figure 3-45. Close the query when you are finished.

**Figure 3-45** **CaryOrSemi query results**

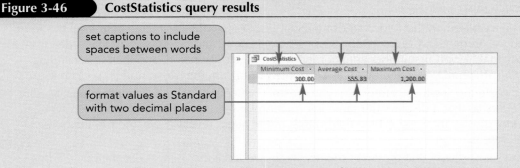

show only records for students from Cary or students taking semi-private sessions
sort in descending order by Contract Date
Total row shows the sum of the Cost values
CaryOrSemi

| Student ID | First Name | Last Name | Contract Date | Cost |
|---|---|---|---|---|
| FRA4045 | Salvador | Francisco | 10/3/2017 | $400 |
| NIV4110 | Christy | Niver | 10/2/2017 | $960 |
| HIC4055 | Hildago | Hickman | 9/18/2017 | $720 |
| FRA4045 | Salvador | Francisco | 9/12/2017 | $300 |
| BAR4018 | Andrew | Bartles | 8/30/2017 | $400 |
| DOR4030 | Barbara | Dorman | 8/15/2017 | $720 |
| PAS4020 | Victor | Pasquez | 7/25/2017 | $360 |
| PER4055 | Rosalyn | Perez | 7/6/2017 | $400 |
| Total | | | | $4,260 |

10. Create and save a query to display statistics for the Cost field, as shown in Figure 3-46. Close the query when you are finished.

**Figure 3-46** **CostStatistics query results**

set captions to include spaces between words
format values as Standard with two decimal places
CostStatistics

| Minimum Cost | Average Cost | Maximum Cost |
|---|---|---|
| 300.00 | 555.83 | 1,200.00 |

11. Copy and paste the CostStatistics query to create a new query named **CostStatisticsByCity**.

12. Modify the CostStatisticsByCity query to display the same statistics grouped by City, with City appearing as the first field. (*Hint*: Add the Student table to the query.) Run the query, and then save and close it.

13. Compact and repair the Programming database, and then close it.

## Case Problem 3

**Data File needed for this Case Problem: Center.accdb** *(cont. from Module 2)*

CHALLENGE

***Diane's Community Center***   Diane Coleman needs to modify some records in the Center database, and then she wants to find specific information about the patrons, donations, and auction items for her not-for-profit community center. Diane asks you to help her update the database and create queries to find the information she needs. Complete the following:

1. Open the **Center** database you created and worked with in previous modules, and then click the Enable Content button next to the security warning, if necessary.

2. In the **Patron** table, delete the record with PatronID 3024. (*Hint*: Delete the related records in the Donation subdatasheet first.) Close the Patron table without saving changes to the table layout.

3. Create a query based on the Auction and Donation tables that includes the AuctionID, DonationID, DonationDate, and Description fields, in that order. Save the query as **AuctionItemsByDate**, and then run it.

4. Modify the AuctionItemsByDate query design so that it sorts records in ascending order first by DonationDate and then by Description. Save and run the query.

5. In the AuctionItemsByDate query datasheet, find the record for the auction item with Auction ID 250, and then change the description for this item to **New scooter**. Close the query.

6. Create a query that displays the PatronID, FirstName, and LastName fields from the Patron table, and the Description and DonationValue fields from the Donation table for all donations over $150. Sort the query in ascending order by donation value. Save the query as **LargeDonations**, run the query, and then close it.

7. Copy and paste the LargeDonations query to create a new query named **LargeCashDonations**.

⊕ **Explore** 8. Modify the LargeCashDonations query to display only those records with donations valued at more than $150 in cash. Do not include the Description field values in the query results. Use the query datasheet to calculate the average cash donation. Save and close the query.

9. Create a query that displays the PatronID, FirstName, and LastName fields from the Patron table, and the AuctionID, AuctionDate, and MinPrice fields from the Auction table. Specify that the results show records for only those items with a minimum price greater than $150. Save the query as **ExpensiveAuctionItems**, and then run the query.

10. Filter the results of the ExpensiveAuctionItems query datasheet to display records with an auction date of 10/14/2017 only.

⊕ **Explore** 11. Format the datasheet of the ExpensiveAuctionItems query so that it does not display gridlines, uses an alternate row Standard Color of Maroon 2, and displays a font size of 12. (*Hint*: Use the Gridlines button in the Text Formatting group on the Home tab to select the appropriate gridlines option.) Resize the columns to display the complete field names and values, if necessary. Save and close the query.

⊕ **Explore** 12. Create a query that displays the PatronID, FirstName, and LastName fields from the Patron table, and the Description, DonationDate, and DonationValue fields from the Donation table. Specify that the query include records for noncash donations only or for donations made in the month of September 2017. Sort the records first in ascending order by the patron's last name, and then in descending order by the donation value. Save the query as **NonCashOrSeptemberDonations**, run the query, and then close it.

13. Copy and paste the NonCashOrSeptemberDonations query to create a new query named **DonationsAfterStorageCharge**.

⊕ **Explore** 14. Modify the DonationsAfterStorageCharge query so that it displays records for noncash donations made on all dates. Create a calculated field named **NetDonation** that displays the results of subtracting $3.50 from the DonationValue field values to account for the cost of storing each noncash donated item. Set the Caption property **Net Donation** for the calculated field. Display the results in ascending order by donation value and not sorted on any other field. Run the query, and then modify it to format both the DonationValue field and the calculated field as Currency with two decimal places. Run the query again, and resize the columns in the datasheet to their best fit, as necessary. Save and close the query.

⊕ **Explore** 15. Create a query based on the **Donation** table that displays the sum, average, and count of the DonationValue field for all donations. Then complete the following:

   a. Specify field names of **TotalDonations**, **AverageDonation**, and **NumberOfDonations**. Then specify captions to include spaces between words.

   b. Save the query as **DonationStatistics**, and then run it. Resize the query datasheet columns to their best fit.

   c. Modify the field properties so that the values in the Total Donations and Average Donation columns display two decimal places and the Standard format. Run the query again, and then save and close the query.

   d. Copy and paste the DonationStatistics query to create a new query named **DonationStatisticsByDescription**.

   e. Modify the DonationStatisticsByDescription query to display the sum, average, and count of the DonationValue field for all donations grouped by Description, with Description appearing as the first field. Sort the records in descending order by Total Donations. Save, run, and then close the query.

16. Compact and repair the Center database, and then close it.

## Case Problem 4

Data Files needed for this Case Problem: Appalachia.accdb *(cont. from Module 2)* and HikeApp.accdb

*Hike Appalachia*   Molly and Bailey Johnson need your help to maintain and analyze data about the hikers, reservations, and tours for their hiking tour business. Additionally, you'll troubleshoot some problems in another database containing tour information. Complete the following:

1. Open the **Appalachia** database you created and worked with in previous modules, and then click the Enable Content button next to the security warning, if necessary.

2. In the **Hiker** table, change the phone number for Wilbur Sanders to **828-910-2058**, and then close the table.

3. Create a query based on the Tour table that includes the TourName, Hours, PricePerPerson, and TourType fields, in that order. Sort in ascending order based on the PricePerPerson field values. Save the query as **ToursByPrice**, and then run the query.

**TROUBLESHOOT**

4. Use the ToursByPrice query datasheet to display the total Price Per Person for the tours. Save and close the query.

5. Create a query that displays the HikerLast, City, and State fields from the Hiker table, and the ReservationID, TourDate, and People fields from the Reservation table. Save the query as **HikerTourDates**, and then run the query. Change the alternate row color in the query datasheet to the Theme Color Blue, Accent 1, Lighter 80%. In Datasheet view, use an AutoFilter to sort the query results from oldest to newest Tour Date. Save and close the query.

6. Create a query that displays the HikerFirst, HikerLast, City, ReservationID, TourID, and TourDate fields for all guests from North Carolina (NC). Do not include the State field in the query results. Sort the query in ascending order by the guest's last name. Save the query as **NorthCarolinaHikers** and then run it. Close the query.

7. Create a query that displays data from all three tables in the database as follows: the HikerLast, City, and State fields from the Hiker table; the TourDate field from the Reservation table; and the TourName and TourType fields from the Tour table. Specify that the query select only those records for guests from West Virginia (WV) or guests who are taking climbing tours. Sort the query in ascending order by Tour Name. Save the query as **WestVirginiaOrClimbing** and then run the query. Resize datasheet columns to their best fit, as necessary, and then save and close the query.

8. Copy and paste the **WestVirginiaOrClimbing** query to create a new query named **SouthCarolinaAndSeptember**.

9. Modify the **SouthCarolinaAndSeptember** query to select all guests from South Carolina (SC) who are taking a tour starting sometime in the month of September 2017. Do not include the State field values in the query results. Run the query. Resize datasheet columns to their best fit, as necessary, and then save and close the query.

10. Create a query that displays the ReservationID, TourDate, and People fields from the Reservation table, and the TourName and PricePerPerson fields from the Tour table for all reservations with a People field value greater than 1. Save the query as **ReservationCosts**. Add a field to the query named **TotalCost** that displays the results of multiplying the People field values by the PricePerPerson field values. Set the Caption property **Total Cost** for the calculated field. Display the results in descending order by TotalCost. Run the query. Modify the query by formatting the TotalCost field to show 0 decimal places. Run the query, resize datasheet columns to their best fit, as necessary, and then save and close the query.

11. Create a query based on the Tour table that determines the minimum, average, and maximum price per person for all tours. Then complete the following:

    a. Specify field names of **LowestPrice**, **AveragePrice**, and **HighestPrice**.

    b. Set the Caption property for each field to include a space between the two words in the field name.

    c. Save the query as **PriceStatistics**, and then run the query.

    d. In Design view, specify the Standard format and two decimal places for each column.

    e. Run the query, resize all the datasheet columns to their best fit, save your changes, and then close the query.

    f. Create a copy of the PriceStatistics query named **PriceStatisticsByTourType**.

    g. Modify the PriceStatisticsByTourType query to display the price statistics grouped by TourType, with TourType appearing as the first field. Save your changes, and then run and close the query.

    h. Compact and repair the Appalachia database, and then close it.

⚙ **Troubleshoot** 12. Open the **HikeApp** database located in the Access1 > Case4 folder provided with your Data Files, and then click the Enable Content button next to the security warning, if necessary. Run the ReservationByDateAndState query in the HikeApp database. The query is not producing the desired results. Fix the query so that the data from the Reservation table is listed first and the data is sorted only by TourDate in ascending order. Save and close the corrected query.

⚙ **Troubleshoot** 13. Run the NCGuestsFewerPeople query, which displays no records in the results. This query is supposed to show data for guests from North Carolina (NC) with fewer than four people in their booking. Find and correct the errors in the query design, run the query, and then close it.

⚙ **Troubleshoot** 14. Run the GeorgiaOrOctStart query. This query should display the records for all guests who are from Georgia (GA) or whose tour date is on or after 10/1/2017. Find and correct the errors in the query design, run the query, and then close it.

15. Compact and repair the HikeApp database, and then close it.

## OBJECTIVES

**Session 4.1**
- Create a form using the Form Wizard
- Apply a theme to a form
- Add a picture to a form
- Change the color of text on a form
- Find and maintain data using a form
- Preview and print selected form records
- Create a form with a main form and a subform

**Session 4.2**
- Create a report using the Report Wizard
- Apply a theme to a report
- Change the alignment of field values on a report
- Move and resize fields in a report
- Insert a picture in a report
- Change the color of text on a report
- Apply conditional formatting in a report
- Preview and print a report

# Creating Forms and Reports

*Using Forms and Reports to Display Owner, Animal, and Visit Data*

## Case | *Riverview Veterinary Care Center*

Kimberly Johnson wants to continue enhancing the Riverview database to make it easier for her staff to enter, locate, and maintain data. In particular, she wants the database to include a form based on the Owner table that staff can use to enter and change data about the owners of the animals that the care center sees. She also wants the database to include a form that shows data from both the Owner and Animal tables at the same time. This form will show the basic information for each owner along with the corresponding animal data, providing a complete picture of Riverview Veterinary Care Center clients and their animals.

In addition, she would like the database to include a report of owner and visit data so that she and other staff members will have printed output when completing analyses of the owners who are clients of the care center and planning strategies for making additional veterinary services available to them. She wants the report to be formatted professionally and easy to use.

In this module, you will create the forms and reports in the Riverview database for Kimberly and her staff.

## STARTING DATA FILES

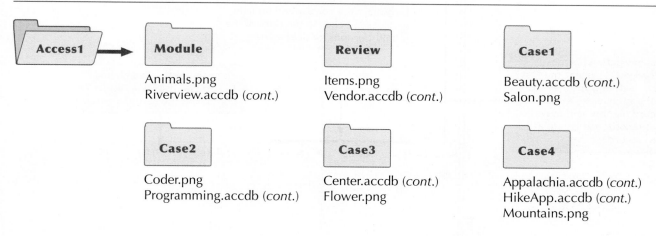

Access1 → Module
Animals.png
Riverview.accdb (*cont.*)

Review
Items.png
Vendor.accdb (*cont.*)

Case1
Beauty.accdb (*cont.*)
Salon.png

Case2
Coder.png
Programming.accdb (*cont.*)

Case3
Center.accdb (*cont.*)
Flower.png

Case4
Appalachia.accdb (*cont.*)
HikeApp.accdb (*cont.*)
Mountains.png

# Session 4.1 Visual Overview:

The form object's name is displayed on the tab for the form.

The form title appears at the top of the form. By default, the form object name is used as the form title, but you can edit the title to display the text you want, as done here—a space was added between the two words for readability.

With the Columnar form layout, the field captions appear in a column on the left side of the form. If captions had not been specified for the fields, the field names would appear here instead.

The navigation buttons allow you to display the first, last, next, or previous record in the form, enter a specific record number and move to that record, and create a new record.

You can add graphic elements, such as a picture, to a form to improve its appearance or add visual appeal.

The Columnar form layout displays the corresponding field values in boxes to the right of the field captions (or field names).

You can use the Search box to find and display a record containing the text you enter.

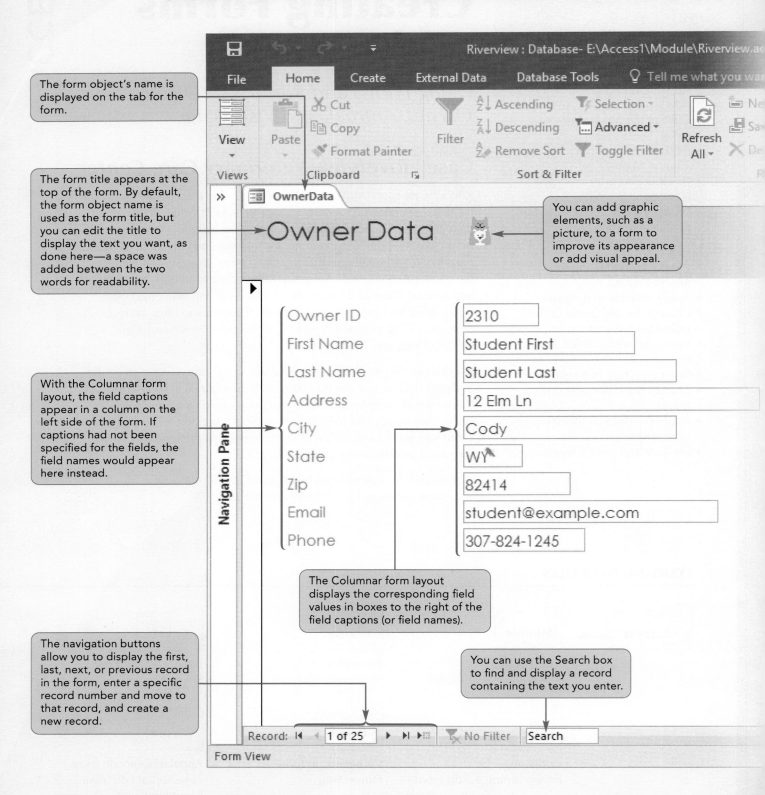

# Form Displayed in Form View

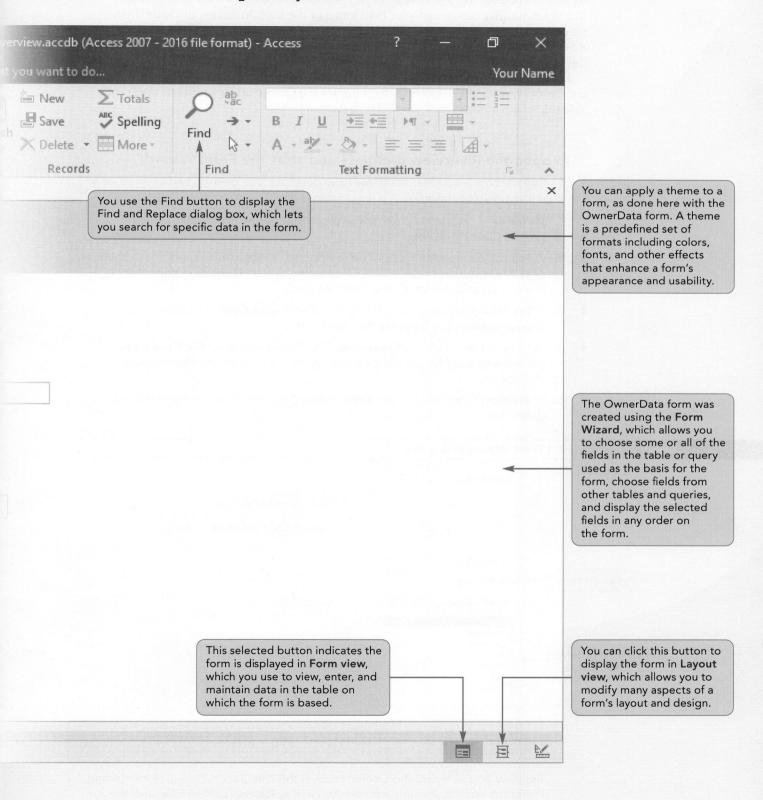

You use the Find button to display the Find and Replace dialog box, which lets you search for specific data in the form.

You can apply a theme to a form, as done here with the OwnerData form. A theme is a predefined set of formats including colors, fonts, and other effects that enhance a form's appearance and usability.

The OwnerData form was created using the **Form Wizard**, which allows you to choose some or all of the fields in the table or query used as the basis for the form, choose fields from other tables and queries, and display the selected fields in any order on the form.

This selected button indicates the form is displayed in **Form view**, which you use to view, enter, and maintain data in the table on which the form is based.

You can click this button to display the form in **Layout view**, which allows you to modify many aspects of a form's layout and design.

# Creating a Form Using the Form Wizard

As you learned earlier, a form is an object you use to enter, edit, and view records in a database. You can design your own forms or use tools in Access to create them automatically. You have already used the Form tool to create the VisitData form in the Riverview database. Recall that the Form tool creates a form automatically, using all the fields in the selected table or query.

Kimberly asks you to create a new form that her staff can use to view and maintain data in the Owner table. To create the form for the Owner table, you'll use the Form Wizard, which guides you through the process.

**To open the Riverview database and start the Form Wizard:**

1. Start Access and open the **Riverview** database you created and worked with in the previous modules.

   **Trouble?** If the security warning is displayed below the ribbon, click the Enable Content button.

2. Open the Navigation Pane, if necessary. To create a form based on a table or query, you can select the table or query in the Navigation Pane first, or you can select it using the Form Wizard.

3. In the Tables section of the Navigation Pane, click **Owner** to select the Owner table as the basis for the new form.

4. On the ribbon, click the **Create** tab. The Forms group on the Create tab provides options for creating various types of forms and designing your own forms.

5. In the Forms group, click the **Form Wizard** button. The first Form Wizard dialog box opens. See Figure 4-1.

| Figure 4-1 | First Form Wizard dialog box |

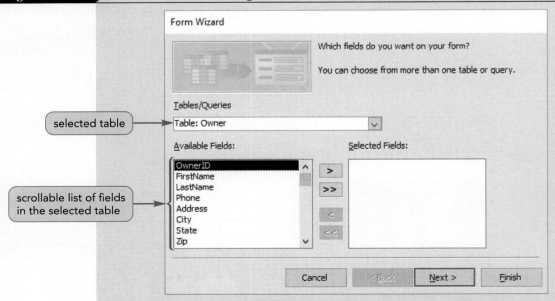

selected table

scrollable list of fields in the selected table

Because you selected the Owner table in the Navigation Pane before starting the Form Wizard, this table is selected in the Tables/Queries box, and the fields for the Owner table are listed in the Available Fields box.

Kimberly wants the form to display all the fields in the Owner table, but in a different order. She would like the Phone field to appear at the bottom of the form so that it stands out, making it easier for someone who needs to call an animal's owner to use the form to quickly locate the phone number.

### To create the form using the Form Wizard:

▶ **1.** Click the `>>` button to move all the fields to the Selected Fields box. Next, you need to position the Phone field so it will appear as the bottom-most field on the form. To accomplish this, you will first remove the Phone field and then add it back as the last selected field.

▶ **2.** In the Selected Fields box, click the **Phone** field, and then click the `<` button to move the field back to the Available Fields box.

Because a new field is always added after the selected field in the Selected Fields box, you need to first select the last field in the list and then move the Phone field back to the Selected Fields box so it will be the last field on the form.

▶ **3.** In the Selected Fields box, click the **Email** field.

▶ **4.** With the Phone field selected in the Available Fields box, click the `>` button to move the Phone field to the end of the list in the Selected Fields box.

▶ **5.** Click the **Next** button to display the second Form Wizard dialog box, in which you select a layout for the form. See Figure 4-2.

**Figure 4-2**    **Choosing a layout for the form**

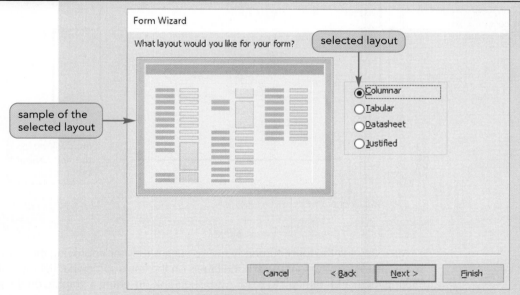

The layout choices are Columnar, Tabular, Datasheet, and Justified. A sample of the selected layout appears on the left side of the dialog box.

▶ **6.** Click each of the option buttons and review the corresponding sample layout.

The Tabular and Datasheet layouts display the fields from multiple records at one time, whereas the Columnar and Justified layouts display the fields from one record at a time. Kimberly thinks the Columnar layout is the appropriate arrangement for displaying and updating data in the table, so that anyone using the form can focus on just one owner record at a time.

▶ **7.** Click the **Columnar** option button (if necessary), and then click the **Next** button.

The third and final Form Wizard dialog box shows the Owner table's name as the default form name. "Owner" is also the default title that will appear on the tab for the form.

You'll use "OwnerData" as the form name, and, because you don't need to change the form's design at this point, you'll display the form.

▶ **8.** Click to position the insertion point to the right of Owner in the box, type **Data**, and then click the **Finish** button.

Close the Navigation Pane to display only the Form window. The completed form is displayed in Form view, displaying the values for the first record in the Owner table. The Columnar layout you selected places the field captions in labels on the left and the corresponding field values in boxes on the right, which vary in width depending on the size of the field. See Figure 4-3.

| Figure 4-3 | OwnerData form in Form view |
|---|---|

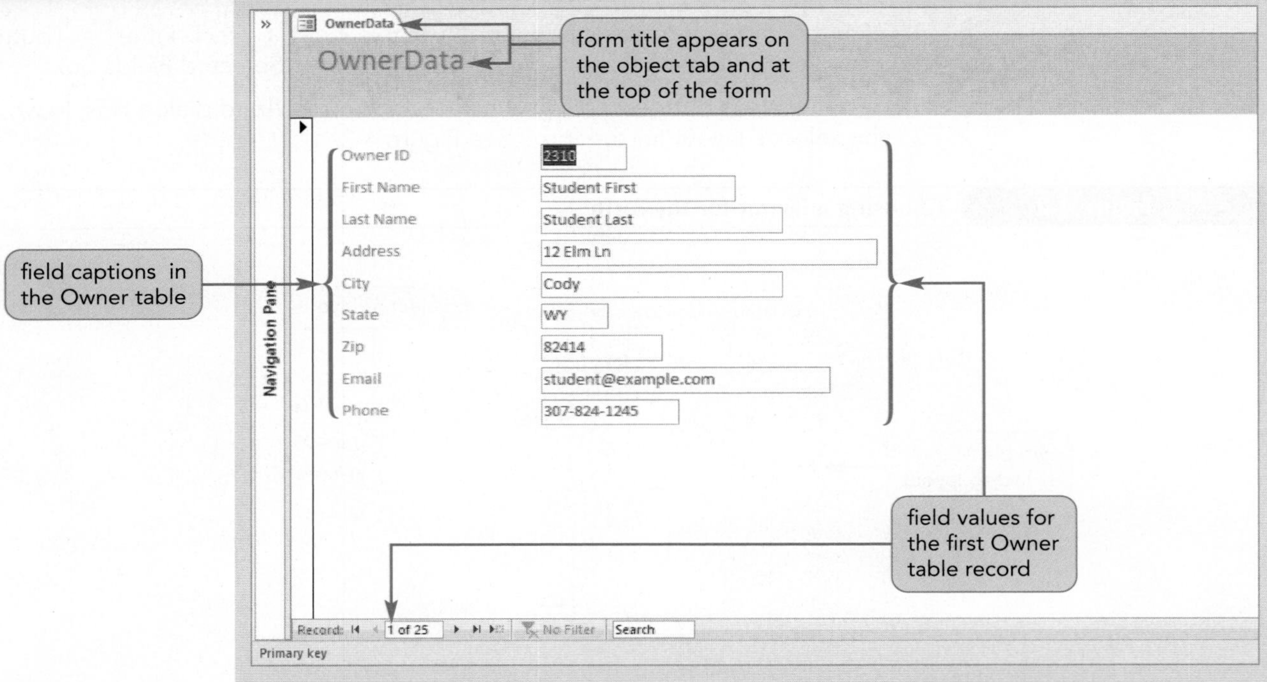

After viewing the form, Kimberly makes suggestions for improving the form's readability and appearance. The font used in the labels on the left is somewhat light in color and small, making them a bit difficult to read. Also, she thinks inserting a graphic on the form would add visual interest, and modifying other form elements—such as the color of the title text—would improve the look of the form. You can make all of these changes working with the form in Layout view.

# Modifying a Form's Design in Layout View

**TIP**

Some form design changes require you to switch to Design view, which gives you a more detailed view of the form's structure.

After you create a form, you might need to modify its design to improve its appearance or to make the form easier to use. You cannot make any design changes in Form view. However, Layout view displays the form as it appears in Form view while allowing you to modify the form's design. Because you can see the form and its data while you are modifying the form, Layout view makes it easy for you to see the results of any design changes you make.

The first modification you'll make to the OwnerData form is to change its appearance by applying a theme.

## Applying a Theme to a Database Object

By default, the objects you create in a database are formatted with the Office theme. A theme provides a design scheme for the colors and fonts used in the database objects. Access, like other Microsoft Office programs, provides many built-in themes, including the Office theme, making it easy for you to create objects with a unified look. You can also create a customized theme if none of the built-in themes suit your needs.

Sometimes a theme works well for one database object but is not as suitable for other objects in that database. Therefore, when applying a theme to an object, you can choose to apply the theme just to the open object or to objects of a particular type, or you can choose to apply the theme to all the existing objects in the database and set it as the default theme for any new objects that might be created.

To change a form's appearance, you can easily apply a new theme to it.

**REFERENCE**

### Applying a Theme to Database Objects

- Display the object in Layout view.
- In the Themes group on the Form Layout Tools Design tab or Report Layout Tools Design tab, click the Themes button.
- In the Themes gallery, click the theme you want to apply to all objects; or, right-click the theme to display the shortcut menu, and then choose to apply the theme to the current object only or to all matching objects.

Kimberly would like to see if the OwnerData form's appearance can be improved with a different theme. To apply a theme, you first need to switch to Layout view.

### To apply a theme to the OwnerData form:

▶ **1.** On the ribbon, make sure the Home tab is displayed.

▶ **2.** In the Views group, click the **View** button. The form is displayed in Layout view. See Figure 4-4.

**Figure 4-4** Form displayed in Layout view

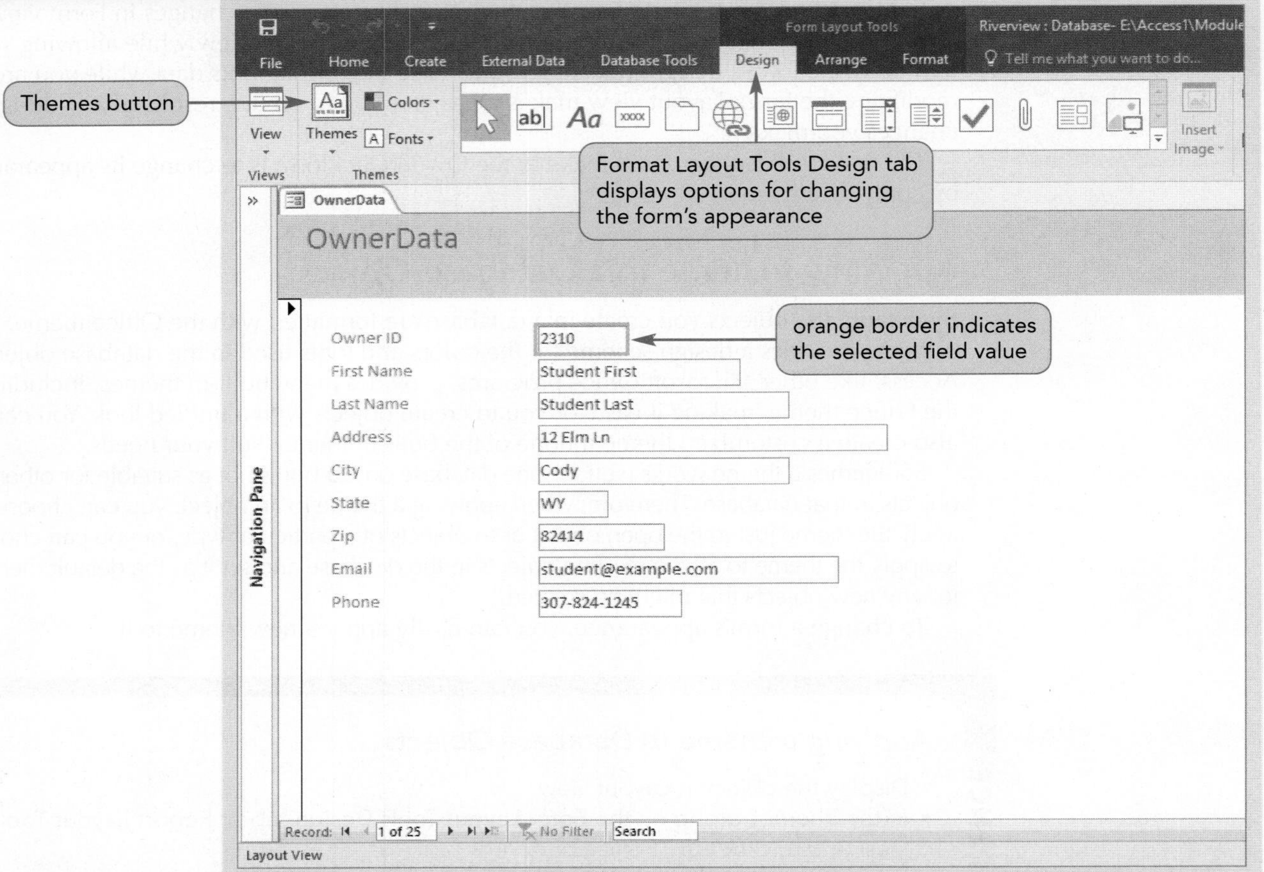

Themes button

Format Layout Tools Design tab displays options for changing the form's appearance

OwnerData

| | |
|---|---|
| Owner ID | 2310 |
| First Name | Student First |
| Last Name | Student Last |
| Address | 12 Elm Ln |
| City | Cody |
| State | WY |
| Zip | 82414 |
| Email | student@example.com |
| Phone | 307-824-1245 |

orange border indicates the selected field value

Record: 1 of 25    No Filter    Search

Layout View

**Trouble?** If the Field List or Property Sheet opens on the right side of the program window, close it before continuing.

In Layout view, an orange border identifies the currently selected element on the form. In this case, the field value for the OwnerID field, 2310, is selected. You need to apply a theme to the OwnerData form.

3. On the Form Layout Tools Design tab, in the Themes group, click the **Themes** button. A gallery opens showing the available themes for the form. See Figure 4-5.

Figure 4-5    Themes gallery

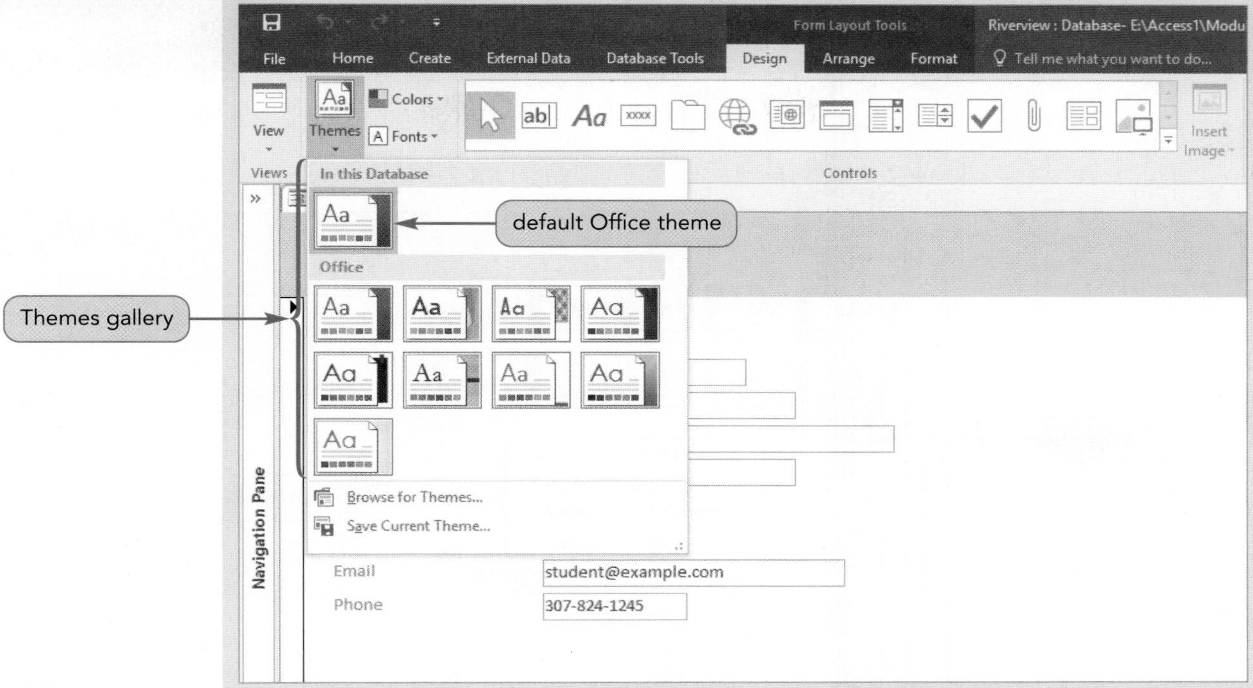

Themes gallery

default Office theme

The Office theme, the default theme currently applied in the database, is listed in the "In this Database" section and is also the first theme listed in the section containing other themes. You can point to each theme in the gallery to see its name in a ScreenTip. Also, when you point to a theme, the Live Preview feature shows the effect of applying the theme to the open object.

**TIP**

Themes other than the Office theme are listed in alphabetical order in the gallery.

4. In the gallery, point to each of the themes to see how they would format the OwnerData form. Notice the changes in color and font type of the text, for example.

   Kimberly likes the Wisp theme because of its light gray color in the title area at the top and its larger font size, which makes the text in the form easier to read.

5. Right-click the **Wisp** theme. A shortcut menu opens with options for applying the theme. See Figure 4-6.

**Figure 4-6** Shortcut menu for applying the theme

Wisp theme

Apply Theme to All Matching Objects
Apply Theme to This Object Only
Make This Theme the Database Default
Add Gallery to Quick Access Toolbar

shortcut menu

Email    student@example.com
Phone    307-824-1245

The menu provides options for applying the theme to all matching objects—for example, all the forms in the database—or to the current object only. You can also choose to make the theme the default theme in the database, which means any new objects you create will be formatted with the selected theme. Because Kimberly is not sure if all forms in the Riverview database will look better with the Wisp theme, she asks you to apply it only to the OwnerData form.

6. On the shortcut menu, click **Apply Theme to This Object Only**.

The gallery closes, and the Wisp theme's colors and fonts are applied to the form.

**Trouble?** If you choose the wrong option by mistake, you might have applied the selected theme to other forms and/or reports in the database. Repeat Steps 3 through 6 to apply the Wisp theme to the OwnerData form. You can also follow the same process to reapply the default Office theme to the other forms and reports in the Riverview database, as directed by your instructor.

Choose this option to avoid applying the theme to other forms in the database.

## Working with Themes

Themes provide a quick and easy way for you to format the objects in a database with a consistent look, which is a good design principle to follow. In general, all objects of a type in a database—for example, all forms—should have a consistent design. However, keep in mind that when you select a theme in the Themes gallery and choose the option to apply the theme to all matching objects or to make the theme the default for the database, it might be applied to all the existing forms and reports in the database as well as to new forms and reports you create. Although this approach ensures a consistent design, it can cause problems. For example, if you have already created a form or report and its design is suitable, applying a theme that includes a larger font size could cause the text in labels and field value boxes to be cut off or to extend into other objects on the form or report. The colors applied by the theme could also interfere with elements on existing forms and reports. To handle these unintended results, you would have to spend time checking the existing forms and reports and fixing any problems introduced by applying the theme. A better approach is to select the option "Apply Theme to This Object Only," available on the shortcut menu for a theme in the Themes gallery, for each existing form and report. If the newly applied theme causes problems for any individual form or report, you can then reapply the original theme to return the object to its original design.

Next, you will add a picture to the form for visual interest. The picture, which is included on various flyers and other owner correspondence for Riverview Veterinary Care Center, is a small graphic of a dog and a cat.

## Adding a Picture to a Form

A picture is one of many controls you can add and modify on a form. A **control** is an item on a form, report, or other database object that you can manipulate to modify the object's appearance. The controls you can add and modify in Layout view for a form are available in the Controls group and the Header/Footer group on the Form Layout Tools Design tab. The picture you need to add is contained in a file named Animals.png, which is located in the Access1 > Module folder provided with your Data Files.

**To add the picture to the form:**

▶ **1.** Make sure the form is still displayed in Layout view and that the Form Layout Tools Design tab is active.

▶ **2.** In the Header/Footer group, click the **Logo** button. The Insert Picture dialog box opens.

▶ **3.** Navigate to the **Access1 > Module** folder provided with your Data Files, click the **Animals** file, and then click the **OK** button. The picture appears on top of the form's title. See Figure 4-7.

**Figure 4-7** | **Form with picture added**

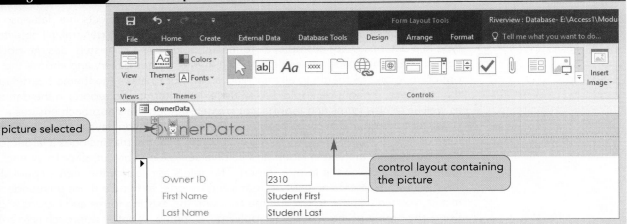

picture selected

control layout containing the picture

A solid orange border surrounds the picture, indicating it is selected. The picture is placed in a **control layout**, which is a set of controls grouped together in a form or report so that you can manipulate the set as a single control. The dotted blue outline indicates the control layout. The easiest way to move the picture off the form title is to first remove it from the control layout. Doing so allows you to move the picture independently.

4. Right-click the picture to open the shortcut menu, point to **Layout**, and then click **Remove Layout**. The dotted blue outline no longer appears, and the picture is removed from the control layout. Now you can move the picture to the right of the form title.

5. Position the pointer ⅍ on the picture, and then drag to the right of the form title. Although the image may not be visible while dragging, you can use the position of the pointer as a guide to where the image will be placed.

6. When the pointer is roughly one-half inch to the right of the form's title, release the mouse button. The picture is positioned to the right of the form title.

7. Click in a blank area to the right of the field values in the form to deselect the picture. See Figure 4-8.

**Trouble?** Don't be concerned if the picture is not in the exact location as the one shown in Figure 4-8. Just make sure the picture is not blocking any part of the form title and that it appears to the right of the form title and within the gray shaded area at the top of the form.

**TIP**

You can resize a selected image by dragging a corner of the orange selection border.

| Figure 4-8 | Form with theme applied and picture repositioned |

Wisp theme colors and fonts applied to the form elements

picture moved to the right of the form title

OwnerData

Owner ID          2310
First Name        Student First
Last Name         Student Last
Address           12 Elm Ln
City              Cody
State             WY
Zip               82414
Email             student@example.com
Phone             307-824-1245

Navigation Pane

Record: I◄ ◄ 1 of 25 ► ►I ►⊡  ⟋⟍ No Filter  Search

Layout View

Next, Kimberly asks you to change the color of the form title to a darker color so that it will stand out more on the form.

## Changing the Color of Text on a Form

The Font group on the Form Layout Tools Format tab provides many options you can use to change the appearance of text on a form. For example, you can bold, italicize, and underline text; change the font, font color, and font size; and change the alignment of text. Before you change the color of the "OwnerData" title on the form, you'll change the title to two words so it is easier to read.

### To change the form title's text and color:

1. Click the **OwnerData** form title. An orange border surrounds the title, indicating it is selected.

**TIP**

Changing the form's title does not affect the form object name; it is still OwnerData, as shown on the object tab.

2. Click between the letters "r" and "D" to position the insertion point, and then press the **spacebar**. The title on the form is now "Owner Data," but the added space caused the words to appear on two lines. You can fix this by resizing the box containing the title.

3. Position the pointer on the right edge of the box containing the form title until the pointer changes to ↔, and then drag to the right until the word "Data" appears on the same line as the word "Owner."

    **Trouble?** You might need to repeat Step 3 until the title appears on one line. Also, you might have to move the picture further to the right to make room for the title.

    Next you will change the title's font color.

▶ **4.** On the ribbon, click the **Form Layout Tools Format** tab.

▶ **5.** In the Font group, click the **Font Color button arrow** $\boxed{\text{A}}$ ▾ to display the gallery of available colors. The gallery provides theme colors and standard colors, as well as an option for creating a custom color. The theme colors available depend on the theme applied to the form—in this case, the colors are related to the Wisp theme. The current color of the title text—Black, Text 1, Lighter 50%—is outlined in the gallery, indicating it is the currently applied font color.

▶ **6.** In the Theme Colors palette, click the **Black, Text 1, Lighter 25%** color, which is the fourth color down in the second column.

▶ **7.** Click a blank area of the form to deselect the title. The darker black color is applied to the form title text, making it stand out more. See Figure 4-9.

**Figure 4-9** **Form title with new color applied**

form title in a darker black font and edited with a space between words

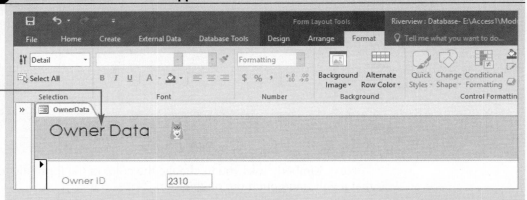

▶ **8.** On the Quick Access Toolbar, click the **Save** button 🖫 to save the modified form.

▶ **9.** On the status bar, click the **Form View** button 🖹 to display the form in Form view.

Kimberly is pleased with the modified appearance of the form. Later, she plans to revise the existing VisitData form and make the same changes to it, so that it matches the appearance of the OwnerData form.

*Written Communication: Understanding the Importance of Form Design*

Similar to any document, a form must convey written information clearly and effectively. When you create a form, it's important to consider how the form will be used, so that its design will accommodate the needs of people using the form to view, enter, and maintain data. For example, if a form in a database is meant to mimic a paper form that users will enter data from, the form in the database should have the same fields in the same order as on the paper form. This will enable users to easily tab from one field to the next in the database form to enter the necessary information from the paper form. Also, it's important to include a meaningful title on the form to identify its purpose and to enhance the appearance of the form. A form that is visually appealing makes working with the database more user-friendly and can improve the readability of the form, thereby helping to prevent errors in data entry. Also, be sure to use a consistent design for the forms in your database whenever possible. Users will expect to see similar elements—titles, pictures, fonts, and so on—in each form contained in a database. A mix of form styles and elements among the forms in a database could lead to problems when working with the forms. Finally, make sure the text on your form does not contain any spelling or grammatical errors. By producing a well-designed and well-written form, you can help to ensure that users will be able to work with the form in a productive and efficient manner.

## Navigating a Form

To view, navigate, and change data using a form, you need to display the form in Form view. As you learned earlier, you navigate a form in the same way that you navigate a table datasheet. Also, the same navigation mode and editing mode keyboard shortcuts you have used working with datasheets can also be used when working with a form.

Kimberly wants to view data in the Owner table. Before using the OwnerData form to display the specific information Kimberly wants to view, you will practice navigating between the fields in a record and navigating between records in the form. The OwnerData form is already displayed in Form view, so you can use it to navigate through the fields and records of the Owner table.

**To navigate the OwnerData form:**

▶ **1.** If necessary, click in the **Owner ID** field value box to make it current.

▶ **2.** Press the **Tab** key twice to move to the Last Name field value box, and then press the **End** key to move to the Phone field value box.

▶ **3.** Press the **Home** key to move back to the Owner ID field value box. The first record in the Owner table still appears in the form.

▶ **4.** Press the **Ctrl+End** keys to move to the Phone field value box for record 25, which is the last record in the table. The record number for the current record appears in the Current Record box between the navigation buttons at the bottom of the form.

▶ **5.** Click the **Previous record** button ◀ to move to the Phone field value box in record 24.

▶ **6.** Press the ↑ key twice to move to the Zip field value box in record 24.

**7.** Click to position the insertion point within the word "Rascal" in the Address field value to switch to editing mode, press the **Home** key to move the insertion point to the beginning of the field value, and then press the **End** key to move the insertion point to the end of the field value.

**8.** Click the **First record** button [◄] to move to the Address field value box in the first record. The entire field value is highlighted because you switched from editing mode to navigation mode.

**9.** Click the **Next record** button [►] to move to the Address field value box in record 2, the next record.

Kimberly wants to find the record for an owner named Thomas. The paper form containing all the original contact information for this owner was damaged. Other than the owner's first name, Kimberly knows only the street the owner lives on. You will use the OwnerData form to locate and view the complete record for this owner.

# Finding Data Using a Form

As you learned earlier, the Find command lets you search for data in a datasheet so you can display only those records you want to view. You can also use the Find command to search for data in a form. You first choose a field to serve as the basis for the search by making that field the current field, and then you enter the value you want Access to match in the Find and Replace dialog box.

**REFERENCE**

### Finding Data in a Form or Datasheet

- Open the form or datasheet, and then make the field you want to search the current field.
- On the Home tab, in the Find group, click the Find button to open the Find and Replace dialog box.
- In the Find What box, type the field value you want to find.
- Complete the remaining options, as necessary, to specify the type of search to conduct.
- Click the Find Next button to begin the search.
- Click the Find Next button to continue searching for the next match.
- Click the Cancel button to stop the search operation.

You need to find the record for the owner Kimberly wants to contact. The owner whose record she needs to find is named Thomas and he lives on Bobcat Trail. You'll search for this record using the Address field.

### To find the record using the OwnerData form:

**1.** Make sure the Address field value is still selected for the current record. This is the field you need to search.

You can search for a record that contains part of the address anywhere in the Address field value. Performing a partial search such as this is often easier than matching the entire field value and is useful when you don't know or can't remember the entire field value.

2. On the Home tab, in the Find group, click the **Find** button. The Find and Replace dialog box opens. The Look In box indicates that the current field (in this case, Address) will be searched. You'll search for records that contain the word "bobcat" in the address.

3. In the Find What box, type **bobcat**. Note that you do not have to enter the word as "Bobcat" with a capital letter "B" because the Match Case check box is not selected in the Find and Replace dialog box. The search will find any record containing the word "bobcat" with any combination of uppercase and lowercase letters.

4. Click the **Match** arrow to display the list of matching options, and then click **Any Part of Field**. The search will find any record that contains the word "bobcat" in any part of the Address field. See Figure 4-10.

| Figure 4-10 | Completed Find and Replace dialog box |
| --- | --- |

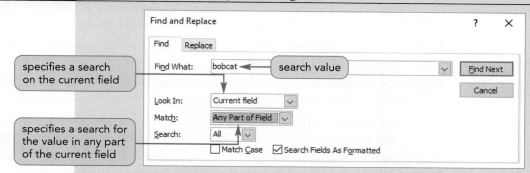

5. Click the **Find Next** button. The Find and Replace dialog box remains open, and the OwnerData form now displays record 13, which is the record for Thomas Jones (OwnerID 2362). The word "Bobcat" is selected in the Address field value box because you searched for this word.

The search value you enter can be an exact value or it can include wildcard characters. A **wildcard character** is a placeholder you use when you know only part of a value or when you want to start or end with a specific character or match a certain pattern. Figure 4-11 shows the wildcard characters you can use when searching for data.

| Figure 4-11 | Wildcard characters |
| --- | --- |

| Wildcard Character | Purpose | Example |
| --- | --- | --- |
| * | Match any number of characters it can be used as the first and/or last character in the character string | th* *finds* the, that, this, therefore, *and so on* |
| ? | Match any single alphabetic character | a?t *finds* act, aft, ant, apt, *and* art |
| [] | Match any single character within the brackets | a[fr]t *finds* aft *and* art *but not* act, ant, *or* apt |
| ! | Match any character not within brackets | a[!fr]t *finds* act, ant, *and* apt *but not* aft *or* art |
| - | Match any one of a range of characters the range must be in ascending order (a to z, not z to a) | a[d-p]t *finds* aft, ant, *and* apt *but not* act *or* art |
| # | Match any single numeric character | #72 *finds* 072, 172, 272, 372, *and so on* |

Next, to see how a wildcard works, you'll view the records for any owners with phone numbers that contain the exchange 824 as part of the phone number. The exchange consists of the three digits that follow the area code in the phone number. You could search for any record containing the digits 824 in any part of the Phone field, but this search would also find records with the digits 824 in any part of the phone number. To find only those records with the digits 824 as the exchange, you'll use the * wildcard character.

### To find the records using the * wildcard character:

▶ **1.** Make sure the Find and Replace dialog box is still open.

▶ **2.** Click anywhere in the OwnerData form to make it active, and then press the **Tab** key until you reach the Phone field value box. This is the field you want to search.

▶ **3.** Click the title bar of the Find and Replace dialog box to make it active, and then drag the Find and Replace dialog box to the right so you can see the Phone field on the form, if necessary. "Current field" is still selected in the Look In box, meaning now the Phone field is the field that will be searched.

▶ **4.** Double-click **bobcat** in the Find What box to select the entire value, and then type **307-824***.

▶ **5.** Click the **Match** arrow, and then click **Whole Field**. Because you're using a wildcard character in the search value, you want the whole field to be searched.

With the settings you've entered, the search will find records in which any field value in the Phone field begins with the area code 307 followed by a hyphen and the exchange 824.

▶ **6.** Click the **Find Next** button. Record 15 displays in the form, which is the first record found for a customer with the exchange 824. Notice that the search process started from the point of the previously displayed record in the form, which was record 13.

▶ **7.** Click the **Find Next** button. Record 16 displays in the form, which is the next record found for a customer with the exchange 824.

▶ **8.** Click the **Find Next** button to display record 18, and then click the **Find Next** button again. Record 19 displays, the fourth record found.

▶ **9.** Click the **Find Next** button two more times to display records 21 and 24.

▶ **10.** Click the **Find Next** button again. Record 1 displays. Notice that the search process cycles back through the beginning of the records in the underlying table.

▶ **11.** Click the **Find Next** button. A dialog box opens, informing you that the search is finished.

▶ **12.** Click the **OK** button to close the dialog box, and then click the **Cancel** button to close the Find and Replace dialog box.

Kimberly has identified some owner updates she wants you to make. You'll use the OwnerData form to update the data in the Owner table.

# Maintaining Table Data Using a Form

Maintaining data using a form is often easier than using a datasheet because you can focus on all the changes for a single record at one time. In Form view, you can edit the field values for a record, delete a record from the underlying table, or add a new record to the table.

Now you'll use the OwnerData form to make the changes Kimberly wants to the Owner table. First, you'll update the record for owner Sandra Pincher, who recently moved from Cody to Powell and provided a new mailing address. In addition to using the Find and Replace dialog box to locate a specific record, you can use the Search box to the right of the navigation buttons. You'll use the Search box to search for the owner's last name, Pincher, and display the owner record in the form.

### To change the record using the OwnerData form:

1. To the right of the navigation buttons, click the **Search** box and then type **Pincher**. As soon as you start to type, Access begins searching through all fields in the records to match your entry. Record 3 (Sandra Pincher) is now current.

   You will first update the address in this record.

   **TIP**

   The pencil symbol appears in the upper-left corner of the form when the form is in editing mode.

2. Select the current entry in the Address field value box, and then type **53 Verde Ln** to replace it.

3. Press the **Tab** key to select the city in the City field value box, and then type **Powell**.

4. Press the **Tab** key twice to move to and select the Zip field value, and then type **82440**. The updates to the record are complete. See Figure 4-12.

**Figure 4-12**    Owner record after changing field values

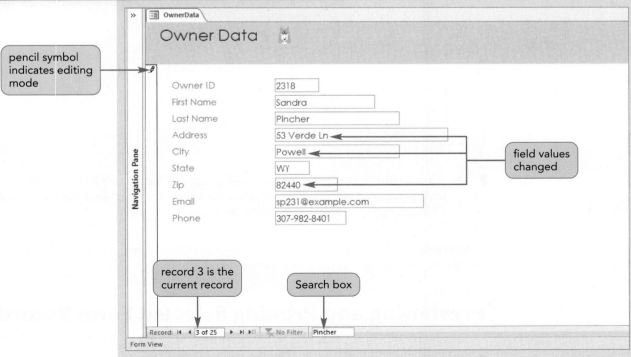

pencil symbol indicates editing mode

field values changed

record 3 is the current record

Search box

Record: 3 of 25    No Filter    Pincher

Access | Module 4 Creating Forms and Reports

Next, Kimberly asks you to add a record for a new owner. This person indicated plans to bring a pet to the care center at a recent adoption fair in which Riverview Veterinary Care Center participated, but the owner has not yet provided information about the animal or scheduled an appointment. You'll use the OwnerData form to add the new record.

### To add the new record using the OwnerData form:

▶ **1.** On the Home tab, in the Records group, click the **New** button. Record 26, the next available new record, becomes the current record. All field value boxes are empty (except the State field, which displays the default value of WY), and the insertion point is positioned in the Owner ID field value box.

▶ **2.** Refer to Figure 4-13 and enter the value shown for each field, pressing the **Tab** key to move from field to field.

| Figure 4-13 | Completed form for the new record |
| --- | --- |

▶ **3.** After entering the Phone field value, press the **Tab** key. Record 27, the next available new record, becomes the current record, and the record for OwnerID 2416 is saved in the Owner table.

Kimberly would like a printed copy of the OwnerData form to show to her staff members. She asks you to print one form record.

## Previewing and Printing Selected Form Records

You can print as many form records as can fit on a printed page. If only part of a form record fits on the bottom of a page, the remainder of the record prints on the next page. You can print all pages or a range of pages. In addition, you can print just the currently selected form record.

Kimberly asks you to use the OwnerData form to print the first record in the Owner table. Before you do, you'll preview the form record to see how it will look when printed.

### To preview the form and print the data for record 1:

1. Click the **First record** button ◄ to display record 1 in the form. This is the record in which you have entered your first and last names.

2. Click the **File** tab to open Backstage view, click **Print** in the navigation bar, and then click **Print Preview**. The Print Preview window opens, showing the form records for the Owner table. Notice that each record appears in its own form and that shading is used to distinguish one record from another. See Figure 4-14.

| Figure 4-14 | Form records displayed in Print Preview |
| --- | --- |

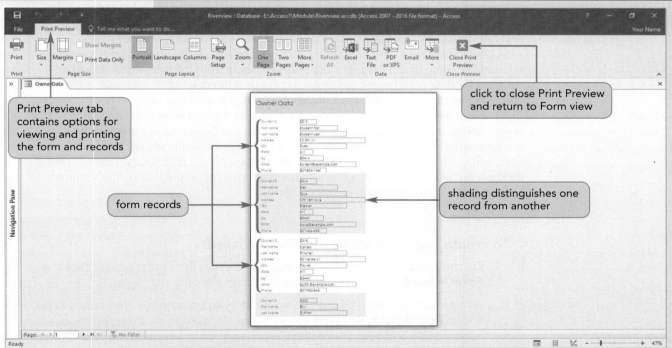

Print Preview tab contains options for viewing and printing the form and records

click to close Print Preview and return to Form view

form records

shading distinguishes one record from another

To print one selected record on a page by itself, you need to use the Print dialog box.

3. On the Print Preview tab, in the Close Preview group, click the **Close Print Preview** button. You return to Form view with the first record still displayed.

4. Click the **File** tab to open Backstage view again, click **Print** in the navigation bar, and then click **Print**. The **Print** dialog box opens.

5. Click the **Selected Record(s)** option button to print the current form record (record 1).

   **Trouble?** Check with your instructor to be sure you should print the form, then continue to the next step. If you should not print the form, click the Cancel button, and then skip to Step 7.

> **6.** Click the **OK** button to close the dialog box and print the selected record.

> **7.** Close the OwnerData form.

After reviewing the printed OwnerData form with her staff, Kimberly realizes that it would be helpful for staff members to also have a form showing information about both owners and their animals. Because this form will need to display information from two different tables, the type of form you need to create will include a main form and a subform.

# Creating a Form with a Main Form and a Subform

To create a form based on two tables, you must first define a relationship between the two tables. Earlier, you defined a one-to-many relationship between the Owner (primary) and Animal (related) tables, so you can now create a form based on both tables.

When you create a form containing data from two tables that have a one-to-many relationship, you actually create a **main form** for data from the primary table and a **subform** for data from the related table. Access uses the defined relationship between the tables to join them automatically through the common field that exists in both tables.

Kimberly would like you to create a form so that she can view the data for each owner and that owner's animals at the same time. Kimberly and her staff will then use the form when contacting the owners about care that their animals are due for. The main form will contain the owner ID, first and last names, phone number, and email address for each owner. The subform will contain the information about that owner's animals. You'll use the Form Wizard to create the form.

### To create the form using the Form Wizard:

> **1.** On the ribbon, click the **Create** tab, and then in the Forms group, click the **Form Wizard** button. The first Form Wizard dialog box opens.

> When creating a form based on two tables, you first choose the primary table and select the fields you want to include in the main form; then you choose the related table and select fields from it for the subform. In this case, the correct primary table, Table: Owner, is already selected in the Tables/Queries box.

> **Trouble?** If Table: Owner is not currently selected in the Tables/Queries box, click the Tables/Queries arrow, and then click Table: Owner.

> The form needs to include only the OwnerID, FirstName, LastName, Phone, and Email fields from the Owner table.

> **2.** Click **OwnerID** in the Available Fields box if necessary, and then click the
> >  button to move the field to the Selected Fields box.

> **3.** Repeat Step 2 for the **FirstName**, **LastName**, **Phone**, and **Email** fields.

> The subform needs to include all the fields from the Animal table, with the exception of the OwnerID field, as that field has been added already for the main form.

> **4.** Click the **Tables/Queries** arrow, and then click **Table: Animal**. The fields from the Animal table appear in the Available Fields box. The quickest way to add the fields you want to include is to move all the fields to the Selected Fields box, and then remove the only field you don't want to include (OwnerID).

TIP

The table name (Animal) is included in the OwnerID field name to distinguish it from the same field in the Owner table.

5. Click the >> button to move all the fields in the Animal table to the Selected Fields box.

6. Click **Animal.OwnerID** in the Selected Fields box, and then click the < button to move the field back to the Available Fields box.

7. Click the **Next** button. The next Form Wizard dialog box opens. See Figure 4-15.

| Figure 4-15 | Choosing a format for the main form and subform |

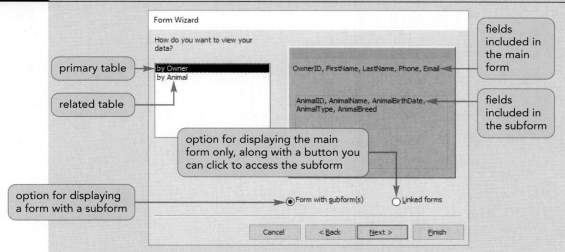

In this dialog box, the section on the left shows the order in which you will view the selected data: first by data from the primary Owner table, and then by data from the related Animal table. The form will be displayed as shown on the right side of the dialog box, with the fields from the Owner table at the top in the main form, and the fields from the Animal table at the bottom in the subform.

8. Click the **Next** button. The next Form Wizard dialog box opens, in which you choose the subform layout.

The Tabular layout displays subform fields as a table, whereas the Datasheet layout displays subform fields as a table datasheet. The layout choice is a matter of personal preference. You'll use the Datasheet layout.

9. Click the **Datasheet** option button to select it if necessary, and then click the **Next** button. The next Form Wizard dialog box opens, in which you specify titles for the main form and the subform. You'll use the title "OwnerAnimals" for the main form and the title "AnimalSubform" for the subform. These titles will also be the names for the form objects.

10. In the Form box, click to position the insertion point to the right of the last letter, and then type **Animals**. The main form name is now OwnerAnimals.

11. In the Subform box, delete the space between the two words so that the subform name appears as **AnimalSubform**, and then click the **Finish** button. The completed form opens in Form view. See Figure 4-16.

| Figure 4-16 | Main form with subform in Form view |

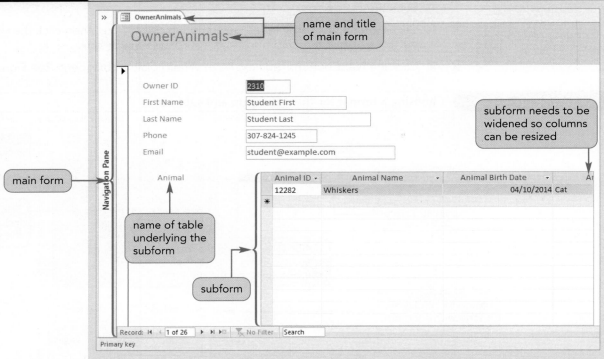

The main form displays the fields from the first record in the Owner table in a columnar format. The records in the main form appear in primary key order by OwnerID. OwnerID 2310 has one related record in the Animal table; this record, for AnimalID 12282, is shown in the subform, which uses the datasheet format. The main form name, "OwnerAnimals," appears on the object tab and as the form title. The name of the table "Animal" appears to the left of the subform indicating the underlying table for the subform. Note that only the word "Animal" and not the complete name "AnimalSubform" appears on the form. Only the table name is displayed for the subform itself, but the complete name of the object, "AnimalSubform," is displayed when you view and work with objects in the Navigation Pane. The subform designation is necessary in a list of database objects so that you can distinguish the Animal subform from other objects, such as the Animal table, but the subform designation is not needed in the OwnerAnimals form. Only the table name is required to identify the table containing the records in the subform.

Next, you need to make some changes to the form. First, you'll edit the form title to add a space between the words so that it appears as "Owner Animals." Then, you'll resize the subform so that it is wide enough to allow for all the columns to be fully displayed. To make these changes, you need to switch to Layout view.

### To modify the OwnerAnimals form in Layout view:

1. Switch to Layout view.

2. Click **OwnerAnimals** in the gray area at the top of the form. The form title is selected.

▶ **3.** Click between the letters "r" and "A" to place the insertion point, and then press the **spacebar**. The title on the form is now "Owner Animals."

▶ **4.** Click in a blank area of the form to the right of the field value boxes to deselect the title. Next, you'll increase the width of the subform.

▶ **5.** Click the **subform**. An orange border surrounds the subform, indicating it is selected.

▶ **6.** Position the pointer on the right border of the selected subform until the pointer changes to ↔, and then drag to the right approximately three inches. The wider subform makes all the columns visible. See Figure 4-17.

| Figure 4-17 | Modified form in Layout view |

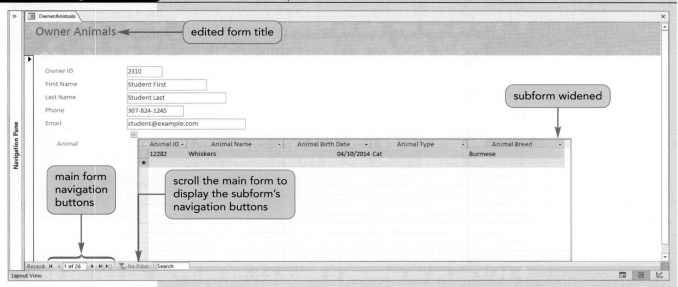

▶ **7.** On the Quick Access Toolbar, click the **Save** button 🖫 to save both the main form and the subform.

▶ **8.** Switch to Form view, and then if necessary, scroll up to view all the fields in the main form.

The form includes two sets of navigation buttons. You use the set of navigation buttons at the bottom of the Form window to select records from the primary table in the main form (see Figure 4-17). The second set of navigation buttons is currently not visible; you need to scroll down the main form to see these buttons, which appear at the bottom of the subform. You use the subform navigation buttons to select records from the related table in the subform.

You'll use the navigation buttons to view different records.

## To navigate to different main form and subform records:

▶ **1.** In the main form, click the **Next record** button ▶ six times. Record 7 of 26 total records in the Owner table (for Joey Smith) becomes the current record in the main form. The subform shows that this owner has one animal, a cat. Note that the Animal Name, Animal Birth Date, and Animal Type columns are much wider than necessary for the information displayed.

▶ **2.** Double-click the ✛ pointer on the right column divider of the Animal Name column in the subform to resize this field to its best fit.

▶ **3.** Repeat Step 2 to resize the Animal Birth Date and Animal Type columns in the subform.

▶ **4.** Use the main form navigation buttons to view each record, resizing any subform column to fully display any field values that are not completely visible.

▶ **5.** In the main form, click the **Last record** button ▶|. Record 26 in the Owner table (for Mei Kostas) becomes the current record in the main form. The subform shows that this owner currently has no animals; recall that you just entered this record using the OwnerData form. Kimberly could use the subform to enter the information on this owner's animal(s), and that information will be updated in the Animal table.

▶ **6.** In the main form, click the **Previous record** button ◀. Record 25 in the Owner table (for Taylor Johnson) becomes the current record in the main form. The subform shows that this owner has two animals. If you know the number of the record you want to view, you can enter the number in the Current Record box to move to that record.

▶ **7.** In the main form, select **25** in the Current Record box, type **18**, and then press the **Enter** key. Record 18 in the Owner table (for Susan Miller) becomes the current record in the main form. The subform shows that this owner has six animals that are seen by the care center.

▶ **8.** If necessary, use the vertical scroll bar for the main form to scroll down and view the bottom of the subform. Note the navigation buttons for the subform.

▶ **9.** At the bottom of the subform, click the **Last record** button ▶|. Record 6 in the Animal subform, for Animal ID 12440, becomes the current record.

▶ **10.** Save and close the OwnerAnimals form.

▶ **11.** If you are not continuing to Session 4.2, click the **File** tab, and then click **Close** in the navigation bar to close the Riverview database.

Both the OwnerData form and the OwnerAnimals form you created will enable Kimberly and her staff to view, enter, and maintain data easily in the Owner and Animal tables in the Riverview database.

REVIEW

## Session 4.1 Quick Check

1. Describe the difference between creating a form using the Form tool and creating a form using the Form Wizard.

2. What is a theme, and how do you apply one to an existing form?

3. A(n) _____ is an item on a form, report, or other database object that you can manipulate to modify the object's appearance.

4. Which table record is displayed in a form when you press the Ctrl+End keys while you are in navigation mode?

5. Which wildcard character matches any single alphabetic character?

6. To print only the current record displayed in a form, you need to select the _____ option button in the Print dialog box.

7. In a form that contains a main form and a subform, what data is displayed in the main form and what data is displayed in the subform?

# Session 4.2 Visual Overview:

The report object's name is displayed on the tab for the report.

The report title appears at the top of the report. By default, the report object name is used as the report title, but you can edit the title to display the text you want, as done here, with spaces added between words for readability.

Fields from the primary Owner table appear first in the report.

Fields from the related Visit Table appear below the fields from the primary table.

For a **grouped report**, the data from a record in the primary table (the Owner table in this report) appears as a group, followed on subsequent lines of the report by the joined records from the related table (the Visit table in this report).

The navigation buttons allow you to display the first, last, next, or previous page in the report, or to enter a specific page number and move to that page.

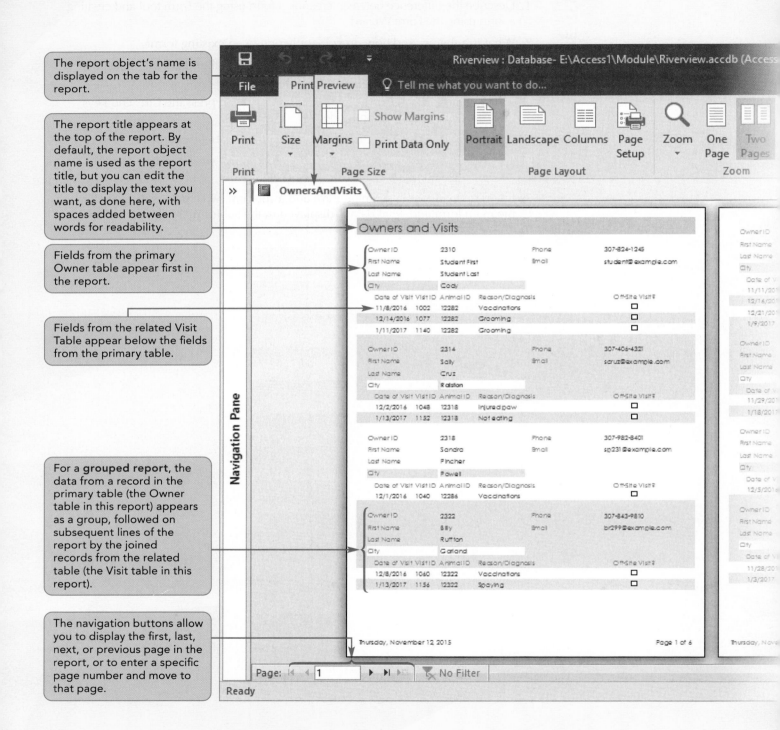

# Report Displayed in Print Preview

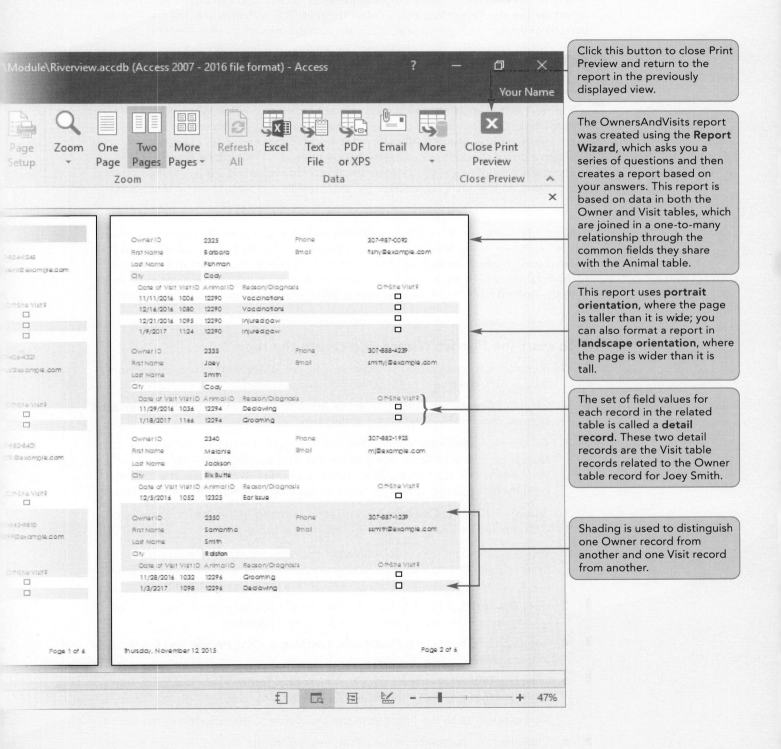

Click this button to close Print Preview and return to the report in the previously displayed view.

The OwnersAndVisits report was created using the **Report Wizard**, which asks you a series of questions and then creates a report based on your answers. This report is based on data in both the Owner and Visit tables, which are joined in a one-to-many relationship through the common fields they share with the Animal table.

This report uses **portrait orientation**, where the page is taller than it is wide; you can also format a report in **landscape orientation**, where the page is wider than it is tall.

The set of field values for each record in the related table is called a **detail record**. These two detail records are the Visit table records related to the Owner table record for Joey Smith.

Shading is used to distinguish one Owner record from another and one Visit record from another.

# Creating a Report Using the Report Wizard

As you learned earlier, a report is a formatted printout or screen display of the contents of one or more tables or queries in a database. In Access, you can create your own reports or use the Report Wizard to create them for you. Whether you use the Report Wizard or design your own report, you can change a report's design after you create it.

INSIGHT

### Creating a Report Based on a Query

You can create a report based on one or more tables or queries. When you use a query as the basis for a report, you can use criteria and other query features to retrieve only the information you want to display in the report. Experienced Access users often create a query just so they can create a report based on that query. When thinking about the type of report you want to create, consider creating a query first and basing the report on the query, to produce the exact results you want to see in the report.

Kimberly wants you to create a report that includes data from the Owner and Visit tables, as shown in the Session 4.2 Visual Overview. Like the OwnerAnimals form you created earlier, which includes a main form and a subform, the report will be based on both tables, which are joined in a one-to-many relationship through common fields with the Animal table. You'll use the Report Wizard to create the report for Kimberly.

### To start the Report Wizard and create the report:

▶ 1. If you took a break after the previous session, make sure that the Riverview database is open and the Navigation Pane is closed.

▶ 2. Click the **Create** tab, and then in the Reports group, click the **Report Wizard** button. The first Report Wizard dialog box opens.

As was the case when you created the form with a subform, initially you can choose only one table or query to be the data source for the report. Then you can include data from other tables or queries. In this case, the correct primary table, Table: Owner, is already selected in the Tables/Queries box.

**Trouble?** If Table: Owner is not currently selected in the Tables/Queries box, click the Tables/Queries arrow, and then click Table: Owner.

You select fields in the order you want them to appear on the report. Kimberly wants the OwnerID, FirstName, LastName, City, Phone, and Email fields from the Owner table to appear on the report, in that order.

▶ 3. Click **OwnerID** in the Available Fields box (if necessary), and then click the ⟩ button. The field moves to the Selected Fields box.

▶ 4. Repeat Step 3 to add the **FirstName**, **LastName**, **City**, **Phone**, and **Email** fields to the report.

▶ 5. Click the **Tables/Queries** arrow, and then click **Table: Visit**. The fields from the Visit table appear in the Available Fields box.

Kimberly wants all the fields from the Visit table to be included in the report.

▶ 6. Click the ⟩⟩ button to move all the fields from the Available Fields box to the Selected Fields box, and then click the **Next** button. The second Report Wizard dialog box opens. See Figure 4-18.

**Figure 4-18**  **Choosing a grouped or ungrouped report**

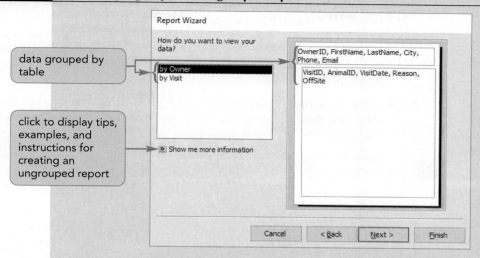

data grouped by table

click to display tips, examples, and instructions for creating an ungrouped report

You can choose to arrange the selected data grouped by table, which is the default, or ungrouped. You're creating a grouped report; the data from each record in the Owner table will appear in a group, followed by the related records for that owner from the Visit table.

▶ **7.** Click the **Next** button. The next Report Wizard dialog box opens, in which you choose additional grouping levels.

Currently the report contains only one grouping level, which is for the owner's data. Grouping levels are useful for reports with multiple levels, such as those containing monthly, quarterly, and annual totals, or for those containing city and country groups. The report requires no further grouping levels, so you can accept the default options.

▶ **8.** Click the **Next** button. The next Report Wizard dialog box opens, in which you choose the sort order for the detail records. See Figure 4-19.

**Figure 4-19**  **Choosing the sort order for detail records**

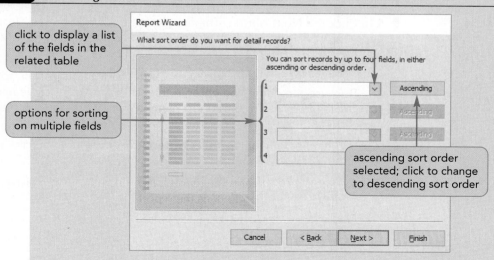

click to display a list of the fields in the related table

options for sorting on multiple fields

ascending sort order selected; click to change to descending sort order

The records from the Visit table for an owner represent the detail records for Kimberly's report. She wants these records to appear in ascending order by the value in the VisitDate field, so that the visits will be shown in chronological order. The Ascending option is already selected by default. To change to descending order, you click this same button, which acts as a toggle between the two sort orders. Also, you can sort on multiple fields, as you can with queries.

▶ **9.** Click the **arrow** on the first box, click **VisitDate**, and then click the **Next** button. The next Report Wizard dialog box opens, in which you choose a layout and page orientation for the report. See Figure 4-20.

**Figure 4-20** **Choosing the report layout**

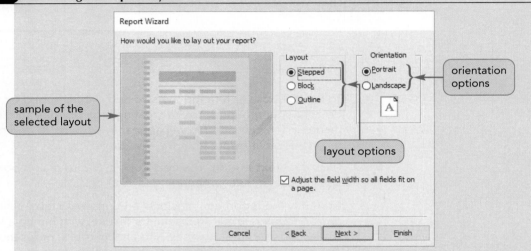

▶ **10.** Click each layout option to view each sample that appears, and then click the **Outline** option button to select that layout for the report.

Because most of the fields in both the Owner and Visit tables contain relatively short field values, the portrait page orientation should provide enough space across the page to display all the field values.

▶ **11.** Click the **Next** button. The final Report Wizard dialog box opens, in which you choose a report title, which also serves as the name for the report object in the database.

Kimberly wants the report title "Owners and Visits" at the top of the report. Because the name you enter in this dialog box is also the name of the report object, you'll enter the report name as one word and edit the title on the report later.

▶ **12.** In the box for the title, enter **OwnersAndVisits** and then click the **Finish** button.

The Report Wizard creates the report based on your answers, saves it as an object in the Riverview database, and opens the report in Print Preview.

After you create a report, you should view it in Print Preview to see if you need to make any formatting or design changes. To view the entire page, you need to change the Zoom setting.

### To view the report in Print Preview:

1. On the Print Preview tab, in the Zoom group, click the **Zoom button arrow**, and then click **Fit to Window**. The first page of the report is displayed in Print Preview.

2. At the bottom of the window, click the **Next Page** button ▶ to display the second page of the report.

   When a report is displayed in Print Preview, you can zoom in for a close-up view of a section of the report.

3. Move the pointer to the center of the report, and then click the ⊕ pointer at the center of the report. The display changes to show a close-up view of the report. See Figure 4-21.

| **Figure 4-21** | **Close-up view of the report** |

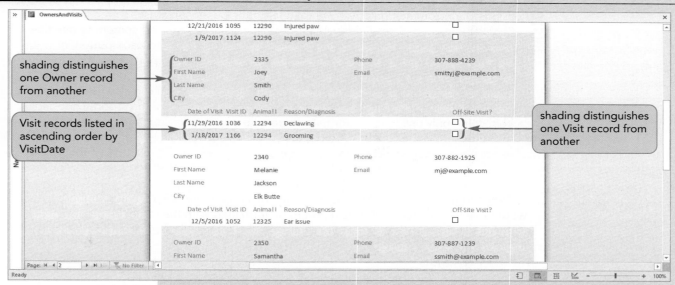

**shading distinguishes one Owner record from another**

**Visit records listed in ascending order by VisitDate**

**shading distinguishes one Visit record from another**

**TIP**

Clicking a report in Print Preview toggles between a full-page display and a close-up display of the report.

Shading is used to distinguish both one Owner record from another and, within a group of each owner's Visit records, one Visit record from another.

**Trouble?** Depending on your computer settings, the shading and colors used in your report might look different. This difference should not cause any problems.

The detail records for the Visit table fields appear in ascending order based on the values in the VisitDate field. Because the VisitDate field is used as the basis for sorting records, it appears as the first field in this section, even though you selected the fields in the order in which they appear in the Visit table.

▶ **4.** Scroll to the bottom of the second page, checking the text in the report as you scroll. Notice the current date and page number at the bottom of the page; the Report Wizard included these elements as part of the report's design.

▶ **5.** Move the pointer onto the report, click the 🔍 pointer to zoom back out, and then click the **Next Page** navigation button ▶ to move to page 3 of the report.

▶ **6.** Continue to move through the pages of the report, and then click the **First Page** button ◀ to return to the first page.

**INSIGHT**

### Changing a Report's Page Orientation and Margins

When you display a report in Print Preview, you can easily change the report layout using options on the Print Preview tab (refer to the Session 4.2 Visual Overview). For example, sometimes fields with longer values cause the report content to overflow onto the next page. You can fix this problem by clicking the Landscape button in the Page Layout group on the Print Preview tab to switch the report orientation to landscape, where the page is wider than it is tall. Landscape orientation allows more space for content to fit across the width of the report page. You can also use the Margins button in the Page Size group to change the margins of the report, choosing from commonly used margin formats or creating your own custom margins. Simply click the Margins button arrow to display the menu of available margin options and select the one that works best for your report.

When you created the OwnerData form, you applied the Wisp theme. Kimberly would like the OwnersAndVisits report to be formatted with the same theme. You need to switch to Layout view to make this change. You'll also make other modifications to improve the report's design.

# Modifying a Report's Design in Layout View

Similar to Layout view for forms, Layout view for reports enables you to make modifications to the report's design. Many of the same options—such as those for applying a theme and changing the color of text—are provided in Layout view for reports.

## Applying a Theme to a Report

The same themes available for forms are also available for reports. You can choose to apply a theme to the current report object only, or to all reports in the database. In this case, you'll apply the Wisp theme only to the OwnersAndVisits report because Kimberly isn't certain if it is the appropriate theme for other reports in the Riverview database.

**To apply the Wisp theme to the report and edit the report name:**

▶ **1.** On the status bar, click the **Layout View** button ⊞. The report is displayed in Layout view and the Report Layout Tools Design tab is the active tab on the ribbon.

▶ **2.** In the Themes group, click the **Themes** button. The "In this Database" section at the top of the gallery shows both the default Office theme and the Wisp theme. The Wisp theme is included here because you applied it earlier to the OwnerData form.

▶ **3.** At the top of the gallery, right-click the **Wisp** theme to display the shortcut menu, and then click **Apply Theme to This Object Only**. The gallery closes and the theme is applied to the report.

The larger font used by the Wisp theme has caused the report title text to be cut off on the right. You'll fix this problem and edit the title text as well.

**Trouble?** After you apply the theme, some VisitDate values may be displayed as a series of # symbols rather than actual date values. You'll fix this later in the session.

▶ **4.** Click the **OwnersAndVisits** title at the top of the report to select it.

▶ **5.** Position the pointer on the right border of the title's selection box until it changes to ↔, and then drag to the right until the title is fully displayed.

▶ **6.** Click between the letters "s" and "A" in the title, press the **spacebar**, change the capital letter "A" to **a**, place the insertion point between the letters "d" and "V," and then press the **spacebar**. The title is now "Owners and Visits."

▶ **7.** Click to the right of the report title in the shaded area to deselect the title.

**TIP**

When you point to the Wisp theme, a ScreenTip displays the names of the database objects that use the theme—in this case, the OwnerData form.

Kimberly views the report and notices some other formatting changes she would like you to make. First, she doesn't like how the VisitDate field values are aligned compared to the other field values from the Visit table. You'll fix this next.

## Changing the Alignment of Field Values

The Report Layout Tools Format tab provides options for you to easily modify the format of various report objects. For example, you can change the alignment of the text in a field value. Recall that Date/Time fields, like VisitDate, automatically right-align their field values, whereas Short Text fields, like VisitID, automatically left-align their field values. Kimberly asks you to change the alignment of the VisitDate field so its values appear left-aligned, which will improve the format of the report.

## To change the alignment of the VisitDate field values:

1. On the ribbon, click the **Report Layout Tools Format** tab. The ribbon changes to display options for formatting the report. The options for modifying the format of a report are the same as those available for forms.

2. In the report, click the **first VisitDate** field value box, which contains the date 11/8/2016. The field value box has an orange border, indicating it is selected. Note that the other VisitDate field value boxes have a lighter orange border, indicating they are selected as well. Any changes you make will be applied to all VisitDate field values throughout the report.

3. On the Report Layout Tools Format tab, in the Font group, click the **Align Left** button ☰. The text in the VisitDate field value boxes is now left-aligned. See Figure 4-22.

| Figure 4-22 | Report after applying a theme and changing field alignment |
| --- | --- |

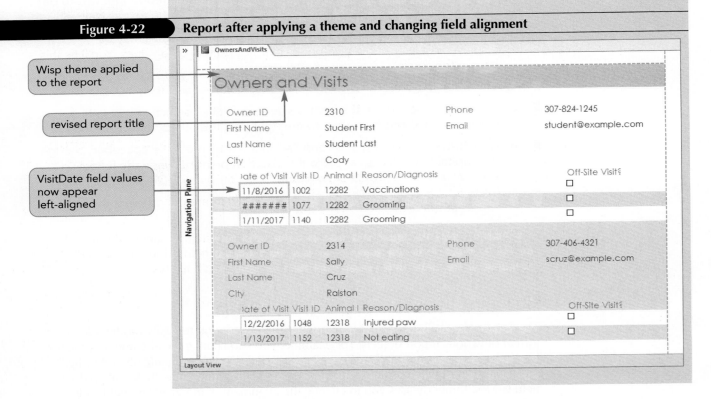

Wisp theme applied to the report

revised report title

VisitDate field values now appear left-aligned

## Moving and Resizing Fields on a Report

Working in Layout view, you can resize and reposition fields and field value boxes to improve the appearance and readability of a report. You resize field value boxes by dragging their borders to the desired size. You can also move field labels and field value boxes by selecting one or more of them and then dragging them to a new location; or, for more precise control over the move, you can use the keyboard arrow keys to move selected objects.

In the OwnersAndVisits report, you need to move and resize the VisitDate, VisitID, and OffSite field labels so that the complete caption is displayed for each. Also, some of the VisitDate field values are not displayed on the report but are instead represented by a series of # symbols. This occurs when a field value box is not wide enough for its content. To fix this, you'll widen the VisitDate field value box. Before addressing these issues, you will move the OffSite field label so it appears centered over its check box.

### To move and resize the OffSite field label:

1. In the report, click the first occurrence of the **Off-Site Visit?** field label. All instances of the label are selected throughout the report.

2. Press the ← key repeatedly until the label is centered (roughly) over its check box.

3. Position the pointer on the right border of the field label's selection box until the pointer changes to ↔, and then drag to the right until the label text is fully displayed.

Next, you need to move the field label and field value box for the Reason and OffSite fields to the right, to make room to widen the Animal ID field label. You also need to make adjustments to the field label and field value box for the VisitDate field.

### To resize and move field labels and field value boxes in the report:

1. In the report, click the first occurrence of the **Reason/Diagnosis** field label, press and hold the **Shift** key, click the first occurrence of the **Reason** field value box, which contains the text "Vaccinations," click the first occurrence of the **Off-Site Visit?** field label, and then click the first occurrence of the **OffSite** field value box. Both field labels and their associated field value boxes are selected and can be moved. See Figure 4-23.

| Figure 4-23 | Report after selecting field labels and field value boxes |

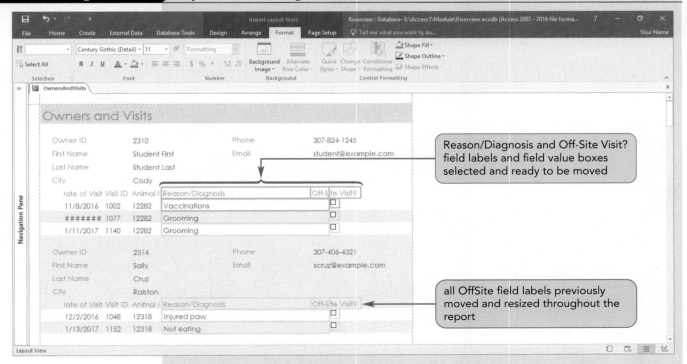

▶ **2.** Press the → key six times to move the field labels and field value boxes to the right.

   **Trouble?** Once you press the right arrow key, the report might jump to display the end of the report. Just continue to press the right arrow key to move the labels and values. Then scroll the window back up to display the beginning of the report.

▶ **3.** Click the **Animal ID** field label to select it and deselect the moved field labels and field value boxes.

▶ **4.** Position the pointer on the right border of the Animal ID field label's selection box until it changes to ↔, and then drag to the right until the Animal ID label is fully displayed.

   Now you need to modify the VisitDate field so that the # symbols that currently appear are replaced with the actual field values. You'll resize the VisitDate field value boxes to fix this problem.

▶ **5.** Scroll to the top of the report if necessary to display the first record in the report, and then click the **#######** symbols that appear in the second VisitDate field value in the first record.

▶ **6.** Using the ↔ pointer, drag the left border of VisitDate field value's selection box to the left until the date value is fully displayed.

▶ **7.** Scroll through the report, resizing the VisitDate field values as necessary until all values are fully displayed, and then scroll back up to display the top of the report.

▶ **8.** Click the **Date of Visit** field label to select it, and then drag the left border of the selection box to the left until the label text is fully displayed.

▶ **9.** Click to the right of the report title in the shaded area to deselect the field label.

▶ **10.** On the Quick Access Toolbar, click the **Save** button 🖫 to save the modified report.

Next, Kimberly asks you to enhance the report's appearance to make it more consistent with the OwnerData form.

## Changing the Font Color and Inserting a Picture in a Report

You can change the color of text on a report to enhance its appearance. You can also add a picture to a report for visual interest or to identify a particular section of the report.

Before you print the report for Kimberly, she asks you to change the report title color to the darker black you applied earlier to the OwnerData form and to include the Animals picture to the right of the report title.

**To change the color of the report title and insert the picture:**

Make sure the title is selected so the picture is inserted in the correct location.

▶ **1.** At the top of the report, click the **Owners and Visits** title to select it.

▶ **2.** Make sure the Report Layout Tools Format tab is still active on the ribbon.

▶ **3.** In the Font group, click the **Font Color button arrow** $\boxed{A}$ ·, and then in the Theme Colors section, click the **Black, Text 1, Lighter 25%** color (fourth color in the second column). The color is applied to the report title.

  Now you'll insert the picture to the right of the report title text.

▶ **4.** On the ribbon, click the **Report Layout Tools Design** tab. The options provided on this tab for reports are the same as those you worked with for forms.

▶ **5.** In the Header/Footer group, click the **Logo** button.

▶ **6.** Navigate to the **Access1 > Module** folder provided with your Data Files, and then double-click the **Animals** file. The picture is inserted in the top-left corner of the report, partially covering the report title.

▶ **7.** Position the ⁺ₖ pointer on the selected picture, and then drag it to the right of the report title.

▶ **8.** Click in a blank area of the shaded bar to deselect the picture. See Figure 4-24.

**Figure 4-24**     Report after changing the title font color and inserting the picture

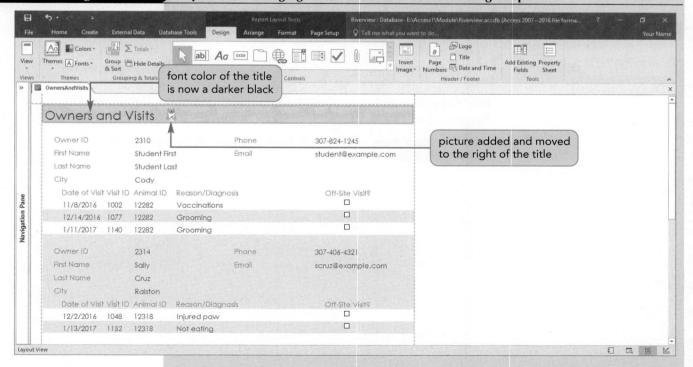

**Trouble?** Don't be concerned if the picture in your report is not in the exact same location as the one shown in the figure. Just make sure it is to the right of the title text and within the shaded area.

Riverview Veterinary Care Center is planning a mobile clinic day in Ralston. Kimberly would like to make it easier to locate the records in the report for owners who live in Ralston by applying unique formatting to their city names. Because you don't need to apply this formatting to the city names in all the records in the report, you will use conditional formatting.

# Using Conditional Formatting in a Report

**Conditional formatting** in a report (or form) is special formatting applied to certain field values depending on one or more conditions—similar to criteria you establish for queries. If a field value meets the condition or conditions you specify, the formatting is applied to the value.

Kimberly would like the OwnersAndVisits report to show a city name of Ralston in a bold, dark red font. This formatting will help to highlight the owner records for owners who live in this location.

### To apply conditional formatting to the City field in the report:

1. Make sure the report is still displayed in Layout view, and then click the **Report Layout Tools Format** tab on the ribbon.

   To apply conditional formatting to a field, you must first make it the active field by clicking any field value in the field's column.

**TIP**

You must select a field value box, and not the field label, before applying a conditional format.

2. Click the first City field value, **Cody**, for OwnerID 2310 to select the City field values in the report. The conditional formatting you specify will affect all the values for the field.

3. In the Control Formatting group, click the **Conditional Formatting** button. The Conditional Formatting Rules Manager dialog box opens. Because you selected a City field value box, the name of this field is displayed in the "Show formatting rules for" box. Currently, there are no conditional formatting rules set for the selected field. You need to create a new rule.

4. Click the **New Rule** button. The New Formatting Rule dialog box opens. See Figure 4-25.

**Figure 4-25**  New Formatting Rule dialog box

specify the condition in these boxes

a preview of the conditional format will appear here

use these options to specify the formatting

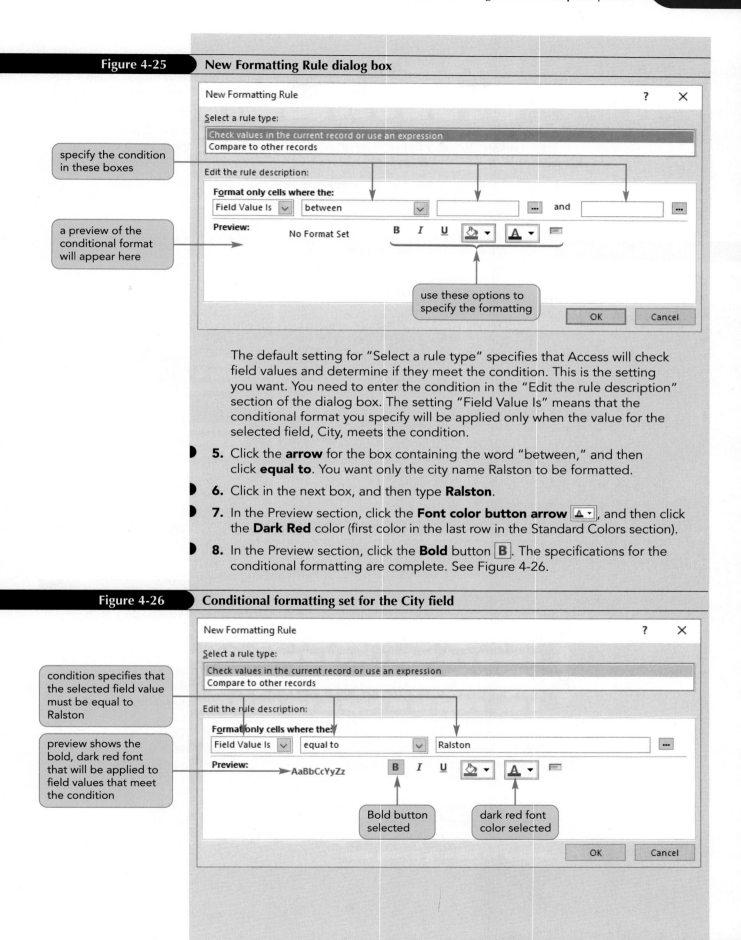

The default setting for "Select a rule type" specifies that Access will check field values and determine if they meet the condition. This is the setting you want. You need to enter the condition in the "Edit the rule description" section of the dialog box. The setting "Field Value Is" means that the conditional format you specify will be applied only when the value for the selected field, City, meets the condition.

> **5.** Click the **arrow** for the box containing the word "between," and then click **equal to**. You want only the city name Ralston to be formatted.

> **6.** Click in the next box, and then type **Ralston**.

> **7.** In the Preview section, click the **Font color button arrow** [A ▾], and then click the **Dark Red** color (first color in the last row in the Standard Colors section).

> **8.** In the Preview section, click the **Bold** button [B]. The specifications for the conditional formatting are complete. See Figure 4-26.

**Figure 4-26**  Conditional formatting set for the City field

condition specifies that the selected field value must be equal to Ralston

preview shows the bold, dark red font that will be applied to field values that meet the condition

Bold button selected

dark red font color selected

**9.** Click the **OK** button. The new rule you specified appears in the Rule section of the Conditional Formatting Rules Manager dialog box as Value = "Ralston"; the Format section on the right shows the conditional formatting (dark red, bold font) that will be applied based on this rule.

**10.** Click the **OK** button. The conditional format is applied to the City field values. To get a better view of the report and the formatting, you'll switch to Print Preview.

**11.** On the status bar, click the **Print Preview** button 🔍. Notice that the conditional formatting is applied only to City field values equal to Ralston. See Figure 4-27.

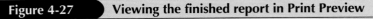

**Figure 4-27** **Viewing the finished report in Print Preview**

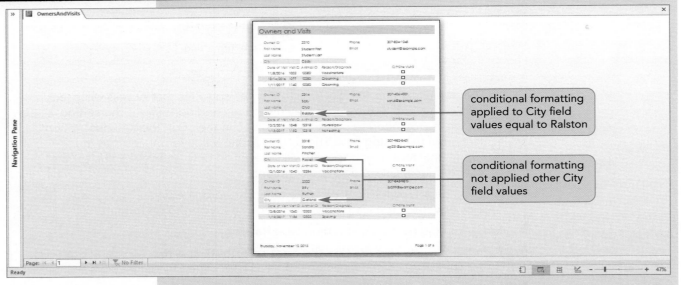

conditional formatting applied to City field values equal to Ralston

conditional formatting not applied other City field values

*Problem Solving: Understanding the Importance of Previewing Reports*

When you create a report, it is a good idea to display the report in Print Preview occasionally as you develop it. Doing so will give you a chance to identify any formatting problems or other issues so that you can make any necessary corrections before printing the report. It is particularly important to preview a report after you've made changes to its design to ensure that the changes you made have not created new problems with the report's format. Before printing any report, you should preview it so you can determine where the pages will break and make any necessary adjustments. Following this problem-solving approach not only will ensure that the final report looks exactly the way you want it to, but will also save you time and help to avoid wasting paper if you print the report.

The report is now complete. You'll print just the first page of the report so that Kimberly can view the final results and share the report design with other staff members before printing the entire report. (*Note*: Ask your instructor if you should complete the following printing steps.)

## To print page 1 of the report:

▶ **1.** On the Print Preview tab, in the Print group, click the **Print** button. The Print dialog box opens.

▶ **2.** In the Print Range section, click the **Pages** option button. The insertion point now appears in the From box so that you can specify the range of pages to print.

▶ **3.** Type **1** in the From box, press the **Tab** key to move to the To box, and then type **1**. These settings specify that only page 1 of the report will be printed.

▶ **4.** Click the **OK** button. The Print dialog box closes, and the first page of the report is printed.

▶ **5.** Save and close the OwnersAndVisits report.

You've created many different objects in the Riverview database. Before you close it, you'll open the Navigation Pane to view all the objects in the database.

## To view the Riverview database objects in the Navigation Pane:

▶ **1.** Open the **Navigation Pane** and scroll down, if necessary, to display the bottom of the pane.

The Navigation Pane now includes the OwnersAndVisits report in the Reports section of the pane. Also notice the OwnerAnimals form in the Forms section. This is the form you created containing a main form based on the Owner table and a subform based on the Animal table. The AnimalSubform object is also listed; you can open it separately from the main form. See Figure 4-28.

| Figure 4-28 | Riverview database objects in the Navigation Pane |

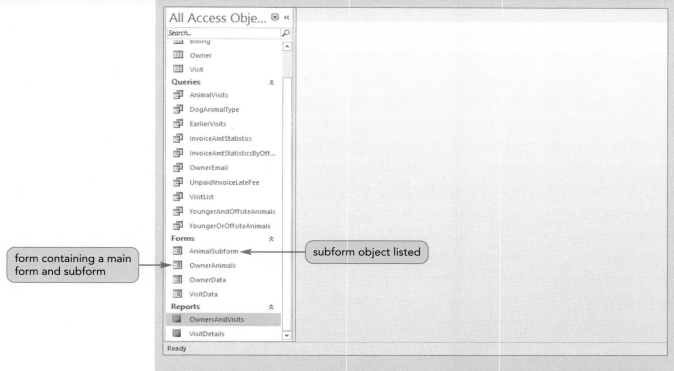

form containing a main form and subform

subform object listed

▶ **2.** Compact and repair the Riverview database, and then close the database.

Kimberly is satisfied that the forms you created—the OwnerData form and the OwnerAnimals form—will make it easier to enter, view, and update data in the Riverview database. The OwnersAndVisits report presents important information about the owners of the animals that the care center treats in an attractive and professional format, which will help Kimberly and other staff members in their work.

**REVIEW**

## Session 4.2 Quick Check

1. In a(n) _____ report, the data from a record in the primary table appears together, followed on subsequent lines by the joined records from the related table.

2. When you create a report based on two tables that are joined in a one-to-many relationship, the field values for the records from the related table are called the _____ records.

3. Identify three types of modifications you can make to a report in Layout view.

4. Describe the process for moving a control to another location on a report in Layout view.

5. When working in Layout view for a report, which key do you press and hold down so that you can click to select multiple controls (field labels, field value boxes, and so on)?

6. _____ in a report (or form) is special formatting applied to certain field values depending on one or more conditions.

## Review Assignments

**PRACTICE**

**Data Files needed for the Review Assignments: Items.png and Vendor.accdb** *(cont. from Module 3)*

Kimberly asks you to enhance the Vendor database with forms and reports. Complete the following steps:

1. Open the **Vendor** database you created and worked with in previous modules, and then click the Enable Content button next to the security warning, if necessary.

2. Use the Form Wizard to create a form based on the Product table. Select all fields for the form and the Columnar layout; specify the title **ProductData** for the form.

3. Apply the Ion theme to the ProductData form *only*.

4. Insert the **Items** picture, which is located in the Access1 > Review folder provided with your Data Files, in the ProductData form. Remove the picture from the control layout, and then move the picture to the right of the form title.

5. Edit the form title so that it appears as "Product Data" (two words), resize the title box as necessary so the title appears on a single line, and then change the font color of the form title to the Gray-25%, Background 2, Darker 75% theme color.

6. Resize the Weight in Lbs field value box so it is the same width (approximately) as the Units/Case field value box above it.

7. Change the alignment of the Price, Units/Case, and Weight in Lbs fields so that their values appear left-aligned in the field value boxes.

8. Save your changes to the form design.

9. Use the ProductData form to update the Product table as follows:

   a. Use the Find command to search for the word "premium" anywhere in the ProductName field, and then display the record for the Premium puppy food (ProductID PF200). Change the Price in this record to **44.00**.

   b. Add a new record with the following field values:
   Product ID: **CT200**
   Supplier ID: **KLS321**
   Product Name: **Cloth tape roll**
   Price: **24.00**
   Units/Case: **10**
   Weight in Lbs: **4**
   Temp Controlled?: **no**
   Sterile?: **no**

   c. Use the form to view each record with a ProductID value that starts with "CT".

   d. Save and close the form.

10. Use the Form Wizard to create a form containing a main form and a subform. Select all fields from the Supplier table for the main form, and select ProductID, ProductName, Price, TempControl, and Sterile—in that order—from the Product table for the subform. Use the Datasheet layout. Specify the title **SuppliersAndProducts** for the main form and **ProductSubform** for the subform.

11. Change the form title text to **Suppliers and Products**.

12. Resize the subform by widening it from its right side, increasing its width by approximately one inch, and then resize all columns in the subform to their best fit, working left to right. Navigate through each record in the main form to make sure all the field values in the subform are completely displayed, resizing subform columns and the subform itself, as necessary. Save and close the SuppliersAndProducts form.

13. Use the Report Wizard to create a report based on the primary Supplier table and the related Product table. Select the SupplierID, Company, City, Category, ContactFirst, ContactLast, and Phone fields—in that order—from the Supplier table, and the ProductID, ProductName, Price, and Units fields from the Product table. Do not specify any additional grouping levels, and sort the detail records in ascending order by ProductID. Choose the Outline layout and Portrait orientation. Specify the title **ProductsBySupplier** for the report.

14. Change the report title text to **Products by Supplier**.

15. Apply the Ion theme to the ProductsBySupplier report *only*.

16. Resize and reposition the following objects in the report in Layout view, and then scroll through the report to make sure all field labels and field values are fully displayed:

    a. Resize the report title so that the text of the title, Products by Supplier, is fully displayed.

    b. Move the ProductName field label and field value box to the right a bit (be sure not to move them too far so that the longest product name will still be completely visible).

    c. Resize the Product ID field label from its right side, increasing its width slightly so the label is fully displayed.

    d. Move the Price field label to the left a bit so the right side of the field label aligns with the right side of the field value below it.

    e. Move the Units/Case field label and field value box to the right a bit; then resize the label on its left side, increasing its width slightly so the label is fully displayed.

    f. Select the field value boxes *only* (not the field labels) for the following four fields: SupplierID, Company, City, and Category. Then move the four field value boxes to the left until their left edges align (roughly) with the "S" in "Supplier" in the report title.

17. Change the color of the report title text to the Gray-25%, Background 2, Darker 75% theme color.

18. Insert the **Items** picture, which is located in the Access1 > Review folder provided with your Data Files, in the report. Move the picture to the right of the report title.

19. Apply conditional formatting so that the Category field values equal to Supplies appear as dark red and bold.

20. Preview each page of the report, verifying that all the fields fit on the page. If necessary, return to Layout view and make changes so the report prints within the margins of the page and so that all field names and values are completely displayed.

21. Save the report, print its first page (only if asked by your instructor to do so), and then close the report.

22. Compact and repair the Vendor database, and then close it.

## Case Problem 1

APPLY

**Data Files needed for this Case Problem: Beauty.accdb** *(cont. from Module 3)* **and Salon.png**

***Beauty To Go***   Sue Miller uses the Beauty database to track and view information about the services her business offers. She asks you to create the necessary forms and a report to help her work with this data more efficiently. Complete the following:

1. Open the **Beauty** database you created and worked with in previous modules, and then click the Enable Content button next to the security warning, if necessary.
2. Use the Form Wizard to create a form based on the Member table. Select all the fields for the form and the Columnar layout. Specify the title **MemberData** for the form.
3. Apply the Slice theme to the MemberData form *only*.
4. Edit the form title so that it appears as "Member Data" (two words); resize the title so that both words fit on the same line; and then change the font color of the form title to the Orange, Accent 5, Darker 25% theme color.
5. Use the Find command to display the record for Maita Rios, and then change the OptionEnds field value for this record to **9/3/2017**.
6. Use the MemberData form to add a new record to the Member table with the following field values:
   Member ID: **2180**
   Option ID: **135**
   First Name: **Risa**
   Last Name: **Kaplan**
   Street: **122 Bolcher Ave**
   City: **Orlando**
   State: **FL**
   Zip: **32805**
   Phone: **212-858-4007**
   Option Begins: **11/11/2017**
   Option Ends: **5/11/2018**
7. Save and close the MemberData form.
8. Use the Form Wizard to create a form containing a main form and a subform. Select all the fields from the Option table for the main form, and select the MemberID, FirstName, LastName, OptionEnd, and Phone fields from the Member table for the subform. Use the Datasheet layout. Specify the title **MembersByOption** for the main form and the title **MemberSubform** for the subform.
9. Change the form title text for the main form to **Members by Option**.
10. Resize all columns in the subform to their best fit, working from left to right; then move through all the records in the main form and check to make sure that all subform field values are fully displayed, resizing the columns as necessary.
11. Save and close the MembersByOption form.
12. Use the Report Wizard to create a report based on the primary Option table and the related Member table. Select all the fields from the Option table, and then select the MemberID, FirstName, LastName, City, Phone, OptionBegin, and OptionEnd fields from the Member table. Do not select any additional grouping levels, and sort the detail records in ascending order by MemberID. Choose the Outline layout and Landscape orientation. Specify the title **MemberOptions** for the report.

13. Apply the Slice theme to the MemberOptions report *only*.

14. Resize the report title so that the text is fully displayed; edit the report title so that it appears as "Member Options" (two words); and change the font color of the title to the Orange, Accent 5, Darker 25% theme color.

15. Change the alignment of the Option Cost field so that its values appear left-aligned in the field value boxes.

16. Resize and reposition the following objects in the report in Layout view, and then scroll through the report to make sure all field labels and field values are fully displayed:

    a. Move the FirstName label and field value box to the right a bit (be sure not to move them too far so that the longest first name will still be completely visible).

    b. Resize the MemberID field label on its right side, increasing its width until the label is fully displayed.

    c. Move the Phone label and field value box to the left; then resize the Option Begins label on its left side, increasing its width until the label is fully displayed.

    d. Scroll to the bottom of the report; note that the page number might not be completely within the page border (the dotted vertical line). If necessary, select and move the box containing the text "Page 1 of 1" until the entire text is positioned to the left of the dotted vertical line marking the right page border.

17. Insert the **Salon** picture, which is located in the Access1 > Case1 folder provided with your Data Files, in the report. Move the picture to the right of the report title.

18. Apply conditional formatting so that any OptionEnds field value less than 3/15/2017 appears as bold and with the Red color applied.

19. Preview the entire report to confirm that it is formatted correctly. If necessary, return to Layout view and make changes so that all field labels and field values are completely displayed.

20. Save the report, print its first page (only if asked by your instructor to do so), and then close the report.

21. Compact and repair the Beauty database, and then close it.

## Case Problem 2

**CREATE**

**Data Files needed for this Case Problem: Coder.png and Programming.accdb** *(cont. from Module 3)*

***Programming Pros***    Brent Hovis is using the Programming database to track and analyze the business activity of his tutoring services company. To make his work easier, you'll create a form and a report in the Programming database. Complete the following:

1. Open the **Programming** database you created and worked with in previous modules, and then click the Enable Content button next to the security warning, if necessary.
2. Create the form shown in Figure 4-29.

**Figure 4-29**    **Completed ContractsByTutor form**

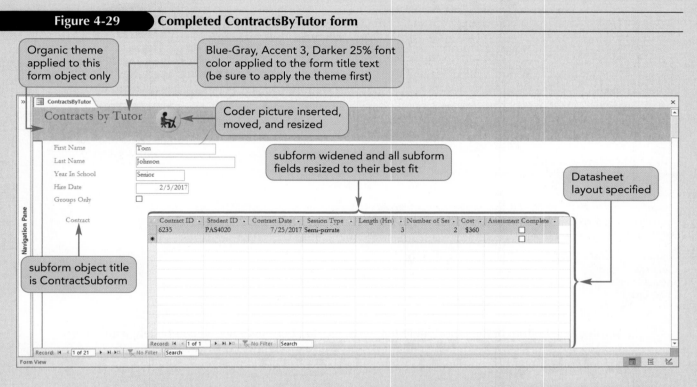

3. Using the form you just created, navigate to the second record in the subform for the eighth main record, and then change the Assessment Complete field value to **yes**.
4. Use the Find command to move to the record for Gail Fordham, and then change the value in the Year In School field to **Senior**.

5. Use the appropriate wildcard character to find all records with a Hire Date field value that begins with the month of February (2). Change the Hire Date field value for Ian Rodriguez (Tutor ID 1020) to **1/17/2017**. Save and close the form.

6. Create the report shown in Figure 4-30.

**Figure 4-30**    **Completed TutorsAndContracts report**

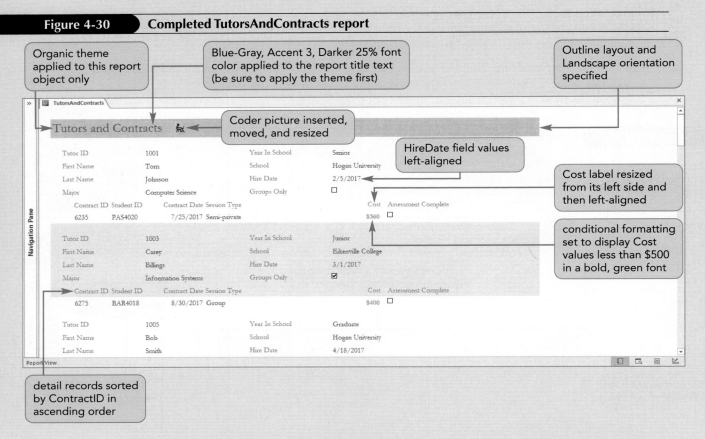

7. Scroll to the bottom of the report; note that the page number might not be completely within the page border (the dotted vertical line). If necessary, select and move the box containing the text "Page 1 of 1" until the entire text is positioned to the left of the dotted vertical line marking the right page border.

8. Preview each page of the report, verifying that all the fields fit on the page. If necessary, return to Layout view and make changes so the report prints within the margins of the page and all field names and values are completely displayed.

9. Save the report, print its first page (only if asked by your instructor to do so), and then close the report.

10. Compact and repair the Programming database, and then close it.

## Case Problem 3

Data Files needed for this Case Problem: Center.accdb *(cont. from Module 3)* and Flower.png

*Diane's Community Center*    Diane Coleman uses the Center database to track, maintain, and analyze data about the patrons, donations, and auction items for her not-for-profit community center. You'll help Diane by creating a form and a report based on this data. Complete the following:

1. Open the **Center** database you created and worked with in previous modules, and then click the Enable Content button next to the security warning, if necessary.

2. Use the Form Wizard to create a form based on the Auction table. Select all the fields for the form and the Columnar layout. Specify the title **AuctionInfo** for the form.

3. Apply the Retrospect theme to the AuctionInfo form *only*.

4. Edit the form title so that it appears as "Auction Info" (two words), and change the font color of the form title to the Brown, Accent 3, Darker 25% theme color.

✛ **Explore** 5. Use the appropriate button in the Font group on the Form Layout Tools Format tab to italicize the form title. Save the form.

6. Use the AuctionInfo form to update the Auction table as follows:

   a. Use the Find command to search for the record that contains the value "240" for the AuctionID field, and then change the MinimumSalesPrice field value for this record to **275**.

   b. Add a new record with the following values:

      Auction ID: **260**

      Donation ID: **5265**

      Date of Auction: **11/11/2017**

      Minimum Sales Price: **125**

      Item Sold at Auction?: [leave blank]

   ✛ **Explore** c. Find the record with AuctionID 245, and then delete the record. (*Hint*: After displaying the record in the form, you need to select it by clicking the right-pointing triangle in the bar to the left of the field labels. Then use the appropriate button on the Home tab in the Records group to delete the record. When asked to confirm the deletion, click the Yes button.) Close the form.

7. Use the Form Wizard to create a form containing a main form and a subform. Select all the fields from the Patron table for the main form, and select all fields except PatronID from the Donation table for the subform. Use the Datasheet layout. Specify the name **PatronsAndDonations** for the main form and the title **DonationSubform** for the subform.

8. Apply the Retrospect theme to the PatronsAndDonations form *only*.

9. Edit the form title so that it appears as "Patrons and Donations." Resize the form title so that the text fits on one line. Change the font color of the title to the Brown, Accent 3, Darker 25% theme color.

10. Insert the **Flower** picture, which is located in the Access1 > Case3 folder provided with your Data Files, in the PatronsAndDonations form. Remove the picture from the control layout, and then move the picture to the right of the form title. Resize the picture so it is approximately double the original size.

✦ **Explore** 11. Use the appropriate button in the Font group on the Form Layout Tools Format tab to apply the theme color Tan, Accent 5, Lighter 80% as a background color for all the field value boxes in the main form. Then use the appropriate button in the Control Formatting group to change the outline of all the main form field value boxes to have a line thickness of 1 pt. (*Hint*: Select all the field value boxes before making these changes.)

12. Resize the subform by extending it to the right, and then resize all columns in the subform to their best fit. Navigate through the records in the main form to make sure all the field values in the subform are completely displayed, resizing subform columns as necessary. Save and close the form.

13. Use the Report Wizard to create a report based on the primary Patron table and the related Donation table. Select all the fields from the Patron table, and select all fields except PatronID from the Donation table. Sort the detail records in *descending* order by DonationValue. Choose the Outline layout and Portrait orientation. Specify the name **PatronsAndDonations** for the report.

14. Apply the Retrospect theme to the PatronsAndDonations report *only*.

15. Resize the report title so that the text is fully displayed; edit the report title so that it appears as "Patrons and Donations"; and change the font color of the title to the Brown, Accent 3, Darker 25% theme color.

16. Move the Donation Value field label and its field value box to the left a bit. Then resize the Donation ID field label on the right to fully display the label. Move the Donation ID field label and its field value box to the left to provide space between the Donation ID and Donation Date fields, and then move the Description field label and its field value box to the right a bit, to provide more space between the Donation Date and Description fields. Widen the Cash Donation? field label so all the text is displayed, and then reposition the field label so it is centered over the CashDonation check boxes below it. Move the AuctionItem check boxes to the right so they are centered below the Possible Auction Item? field label. Finally, resize the Phone and Email field labels from their left sides to reduce the width of the label boxes, moving the words "Phone" and "Email" closer to the field value boxes. Save the report.

17. Insert the **Flower** picture, which is located in the Access1 > Case3 folder provided with your Data Files, in the PatronsAndDonations report. Move the picture to the right of the report title.

✦ **Explore** 18. Use the appropriate button on the Report Layout Tools Format tab in the Background group to apply the theme color Tan, Accent 5, Lighter 60% as the alternate row color for the fields from the Patron table; then apply the theme color Tan, Accent 5, Lighter 80% as the alternate row color for the fields from the Donation table. (*Hint*: You must first select an entire row with no background color for the appropriate fields before applying each alternate row color.) Scroll through the report to find a patron record with multiple donations so you can verify the effect of applying the alternate row color to the Donation fields.

19. Apply conditional formatting so that any DonationValue greater than or equal to 250 is formatted as bold and with the Brown 5 font color.

✦ **Explore** 20. Preview the report so you can see two pages at once. (*Hint*: Use a button on the Print Preview tab.) Check the report to confirm that it is formatted correctly and all field labels and field values are fully displayed. Save the report, print its first page (only if asked by your instructor to do so), and then close the report.

21. Compact and repair the Center database, and then close it.

## Case Problem 4

**TROUBLESHOOT**

**Data Files needed for this Case Problem: Appalachia.accdb** *(cont. from Module 3)*, **HikeApp.accdb, and Mountains.png**

*Hike Appalachia*   Molly and Bailey Johnson use the Appalachia database to maintain and analyze data about the hikers, reservations, and tours for their hiking tour business. You'll help them by creating a form and a report in the Appalachia database. Additionally, you'll troubleshoot some problems in another database containing tour information. Complete the following:

1. Open the **Appalachia** database you created and worked with in previous modules, and then click the Enable Content button next to the security warning, if necessary.

2. Use the Form Wizard to create a form containing a main form and a subform. Select all the fields from the Hiker table for the main form, and select all the fields except HikerID from the Reservation table for the subform. Use the Datasheet layout. Specify the title **HikerReservations** for the main form and the title **ReservationSubform** for the subform.

3. Apply the Integral theme to the HikerReservations form *only*.

4. Edit the form title so that it appears with a space between the two words. Change the font color of the title to the Dark Teal, Text 2, Darker 25% theme color.

5. Insert the **Mountains** picture, which is located in the Access1 > Case4 folder provided with your Data Files, in the HikerReservations form. Remove the picture from the control layout, and then move the picture to the right of the form title. Resize the picture so it is approximately double the original size.

6. Resize all columns in the subform to their best fit so that the subform column titles are fully displayed. Save the form.

7. Use the Find command to search for records that contain "WV" in the State field. Display the record for Sarah Peeler (HikerID 509), and then change the Phone field value for this record to **703-599-2043**. Close the form.

8. Use the Report Wizard to create a report based on the primary Hiker table and the related Reservation table. Select all the fields from the Hiker table, and then select all the fields except HikerID from the Reservation table. Do not select any additional grouping levels, and sort the detail records in ascending order by ReservationID. Choose the Outline layout and Portrait orientation. Specify the title **HikersAndReservations** for the report.

9. Apply the Integral theme to the HikersAndReservations report *only*.

10. Edit the report title so that it appears as "Hikers and Reservations"; then change the font color of the title to the Dark Teal, Text 2, Darker 25% theme color.

11. Left-align the Tour Date field label and field value box, then move the People field label and field value box to the left, to reduce the space between the Tour Date and People columns.

12. Insert the **Mountains** picture, which is located in the Access1 > Case4 folder provided with your Data Files, in the HikersAndReservations report. Move the picture to the right of the report title.

13. Apply conditional formatting so that any People field value greater than or equal to 3 appears as bold and with the Red color applied.

14. Preview the entire report to confirm that it is formatted correctly. If necessary, return to Layout view and make changes so that all field labels and field values are completely displayed.

15. Save the report, print its first page (only if asked by your instructor to do so), and then close the report.

16. Compact and repair the Appalachia database, and then close it.

**Troubleshoot** 17. Open the **HikeApp** database located in the Access1 > Case4 folder provided with your Data Files. Open the HikerData form in the HikeApp database. The form is not formatted correctly; it should be formatted with the Ion Boardroom theme and the theme color Plum, Accent 1, Darker 50% applied to the title. There are other problems with the form title's format as well. Additionally, some of the field labels are not properly formatted with regard to spacing between words. Identify and fix the problems with the form's format. (*Hint*: To fix the spacing between words in the necessary field labels, use the same procedure you use to fix the spacing between words in the form title text.) Save and close the corrected form.

**Troubleshoot** 18. Open the **HikerReservations** form, which is also not formatted correctly. Modify the form so that it matches the corrected format of the HikerData form and has a consistent design, including the correctly placing the logo image and resizing it to approximately double its original size. Fix the formatting problems with the subform as well, and then save and close the corrected form with subform.

**Troubleshoot** 19. Open the **HikersAndReservations** report. This report should have a consistent format in terms of theme, color, and so on as the two forms. Additionally, some of the field labels are not properly formatted with regard to spacing between words. (*Hint*: To fix the spacing between words in the necessary field labels, use the same procedure you use to fix the spacing between words in the report title text.) Find and fix these formatting errors. The report also has several problems with field labels and field value boxes, where the labels and values are not fully displayed. Locate and correct all of these problems, being sure to scroll through the entire report. Also, the conditional formatting applied to the People field is supposed to use a bold Red font. Edit the rule to correct the conditional formatting. Save the corrected report, and then preview it to identify and correct any remaining formatting problems.

20. Compact and repair the HikeApp database, and then close it.

# INDEX